The European Union and Member State Territories: A New Legal Framework Under the EU Treaties

Fiona Murray

The European Union and Member State Territories: A New Legal Framework Under the EU Treaties

T·M·C·ASSER PRESS

Springer

Dr. Fiona Murray
Rue de la Poste 214
1030 Brussels
Belgium
e-mail: fiona@schumanassociates.com

ISBN 978-90-6704-825-5 e-ISBN 978-90-6704-826-2
DOI 10.1007/978-90-6704-826-2

Library of Congress Control Number: 2011945152

Published by T.M.C. ASSER PRESS, The Hague, The Netherlands http://www.asserpress.nl
Produced and distributed for T.M.C. ASSER PRESS by Springer-Verlag Berlin Heidelberg

Cover design: eStudio Calamar S.L.

Printed on acid-free paper

Springer is part of springer Science+Business Media (www.springer.com)

For my husband, Barry O'Halpin

Foreword

Dr. Fiona Murray's book on *The European Union and Member State Territories* should be praised as a major contribution in the English language literature to an important topic which had been almost only covered until 2011 by literature in French or Spanish. It is worthwhile quoting the preface that has been written for the only other English language book dealing with this topic (DimitryKochenov, *EU Law of the Overseas*, 2011) by the Honourable Sir Richard Plender, Justice of the High Court of England and Wales, to which he was appointed in 2007, as it also applies to Dr. Murray's work:

> "The study of European Union (EU) law has become too Eurocentric. Essays on interpersonal and commercial exchanges within the EU abound, but rarely do they consider the impact of the Union's laws in non-European territories. Even the treaty-making capacity of the Union is more frequently examined from a constitutional than from an international perspective. This is much to the disadvantage of those who have to address the EU's external impact: a disadvantage that I experienced at first hand, when required to deal with the status of the Faeroe Islands [...] and in my years as legal adviser to the States (parliament) of the Bailiwick of Jersey".

Differently from Kochenov's book, which is a collection of essays by some twenty leading experts—mainly academics—Dr. Murray's book is the work of a single author, who researched her topic with passion during the years which led to her being awarded the grade of Ph.D at the Erasmus university, Rotterdam. The book is proposing a thesis, namely that the clauses of the EU treaties dealing with the differentiated statuses of Member States' Territories which are not part of mainland Europe or the British Isles (Channel Islands and Isle of Man excepted) are not adapted to the present and future situation and should be redrafted. Arguing a thesis does not necessarily mean developing abstract reasoning: on the contrary, Dr. Murray's book is firmly rooted in reality.

The major contribution of Dr. Murray's book, which should open it a large readership, is the extremely precise and detailed study of the different EU Member States' Territories which enjoy a differentiated status: European territories for whose external relations a Member State is responsible, EU outermost regions which are non-European territories forming part of France, Portugal and Spain, and the overseas countries and territories associated with the union, which are non-European territories constitutionally bound to Denmark, France, the Netherlands, or the United Kingdom.

Far from being a dull legal work, Dr. Murray's book is therefore also an invitation to travel around the world, which the reader will certainly enjoy.

Jacques Ziller, Ph.D.
Professor of EU law at the University of Pavia, formerly professor at the European University Institute (Florence), at Sorbonne University (Paris) and at the University of the French West Indies and Guyana

Preface

During the 20 years I have been working in the area of EU law and policy, a considerable part of this experience has been devoted to advising and assisting EU Member State territories, both Governments and private sector. In working with these territories from an EU perspective, a number of factors have struck me, notably:

- The disparate nature of their relationships with the EU; whilst some territories chose to join the EU, others opted to remain outside; all, however, had negotiated derogations or special arrangements from the TEC
- The absence of any coherent overall EU policy in relation to these territories, despite their many broad similarities
- The piecemeal nature of their evolution *vis à vis* the EU.

In general, in my work for these territories, it was not always easy to find source materials that would, for example, clarify the precise nature of their legal relations with the EU or facilitate comparisons between territories or groups of territories in the context of the EU.

It was in order to address the dearth of source materials on EU Member State Territories as a whole that I wrote and published a book in 2004 on "*EU and Member State Territories: The Special Relationship under Community Law*".[1] The then European Commissioner for Development, Poul Nielsen acknowledged in a foreword to the book the "information deficit" on the subject.

Having written what was intended to be a straightforward reference book about the territories, I then began to consider the Treaty's basic legal framework for relations between Member State Territories and the EU as set out (until the recent entry into force of the Lisbon Treaty) in Article 299 TEC. Once I had reviewed the individual relations with the EU particularly in the context of their evolution since 1957, I observed that Article 299 seemed somewhat incongruous as a broad legal framework for relations between Member States Territories and the EU, due

[1] Murray 2004.

particularly to the many developments that had taken place since the TEC was signed in 1957 which no longer seemed to fit appropriately into the current Article 299 framework. Therefore, I decided to investigate further:

- The origins of Article 299 as a legal framework for relations between the EU and territories as drafted in 1957
- The various developments that have taken place since 1957, including Member State accessions, the addition of new territories and the departure of former territories with independence, the emergence of new groups or associations of territories, the impact of the changing political and economic setting as compared to 1957, Treaty amendments including those that resulted from the Lisbon Treaty.
- On the basis of the first two elements above, to re-examine Article 299 and the current EU Treaties framework for EU/Member State territories and to argue the case for and propose a new model Treaties framework for relations between the EU and the relevant Member State Territories.

Many people have helped me in my research for this book, to whom I extend a general heartfelt thank you. I would like to extend my particular gratitude, however, to the following: to Professor Dr. Jaap W. De Zwaan for his unfailing patience, kindness, commitment and incisive comment throughout the period of research for this book. It has been a pleasure to know and to work with you. To Associate professor Dr. Flora Goudappel, thank you for generously giving of your time and experience. To Professor Dr. Jacques Ziller for his expert and helpful comments and especially for graciously agreeing to prepare the foreword to this book. To my publishers, particularly Philip van Tongeren, Marjolijn Bastiaans and Antoinette Wessels for their kind, patient and experienced guidance in the editing of this book. To my three sons, Fionn, Oisín and Áengus who provided tireless love, inspiration and encouragement to keep me going. And, last but not least, to my husband, Barry, who has supported and encouraged me unceasingly in this project and to whom I dedicate this work. I love you and thank you.

Reference

Murray F (2004) EU and Member State Territories: The Special Relationship under Community Law, Sweet & Maxwell

Contents

Part III Assessment of Article 299 and Lisbon Treaty Amendments as a Legal Framework for EU/Territories Relations Proposed New Model EU Treaties Framework

Abbreviations

ACP	African, Caribbean and Pacific States
CAP	Common Agricultural Policy
CCP	Common Commercial Policy
CCT	Common Customs Tariff
CFI	European Court of First Instance
DOMS	Départements d'outre-mer (French Overseas Departments)
ECJ	European Court of Justice
ECSC	European Coal and Steel Community
EDF	European Development Fund
EPA	European Partnership Agreements
ERDF	European Regional Development Fund
ESF	European Social Fund
EU	European Union
EUR	Euro
EURATOM	European Atomic Energy Treaty
FPA	Fisheries Partnership Agreement
GDP	Gross Domestic Product
OCTs	Overseas Countries and Territories
OJ	Official Journal
OP	Operational Programme
POSEIDOM	Programmes of options specific to the remote and insular nature of the DOMs
POSEICAN	Programmes of options specific to the remote and insular nature of the Canary Islands
POSEIMA	Programmes of options specific to the remote and insular nature of Madeira and the Azores
R&D	Research and Development
SBAs	Sovereign Base Areas of the UK in Cyprus
TCE	Treaty establishing a Constitution for Europe
TEC	Treaty on the European Community
TEU	Treaty on the European Union

TFEU	Treaty on the Functioning of the European Union
TOMs	Territoires d'outre mer (French Overseas Territories)
VAT	Value Added Tax
UK	United Kingdom

Chapter 1
General Introduction

Abstract This chapter sets out a general introduction to the present EU Treaties framework governing relations between the EU and Member State territories including key developments leading up to the adoption of the Lisbon Treaty provisions. The scope of this book is clarified, including territories concerned, main objectives, methodology used, structure and content of publication. Finally, an overview of the currently applicable EU Treaties provisions is provided.

1.1 Overview

Certain of the EU Member States have autonomous and semi-autonomous territories. Examples include the French overseas departments, the UK Crown Dependencies and the former Netherlands Antilles. All of these territories have particular constitutional links with their Member States, some more integrated into their Member States; others are virtually independent.

Likewise, their relations with the EU vary: whilst some territories, like the French departments (*Départements d'outre-mer*, DOMs) and the Portuguese Azores and Madeira, chose to join the EU when their Member States acceded to the EU, others, such as the UK Crown Dependencies and the French overseas collectivities (*Collectivités d'outre-mer*, COMs), opted to remain outside the EU, thus essentially assuming the status of non-EU third countries. Still others have altered their original arrangements with the EU. Greenland, for instance, once part of the EU, is now formally outside the EU as one of the Overseas Countries and Territories (OCTs). For all of these territories, however, whether in or out of the EU, special arrangements were negotiated at the time of their Member State accession.

F. Murray, *The European Union and Member State Territories: A New Legal Framework Under the EU Treaties*, DOI: 10.1007/978-90-6704-826-2_1,

1.2 Current EU Treaties Framework: EU/Member State Territories

1.2.1 Background

Until the recent entry into force of the Lisbon Treaty, the Treaty provision governing relations between the EU and Member State territories was Article 299 of the Treaty of the European Community (TEC), which defined in broad terms the territorial scope of the Treaty. As a result of the entry into force of the Lisbon Treaty, the EU Treaties framework governing EU and Member State territories falls primarily under Article 52 (1) and (2) of the Treaty on the European Union (TEU) with the detailed provisions set out in Article 355 and, in relation specifically to Outermost Regions, Article 349 of the Treaty on the Functioning of the European Union (TFEU).

When the original version of Article 299 (ex Article 227 TEC) was drafted in 1957, there existed a very different geographical, political and economic landscape compared with today. One obvious difference was that there were only 6 Member States, the only one of which had any significant number of territories was France. Whilst the first paragraph of Article 227 provided that the Treaty was to apply to all Member States, which as we shall see by definition included their territories, it was to address mainly the situation of the French territories, at the request of France, that subparagraphs two and three of Article 227 were drafted. Article 227(2) made provision for the qualified application of the Treaty to the French DOMs to take account of their social and economic backwardness compared with the rest of France. Article 227(3) created a special arrangement for the French TOMs which had less close links to France. As we shall note, Article 227(2) paved the way for the emergence of today's policy on Outermost Regions while Article 227(3) provided the basis for today's EU/OCT association.

Article 227(4), however, (and the equivalent provision under the Lisbon Treaty, Article 355(3) TFEU), remains something of an anomaly. It provided that the Treaty should apply to all European territories for whose external relations a Member State is responsible. The text of this subparagraph was borrowed from the equivalent provision in the European Coal and Steel Community (ECSC) Treaty. The latter was aimed at the Saar region over whose jurisdiction Germany and France were in dispute. When, however, the TEC was signed in 1957, the dispute over the Saar's jurisdiction had ended (in favour of Germany) with the result that Article 227(4) was in fact redundant when the TEC was signed and remained redundant until the UK (and Gibraltar) joined the Community in 1972.

1.2.2 Developments Since 1957

At the time of writing, just after the 50th anniversary of the TEC, the geo-political and economic backdrop to the Treaties is quite different to that which existed in

1957. For one thing, in terms of Article 52 TEU and the territorial reach of the EU, there are many more Member States and there has been an ebb and flow in the numbers of territories since 1957. One notable change is that many of the early overseas territories gained independence and most now fall under the EU/African Caribbean and Pacific (ACP) association which developed out of the EU/OCT framework. Another is the development of a new group of overseas territories, known as the Outermost Regions, which are part of the EU but for which special provision is made due to their economic, social and geographic handicaps.

The predicament of territories whose Member States joined the EU post-1957 has rarely if ever been straightforward. The process has almost always necessitated the negotiation of special arrangements, sometimes ill-fitting to accommodate the EU Treaties framework, but has also led to anomalies and inconsistencies. Thus, to give a few examples, when Denmark joined the EU, Greenland as a colony was assumed to form part of the EU under Article 52(1) TEU (ex Article 299(1)) and no special provision was made for it other than a short Protocol. In contrast, Gibraltar is considered to be part of the EU by virtue of Article 355(3) (ex Article 299(4)), rather than Article 52(1) and in that case, special derogations were agreed for it. Later, when Greenland opted for 'home rule', as it was still officially a Danish territory, Greenland was granted the status of OCT. However, rather than being subject to the OCT Decision and therefore being eligible for financial and technical assistance from the EU, Greenland entered into a fisheries agreement with the EU. Likewise, Bermuda, a UK territory, though officially one of the OCTs, opted not to be subject to the OCT Decision.

The overall resulting picture today is one of several more Member States and a great variety of territories, some of which despite similar characteristics and status *vis à vis* the EU are treated and 'classified' in very different ways under the EU Treaties.

Another general issue with the current EU Treaties framework for EU/territories' relations is the scarcity of literature or expertise on this subject. Whilst there are ample source materials and persons with knowledge on individual territories or groups of territories and their relations with the EU and even on the specific topic of the territorial scope of the treaties, there are comparatively few materials or specialists with an overall perspective on the relevant territories and/or particular insight into the EU Treaties framework for their relations with the EU. It was this dearth of knowhow which I remarked upon whilst working with some of these territories that led me to write a book on the subject, published in 2004.[1] Whilst my book was intended as a general reference source on the territories themselves, this book seeks to provide a new and original perspective on this topic in the following ways:

- first, by providing a deeper, more comprehensive focus on the relevant territories, including their evolution *vis à vis* the EU and their current relations with the EU, a little-researched and written about subject in itself;
- second, by focusing in particular on the pre Lisbon Treaty framework for EU/territories relations, tracing the origins of these provisions from 1957 to the

[1] Murray 2004.

present day and examining the adequacy of Article 299 and the changes introduced by the Lisbon Treaty both in the context of 1957 and today. Whilst there is ample commentary on the broader subject of the territorial scope of the EU Treaties, there is very little, if indeed any comprehensive literature on Article 299 TEC or indeed the general EU Treaties framework governing the EU/territories' relationship;
- finally, in the light of the foregoing examination and analysis, by positing, in place of the existing one, a new model Article as a more adequate EU Treaties framework for EU/Member State territories relations.

1.2.3 Lisbon Treaty Changes to Article 299 TEC

The Lisbon Treaty entered into force on 1 December 2009. Its broad objective is to reform the functioning of the EU following the two waves of enlargement which took place since 2004 and which increased the number of EU Member States from 15 to 27. The Lisbon Treaty was drafted to replace the Treaty establishing a Constitution for Europe (TCE), which was rejected by French and Dutch voters in 2005. It aims to streamline the decision-making process without making substantive changes to the detailed Treaty provisions including Article 299 TEC.

The substance of the Lisbon Treaty changes to the EU Treaty framework governing EU/territories will be examined in more detail later in this text. However, for the purposes of introduction and for structure, it is important to note here that much of this book is focused on the pre-Lisbon Treaty framework for EU/territories relations, namely Article 299 TEC (and its predecessor Article 227 TEC). There are two main reasons for focusing more on the structure of Article 299 rather than the present applicable Lisbon Treaty framework. Firstly, there is the relative familiarity of Article 299 TEC compared to the Lisbon Treaty framework, thus making it easier for the reader to follow both the developments to Article 299 through to the present day and also to contrast and compare the changes to the framework brought about by the Lisbon Treaty. In the final analysis, this in turn will help to highlight the ongoing inadequacies of the current EU Lisbon Treaty framework for EU/Member State territories and set the basis for the new model EU Treaties framework proposed by this book. For similar reasons to those outlined above, in proposing this model, this book takes as its basis the structure of the former Article 299 TEC rather than that of the Lisbon Treaty framework.

The second main reason for drafting the proposed model framework by reference to Article 299 TEC rather than to the Lisbon Treaty provisions is that this book will argue that like Article 299, the model EU Treaties framework for relations between the EU and Member State territories should be grouped under a single framework provision, rather than the Lisbon Treaty approach which spreads the relevant provisions for EU territories over three principle Articles in two different Treaties.

1.3 Introduction to Current EU Treaties Framework: EU/Member State Territories

Having examined above the general background to the EU Treaties framework governing relations between the EU and Member State territories, there now follows an overview of the current EU Treaties framework, following the entry into force of the Lisbon Treaty. This will help bridge the link between the previous Article 299 TEC framework and the proposed new model Treaties framework set out in Part III of this book.

1.3.1 Overview of Current Relevant Lisbon Treaty Provisions

Although for reasons outlined in the previous section, this book will focus mainly on the pre-Lisbon Treaty Article 299 TEC, it is helpful here to summarise the current EU Treaties framework for EU/Member State territories as a result of the entry into force by the Lisbon Treaty. For ease of reference and where applicable, the corresponding provisions of Article 299 TEC are bracketed.

Following the entry into force of the Lisbon Treaty in December 2009, the core provisions governing EU/Member State territories are set out in two parts of the Treaties—the Treaty on the European Union (TEU) which sets out the broad principles of the EU, and the Treaty on the Functioning of the European Union (TFEU) which covers the operational aspects of the former TEC.

Article 52(1) and (2) TEU (ex Article 299(1) TEC) set down the general principle that the Treaties apply to all Member States and that the territorial scope of the Treaties is specified in Article 355 TFEU.

Article 355(1) TEU (ex Article 299(2) first subparagraph) provides that the Treaties apply to the Outermost Regions and that the detailed provisions concerning them are set out in Article 349 TFEU.

Subparagraph (2) (ex Article 299(3)) deals with the OCTs.

Subparagraph (3) (ex Article 299(4)) provides that the Treaty applies to all European territories for which a Member State is responsible.

Subparagraph (4) (ex Article 299 (5)) concerns the application of the Treaties to the Aland Islands.

Subparagraph (5) (ex Article 299 (6)) covers those Member State European territories—exceptions to the rule in (3)—which have chosen to remain outside the EU, namely, the Danish Faroe Islands, the UK SBAs in Cyprus, Channel Islands and the Isle of Man.

Subparagraph (6) (new—no equivalent under Article 299 TEC) facilitates a status change to Danish, French or Dutch OCTs or Outermost Regions referred to in subparagraphs(1) and (2) on the basis of a Council decision.

Article 349 TFEU (ex Article 299(2) second, third and fourth subparagraphs) sets out the more detailed provisions governing relations with the Outermost Regions.

1.3.2 Background to the Current EU Treaties Framework and Developments Since 1957

The political and economic context in which the present EU Treaties provisions for EU Member State territories was originally conceived and drafted is very different to today's political and economic reality. Some of the key changes since 1957 are:

- more Member States
- a greater variety of territories often with very different constitutional relations with their Member States
- a wider range of arrangements and derogations negotiated for these territories *vis à vis* the EU, including the emergence of the Outermost Regions
- structural and textual changes introduced by major Treaty amendments such Maastricht, Amsterdam and also latterly the Lisbon Treaty
- impact of globalization and the Internet.

Despite these and other changes, the EU Treaties framework has never undergone an overall review process. Rather, it has been added to and adapted in piecemeal fashion as new Member States have joined, to accommodate the specific requirements and requests of individual territories or to adapt to emerging groups like the Outermost Regions but also the OCTs. The result of this lack of review is a framework for relations between the EU and Member State territories which is incoherent, inconsistent and anomalous.

1.4 Scope

1.4.1 Territories Concerned

At the outset, it is important to determine the precise scope and purpose of this book, including specifically the meaning of territories for the purpose of this publication. Firstly, before delineating which territories fall within the scope of this book, it is worth emphasizing at this point that, though relevant and commented on, this book is not focused on the broader subject of territorial scope of the Treaty about which much has already been written.[2] Nor does it focus on specific EU policy areas which may be

[2] For example: Dewost 1979; Groux 1987; Ziller 2007.

the subject of derogations or special arrangements between the EU and the relevant territories. Rather, this book takes as its primary focus the territories of the Member States, their evolving relations with the EU and, in the light of this relationship, the adequacy of the Article 299 TEC and the current EU Treaties framework for the EU/Member State territories relationship.

As to the question which territories fall within the scope of this book, such territories fulfill the following requirements:

- With the exception of Gibraltar and Ceuta and Melilla, all of these territories, whether individually or as part of a group, are specifically mentioned in the main provisions of the EU Treaties framework for EU/Member State territories
- All are covered by special provisions or protocols in their Member States Treaties of Accession with the EU
- All of the territories concerned have a constitutional link with a Member State
- All are either autonomous or semi-autonomous.

This book will also, however, address the position of specific Member State territories whose status *vis à vis* the EU is uncertain, for example, the French territories of Clipperton and the scattered islands of the Indian Ocean. In this context it is also worth noting that none of the EU's candidate countries or 12 "new" Member States has autonomous or semi-autonomous territories for which their Treaties of Accession make special provision.

Currently, the EU Treaties refer specifically to the following territories or groups of territories:

- Outermost Regions:
  - French Overseas Departments and collectivities (Guadeloupe, Martinique, French Guiana, Réunion, Saint Barthélemy, Saint Martin)
  - Portuguese Azores and Madeira
  - Spanish Canary Islands
- Overseas Countries and Territories:
  - Danish Greenland
  - French New Caledonia and Dependencies, French Polynesia, French Southern and Antarctic Territories, Wallis and Futuna Islands, Mayotte, Saint Pierre and Miquelon
  - Dutch autonomous countries of Aruba, Curaçao, and Sint Maarten. Bonaire, Saba and Sint Eustatius are special municipalities of the Netherlands
  - British Anguilla, Cayman Islands, Falkland Islands, South Georgia and the South Sandwich Islands, Montserrat, Pitcairn, Saint Helena and Dependencies, British Antarctic Territory, British Indian Ocean Territory, Turks and Caicos Islands, British Virgin Islands, Bermuda
- Other territories:
  - British Gibraltar
  - Finnish Aland Islands

Table 1.1 Territories which are part of the EU and those which are not

Territory/Group of territories	Part of EU	Not part of EU
Outermost Regions	X	
OCTs		X
Gibraltar	X	
Aland Islands	X	
Faroe Islands		X
UK SBAs in Cyprus		X
Channel Islands and Isle of Man		X
Ceuta and Melilla	X	

- Danish Faroe Islands
- British UK Sovereign Base Areas in Cyprus
- British Channel Islands and Isle of Man

As shown in the table below, broadly half of these territories form part of the EU. The other half are outside the EU, effectively in the position of third, non-EU countries (Table 1.1).

1.4.2 Territorial Scope of Treaties

Some of the key issues in the debate on the territorial scope of the Treaties include the following:

- territorial scope of the original EC, ECSC and Euratom Treaties
- impact of Maastricht Treaty amendments, in particular the definition of territorial scope of the EU Treaty and of territorial scope of the second and third pillars
- impact of the Lisbon Treaty including the merging of the three pillars for the territorial scope
- territorial scope of specific subject areas e.g. Common Customs Tariff (CCT)

All of these issues will be addressed in this book only in so far as they are relevant to the central theme of the EU Treaties framework for relations between the EU and Member State territories.

1.5 Aims

The basic contention of this study is that the current EU Treaties framework is inadequate for relations between the EU and Member State territories. The issues with the current framework can be traced back to the original drafting of Article 227 TEC when an overall structured approach to the drafting of this provision was lacking at the outset, and to the general failure to review the EU Treaties framework governing EU/Member State territories' relations in the light of the many political, socio-economic, constitutional and legal developments that have taken place since the original Article 227 TEC was adopted in 1957.

Some of the key issues are:

- in the original 1957 version of Article 227 TEC, a framework that was drafted to fit the demands of mainly one Member State's territories (France), but which lacked adaptability to incorporate and apply to new territories with different structures and constitutional relations with their Member States
- a provision—the current Article 355(3) TEFU on European Member State territories–which was obsolete from the start and which ever since has sat uncomfortably within the EU Treaties framework
- the piecemeal way in which the original provisions have been added to in order to accommodate new Member State territories and new groups of territories resulting in an inconsistent approach to categorizing territories and to incorporating future territories
- the absence of any overall review of the EU Treaties framework for relations with Member State territories in order to bring the provisions up to date with the current socio-political and constitutional landscape despite a succession of major overall Treaty revisions including Maastricht, Amsterdam and latterly, Lisbon, which would have afforded opportunities for a comprehensive review.

The result of these and many more issues and anomalies, which will be examined in detail in this paper, is that the Article 299 framework—including the changes to structure introduced by the Lisbon Treaty—is ill-matched to the current reality of EU/Member States relations. The current Treaties framework lacks consistency, transparency and adaptability to accommodate ongoing future changes.

- propose a new model Treaties framework for the EU/territories' relationship in the light of the foregoing analysis.

1.6 Methodology

Some further general comments:

First, for ease of reference and cross-reference, the full texts of relevant Treaty provisions and key supporting legislation have been added as annexes to this book. The commentaries on these legal provisions are for the most part brief and are reviewed and analysed only insofar as they are relevant to the overall objective of analysing the adequacy of the EU/Member State territories Treaty framework.

Second, as mentioned already, this publication includes a general overview of the relevant territories. These profiles do not intend to examine in any depth each territory as any such detail would not contribute to the overall objective of the book as regards the adequacy or otherwise of the Treaty framework for these territories. Nevertheless, it is important to include an overview of the relevant territories so as to be better able to assess the effectiveness of the Treaties framework.

Third, when referring to the European Union in general and to specific relations such as with the OCTs and ACP, the generic EU is used.

Finally, in Part III of this book, a review and comparative analysis of the corresponding provisions of the Lisbon Treaty and its predecessor, the TCE, is also undertaken to see whether the changes proposed to Article 299 in the TCE might have offered a better solution to the inadequacies of Article 299.

Box 1.1 Lisbon Treaty Provisions Governing EU/Member State Territories

Article 52 (1) and (2) TEU

1. *The Treaties shall apply to the Kingdom of Belgium, Republic of Bulgaria, the Czech Republic, the Kingdom of Denmark, the Federal Republic of Germany, the Republic of Estonia, the Hellenic Republic, the Kingdom of Spain, the FrenchRepublic, Ireland, the Italian Republic, the Republic of Cyprus, the Republic of Latvia, the Republic of Lithuania, the Grand Duchy of Luxembourg, the Republic of Hungary, the Republic of Malta, the Kingdom of the Netherlands, the Republic of Austria, the Republic of Poland, the Portuguese Republic, Romania, the Republic of Slovenia, the Slovak Republic, the Republic of Finland, the Kingdom of Sweden and the United Kingdom of Great Britain and Northern Ireland. The territorial scope of the Treaties is specified in Article 355 of the Treaty on the Functioning of the European Union.*

Article 349 TFEU

Taking account of the structural social and economic situation of Guadeloupe, French Guiana, Martinique, Réunion, Saint-Barthélemy, Saint-Martin, the Azores, Madeira and the Canary Islands, which is compounded by their remoteness, insularity, small size, difficult topography and climate, economic dependence on a few products, the permanence and combination of which severely restrain their development, the Council, acting by a qualified majority on a proposal from the Commission and after consulting the European Parliament, shall adopt specific measures aimed, in particular, at laying down the conditions of application of the present Treaty to those regions, including common policies. Where the specific measures in question are adopted by the Council in accordance with a special legislative procedure, it shall also act on a proposal from the Commission and after consulting the European Parliament.

The measures referred to in the first paragraph concern in particular areas such as customs and trade policies, fiscal policy, free zones, agriculture and fisheries policies, conditions for supply of raw materials and essential consumer goods, State aids and conditions of access to structural funds and to horizontal Union programmes.

The Council shall adopt the measures referred to in the first subparagraph taking into account the special characteristics and constraints of the Outermost Regions without undermining the integrity and the coherence of the Union legal order, including the internal market and common policies.

Article 355 TFEU

In addition to the provisions of Article 52 of the Treaty on European Union relating to the territorial scope of the Treaties, the following provisions shall apply:

1. *The provisions of the Treaties shall apply to Guadeloupe, French Guiana, Martinique, Réunion, Saint-Barthélemy, Saint-Martin the Azores, Madeira and the Canary Islands in accordance with Article 349.*
2. *The special arrangements for association set out in part four of this Treaty shall apply to the overseas countries and territories listed in Annex II to the Treaties*
   This Treaty shall not apply to those overseas countries and territories having special relations with the United Kingdom of Great Britain and Northern Ireland which are not included in the aforementioned list.
3. *The provisions of the Treaties shall apply to the European territories for whose external relations a Member State is responsible.*
4. *The provisions of the Treaties shall apply to the Åland Islands in accordance with the provisions set out in Protocol 2 to the Act concerning the conditions of accession of the Republic of Austria, the Republic of Finland and the Kingdom of Sweden.*
5. *Notwithstanding Article 52 of the Treaty on European Union and paragraphs 1 to 4 of this Article:*
   (a) *the Treaties shall not apply to the Faroe Islands;*
   (b) *the Treaties shall not apply to the sovereign base areas of the United Kingdom of Great Britain and Northern Ireland in Cyprus;*
   (c) *the Treaties shall apply to the Channel Islands and the Isle of Man only to the extent necessary to ensure the implementation of the arrangements for those islands set out in the Treaty concerning the accession of new Member States to the European Economic Community and to the European Atomic Energy Community signed on 22 January 1972.*
6. *The European Council may, on the initiative of the Member State concerned, adopt a decision amending the status, with regard to the Union,*

of a Danish, French or Netherlands country or territory referred to in paragraphs 1 and 2. The European Council shall act unanimously after consulting the Commission.

References

Dewost J L (1979) L'Application Territoriale du Droit Communautaire: disparition et resurgence de la notion de frontière, Société Française pour le Droit International, Colloque de Poitiers

Groux J (1987) Territorialité et droit communautair, RTD eur

Murray F (2004) EU and Member State Territories: The Special Relationship under Community Law, Sweet & Maxwell

Ziller J (2007) The European Union and the Territorial Scope of the European Territories, 38 Vict. U. Wellington L. Rev 51

Part I
Background to Article 299 (ex Article 227) at the Time the Provision was Drafted in 1957

Chapter 2
General Introduction to Original Art 227 TEC

Abstract This chapter provides a general overview of the original version of Article 227 TEC, as included in the 1957 text of the Treaty. The background to and reasons for the Article, relevant territories and general aims of the provision are examined. A brief comparison with the corresponding provisions of the ECSC and Euratom Treaties is also given.

Box 2.1 1957 TEC—Article 227 (original version)

(Part Six: General and Final Provisions)
Article 227:

1. *This Treaty shall apply to the Kingdom of Belgium, the Federal Republic of Germany, the French Republic, the Italian Republic, the Grand Duchy of Luxembourg and the Kingdom of the Netherlands.*
2. *With regard to Algeria and the French overseas departments, the general and particular provisions of this Treaty relating to:*

- *the free movement of goods;*
- *agriculture, save for Article 40(4);*
- *the liberalisation of services;*
- *the rules of competition;*
- *the protective measures provided for in Articles 108, 109 and 226;*
- *the institutions,*

Shall apply as soon as this Treaty enters into force.

The conditions under which the other provisions of this Treaty are to apply shall be determined, within two years of the entry into force of this Treaty, by decisions of the Council, acting unanimously on a proposal from the Commission.

F. Murray, *The European Union and Member State Territories: A New Legal Framework Under the EU Treaties*, DOI: 10.1007/978-90-6704-826-2_2,

The institutions of the Community will, within the framework of the procedures provided for in this Treaty, in particular Article 226, take care that the economic and social development of these areas is made possible.

3. *The special arrangements for association set out in Part Four of this Treaty shall apply to the overseas countries and territories listed in Annex IV to this Treaty.*
4. *The provisions of this Treaty shall apply to the European territories for whose external relations a Member State is responsible.*

2.1 Introduction to Article 227 TEC (1957)

The original version of Article 299, of the TEC, signed in 1957 by the first 6 Member States, was set out in Part Six of the Treaty headed 'General and Final Provisions'.[1] Although not specifically entitled as such, Article 227 was intended to set out in the broadest terms the territorial scope of the Treaty. In essence, Article 227 provided that the Treaty applied to the 6 original Member States (in subparagraph (1)) and then addressed, in the remaining three subparagraphs, the 'exceptions' to this general principle, namely,

- (subparagraph (2)): the French overseas dependencies, which were an integral part of France i.e. Algeria and the French DOMs,
- (subparagraph (3)): the overseas countries and territories including the French TOMs and other Member States territories which had a large degree of autonomy and the specifics of whose relationship with the EU was defined in Part Four of the Treaty,
- (subparagraph (4)): those European territories for whose external relations a Member State is responsible—as we will see, when the Treaty was signed, no European territories fell within this provision.

2.2 Pre 1957: Political and Economic Backdrop

The origins of the EU lie in the Second World War in the aftermath of which Europeans were determined to take collaborative action to try to prevent a recurrence of such conflict. In addition, the 1950s was dominated by the cold war between east and west. The creation of the Council of Europe in 1949 was a first

[1] See Annex II *infra*, Article 227 TEC 1957.

step towards cooperation, the broad aim of which was to defend human rights, promote democracy and the rule of law.

Six European countries, however, wanted to go further and in April 1951 the six original members of the EU—France, Germany, Italy, Luxembourg, Belgium and the Netherlands—signed a treaty to run their coal and steel industries under common management. In so doing, the aim was to ensure that none of the members could make their own weapons of war to turn against the other. In March 1957, building on the success of the Coal and Steel Treaty, the six countries created a 'European Economic Community' or 'common market'. The intention was to permit people, goods, services and capital to move freely across their borders.

In 1957 associated and sometimes forming an integral part of these six countries were many overseas territories, some of which had close ties to their mother country, others had less close ties. The Treaty sought to address the position of these territories *vis à vis* the European Community under Article 227 and in Part Four of the Treaty (Articles 131 to 136).

2.3 Relevant Member States and Territories

The 1957 TEC was signed by the following six Member States:

- Belgium
- Germany
- France
- Italy
- Luxembourg
- The Netherlands.

It is by reference to these six Member States that Article 227(1) defined the scope of the Treaty.

The broad definition set out in Article 227(1) was intentional. It was meant to cover in general Member States and the territories over which they had jurisdiction. However, it was acknowledged and agreed that special provision should be made for the overseas territories of the Member States, particularly France, and so Article 227 went onto to specify and therefore act as a legal framework for relations between the EU and these territories. At the time of the signing of the Treaty in 1957, these territories were:

- Article 227(2):
  - French

  - Algeria
  - French DOMs (Guadeloupe, Martinique, French Guiana, Réunion)

- French:
  - French West Africa comprising Senegal, French Sudan, French Guinea, Ivory Coast, Dahomey, Mauritania, Niger and Upper Volta;
  - French Equatorial Africa comprising Middle Congo, Ubangi-Shari, Chad and Gabon;
  - Saint Pierre et Miquelon, the Archipelago of the Comores, Madagascar and dependencies, the French Somali Coast, New Caledonia and dependencies, French settlements in Oceania and French Southern and Antarctic Territories;

- French/British:

- Autonomous Republic of Togo
- The trust territory of the Cameroons under French administration
- The British/French condominium of the New Hebrides

- Belgian:
  - The Belgian Congo and Rwanda-Urundi

- Italian:
  - The trust territory of Somaliland under Italian administration

- Dutch:
  - Netherlands New Guinea

- Article 227(4):

As we shall see below, although originally conceived for the Saar region over whose jurisdiction France and Germany had been in dispute prior to the signing of the TEC, since that dispute had been resolved just before the Treaty was signed in 1957, Article 227(4) in fact was redundant at the time the Treaty was signed—until UK accession on 1 January 1972.

The ensuing chapters will examine in more detail each of the original sub-paragraphs of Article 227 as set out in the TEC, with a particular focus on the aims and intentions of the drafters of these provisions.

2.4 General Aims of Article 227, 1957 TEC

Concerning Article 227 specifically, this was set out in Part Six of the 1957 Treaty dealing with 'General and Final Provisions'. The intention of Article 277 was to set out the territorial scope of the Treaty in very general terms and within that to clarify the position of the many Member States territories, broadly those overseas (French) territories forming an integral part of metropolitan France and the remaining Member State overseas territories with less close ties to their 'mother' country. Many of the latter were also in a state of flux facing and eventually opting for independence.

Regarding the former category, the French DOMs had been given full equality with other regions in France, and Algeria had its own regime but was very close to France. Thus, Article 227(2)—applicable to the French DOMs and Algeria and reflecting these territories' constitutional relationship with France—was set up.

Concerning those territories with less close ties to their mother country, Article 227(3) was established to cover those overseas territories which had not yet opted for independence. The OCTs were not included in the Common Market as they did not form part of the domestic markets of their Member States. For overseas Member State territories falling under Article 227(3) (and eventually for those territories choosing independence), Part Four (Articles 131 to 136) of the 1957 Treaty provided for the setting up of a special development fund—the European Development Fund (EDF)—aimed at giving technical and financial assistance to African—and later, Caribbean and Pacific—countries still colonized at the time. This first EDF lasted for the 5 year period from 1958 to 1963 and in subsequent cycles became successively the Yaoundé and Lomé Conventions and finally the Cotonou Agreement providing EU development aid to ACP territories, former colonies of EU Member States.

2.5 ECSC and Euratom Treaties

It is worth noting here the application of the other two original EC Treaties—the ECSC and Euratom. Briefly, the ECSC Treaty, signed in Paris in 1951, created a framework of production and distribution of the key coal and steel industries and set up an institutional system to manage it. The Treaty expired in 2002. The objective of the Euratom Treaty, issued in Rome in 1957, was to contribute to the formation and development of Europe's nuclear industries.

All three Treaties—EC, ECSC and Euratom—had different fields of application to Member States and their territories specifically. The scope of these three treaties in relation to Member State territories reflects the different political and economic background at the time they were signed. In 1951, when the ECSC Treaty was signed, the many Member State overseas territories having a great variety of legal and constitutional relations with their mother countries, not to mention economic and political diversity, would have made it extremely difficult to create a uniform EU legal framework for them. Thus, the application of the ECSC Treaty was limited to European territories of Member States, as set out in Article 79 ECSC.

By 1957, when the EC and Euratom Treaties were signed, the process of decolonisation was well under way. Only the territories of France and Belgium were economically important to their mother countries. Thus, the scope of both Treaties in respect to territories, was significantly broader than the ECSC Treaty. The ECSC expired in July 2002, bringing the products the ECSC Treaty covered into the scope of EC rules. The Euratom has the widest territorial scope as it applies both to European territories and to non-European territories within their jurisdiction with some exceptions for Danish and UK territories—Article 198.[2]

The common denominator was therefore the principle of the integral application of European territories for whose external relations a Member State is responsible. Article 227(4) was transposed from the corresponding provision in the ECSC Treaty which had been devised to address the position of the Saarland and also possibly Berlin which was then under the joint sovereignty of France, Great Britain, the Soviet Union and the United States.[3]

2.6 Conclusions

Article 277 was set out in Part Six of the Treaty on General and Final Provisions so was not part of the core operational part of the Treaty, nor of Parts One and Two of the 1957 Treaty dealing with respectively the basic Principles and Foundations of the Community. Nevertheless, it is noteworthy that Article 227 was drafted in the broadest terms. Explicitly, all six Member States (and implicitly their territories) are covered whereas those with special provisions are mentioned in subparagraphs (2) and (3).

The only Member State with a significant number of territories at the time was France which requested these special provisions for its more integrated DOMs and Algeria and its more distant TOMs. Thus, subparagraph (2) was drafted to accommodate specifically the French territories of Algeria and the DOMs, whereas those territories with less close ties were intended to be covered by Article 227(3). In general, both subparagraphs (2) and (3) were drafted with specific territories in mind and with little or no foresight given to how to accommodate possible future territories.

Subparagraph (4) was anomalous from the beginning in that it did not apply to any specific territory or territories. Its redundancy is reflective of the general absent-minded approach to Article 299 that has persisted to the present day.

The overall structure and aims of Article 227 thus were broad, all-encompassing and uncomplicated with special general provisions for the French 'integrated'

---

[2] The Danish Faroe Islands and Greenland, and the UK Sovereign Base Areas in Cyprus are exempt. The UK Crown Dependencies are mainly exempt.

[3] European Commission Press Note JUR/2827/72/JA, 16 November 1972, *Territories of the Member States.*

territories. It was not intended to be any more than that. It is important to keep this broad original objective foremost when considering in Part II the various developments and Treaty amendments and in the light of the proposed new model provision in Part III.

Chapter 3
Article 227(1): Territorial Scope of the TEC

Abstract This chapter provides an introduction and background to the original version of the first paragraph of Article 227 TEC 1957, establishing the broad territorial scope of the Treaty including relevant Member States and territories.

3.1 Introduction and Background

Article 227(1) established the general principle that the TEC applied to all Member States and, by implication, their territories. Thus, the original version of Article 227(1) simply provides: "This Treaty shall apply to the Kingdom of Belgium, the Federal Republic of Germany, the French Republic, the Italian Republic, the Grand Duchy of Luxembourg and the Kingdom of the Netherlands." It is notable therefore that this first subparagraph of Article 227 delineated the territorial scope of the Treaty, not by reference to territories, but to the Member States themselves. It simply provided that the Treaty should apply to all 6 Member States. This same principle was reflected in other provisions of the Treaty, for example, former Articles 48 and 51 (now Articles 45 and 48 TFEU) concerning the free movement of workers, Article 52 and 53 (now Article 49 TFEU) relating to the right of establishment and Article 75 (now Article 91 TFEU) dealing with transport, all of which referred to the "territory of a Member State" or "territories of Member States". The general rule, therefore, set out in Article 227 (1) was that the TEC applied to all Member States and their territories unless otherwise provided in the Treaty itself. That Article 227(1) was intended to apply to Member State territories is further supported by the fact that the remaining subparagraphs

F. Murray, *The European Union and Member State Territories: A New Legal Framework Under the EU Treaties*, DOI: 10.1007/978-90-6704-826-2_3,

address the "exceptions" i.e those territories which have derogated and/or negotiated special arrangements.[1]

3.2 Relevant Member States and Territories

As already remarked on, Article 227(1) applied to the 6 original signatory countries, namely:

- Belgium
- Germany
- France
- Italy
- Luxembourg
- The Netherlands.

As the only relevant territories (as the term is understood for the purposes of this thesis), in 1957 were the French overseas territories for which special provision was made in subparagraphs (2) and (3) and the disparate territories and protectorates of Belgium, Italy and The Netherlands (also covered by subparagraph (3)), there appear to be no other specific territories covered by Article 227(1) in 1957 when Treaty was signed.

3.3 Conclusions

Article 227(1) was drafted in very broad, general terms. No specific mention was made of territories. This would tend to lend support to the argument that the Treaty was intended to have general application to all Member States and their territories. The fact that the subsequent paragraphs set out exceptions would confirm this interpretation.[2]

Reference

Dewost J L (1979) L'Application Territoriale du Droit Communautaire: disparition et resurgence de la notion de frontière, Société Française pour le Droit International, Colloque de Poitiers

[1] See for example: DEWOST 1979 in which he refers to subparagraphs (2) et seq as setting out the exceptions to Article 299.

[2] For a more detailed commentary and jurisprudence on the meaning and scope of Article 227(1) (later Article 299(1)), see commentary on Article 299(1) in Part II *infra*.

Chapter 4
Article 227(2): Algeria, French DOMS

Abstract This chapter provides an introduction and background to the original version of the second paragraph of Article 227 TEC 1957, addressing broadly those—mainly French—territories having close ties with their mother country. The aims and scope of Article 227 (2) are also examined.

4.1 Introduction and Background

It has already been noted above that Article 227(1) established the principle, both in territorial and general terms that the TEC applies to all Member States and their territories unless specific provision was made to the contrary. By contrast, the remaining provisions of Article 227 (subparagraphs (2)–(4)), setting out the exceptions to this general principle, were drafted and applied in a strictly territorial sense.

The first exception to the general principle in Article 227(1) that the Treaty applies to all Member States was set out in Article 227(2) providing for the application of the Treaty to Algeria and the French DOMs. Article 227(2) was drafted specifically with these territories in mind. At the time of signing the TEC, unlike the other Member State territories, Algeria and the French DOMs were, for historical reasons, by and large a part of metropolitan France, having the status of "departments *d'outre-mer*". Algeria had its own particular status but was likewise an integral part of metropolitan France. This contrasted with other mainly French overseas territories which were not an integral part of the mother country and, in the case of the French territories, were called *"territoires d'outre-mer"*.

Therefore, the Treaty had broadly to be applied to these territories. However, since these regions lagged behind the rest of France in economic and social terms, it was felt (by the French) that special provision should be made for them.

F. Murray, *The European Union and Member State Territories: A New Legal Framework Under the EU Treaties*, DOI: 10.1007/978-90-6704-826-2_4,

Therefore, in parallel with equivalent provisions in the French Constitution, Article 227 (2) was devised to address and make special provision for their different level of development.[1] Following Algerian independence in 1962, Article 227(2) ceased to apply to Algeria and only to the DOMs—although Article 299(2) was only amended to reflect this by the Maastricht Treaty in 1992 to refer only to the DOMs.[2]

4.2 Relevant Member States and Territories

As noted, the only relevant Member State for the purpose of Article 227(2) when originally drafted was France. In consequence, the only territories to which subparagraph (2) applied were the French DOMs and Algeria.

4.3 Aims and Scope of Article 227(2)

Article 227(2) first paragraph provides simply that certain specific core provisions of the Treaty shall apply to the French DOMs and Algeria as soon as the Treaty entered into force, namely:

- the free movement of goods,
- agriculture (except for those of Article 40(4) on the European Agricultural Guidance and Guarantee Fund),
- free movement of services,
- competition rules,
- the safeguard measures of Articles 108, 109 and 226
- Community institutions

This extension to the DOMs and Algeria as far as possible of French national legislation was reflected in the French Constitution.[3] The principle in the Constitution did not preclude adaptations considered necessary by the geographical situation or the economic and social development of these departments. This same notion was reflected in Article 227(2) of the TEC which foresaw the broad application to these territories of the Treaty whilst providing for the possibility of

[1] For French dependent territories with less close ties to their mother country, it was less feasible to apply the Treaty in its entirety to them. Therefore, special rules governing their relationship with the Community were devised and let out in Part Four of the Treaty dealing with the Association of Overseas Countries and Territories—see Chapter 5 on Article 227(3).

[2] Amendment of Article 299(2) by the Treaty on European Union (Maastricht Treaty) OJ C 191, 29 July 1992 (entered into force November 1993).

[3] Article 73 of the French Constitution of 27 October 1946 and Article 73 of the French Constitution of 4 October 1958.

adaptations to take account of the peculiarities of their situation and their different level of development.

Regarding the application to the DOMs and Algeria of other provisions of the Treaty Article 227(2), second paragraph further provided that the Council would decide by unanimity within two years of entry into force of the Treaty (i.e. by 31 December 1959) the conditions under which other Treaty provisions should apply to these territories.

Article 227(2), third paragraph obliged the Community institutions, particularly by reference to Article 226 TEC (dealing with emergency protection measures), to ensure that the economic and social development of these areas was made possible.[4] Article 226 permitted Member States, during the transitional period to adopt protective measures to address difficulties in its economic sector. Such measures could involve derogations from the Treaty for limited periods. Article 226 permitted Member States to take emergency protective measures in order to deal with difficulties that threaten the economy in a particular area. Such measures could include derogations from the Treaty for limited periods. Article 226 specified that priority would be given to measures which would least disturb the functioning of the common market. Thus, whilst Article 227(2), second paragraph envisaged permanent derogations from the Treaty, the third paragraph provided for the possibility of temporary emergency derogations to address economic crises.[5]

4.4 Conclusions

Article 227(2) provided for the immediate application to the DOMs and Algeria of the core principles of the Common Market and for the adaptation of other Treaty provisions. Such adaptations were meant to have been made during the transitional period i.e before 1 January 1960. As we shall note later in Part II, few such adaptations were made during this period. These came later.

Normally all Member State territories should have been deemed to be part of the EU by virtue of Article 227(1). However, at France's request, special exceptions were made for these territories. For those with closer ties to the mother country, notably the DOMs and Algeria, this meant a separate subparagraph defining and confirming this special relationship *vis à vis* the EU.

Article 227(2) was therefore drafted specifically for these French territories and did not envisage any other French or other Member States territories. It was thus not drafted in such a way as to accommodate future territories with constitutional

---

[4] See Annex III *infra*, Article 226 TEC 1957.

[5] Megret 1987, 484. For example, Case 212/96 where the European Court of Justice upheld a Council Decision (89/688) authorising temporary exemptions for the French DOMs (Réunion) from the dock dues (*octroi de mer*) as permitted by Article 227(2) read in conjunction with Article 226 of the TEC, Case C-212/96 *Paul Chevassus-Marche v Conseil régionale de la Réunion*, [1998] ECR I-743.

relations with their Member States. This is evidence of the piecemeal approach to the EU/Member State territories framework from the beginning and of a rigidity that has left the present equivalent Treaty provisions (Articles 349 and 355(1) TFEU) ill-suited to easy adaptation to future territories and different structures.

Reference

Megret J (1987) Le Droit de la Communauté Economique Européene, Editions de L'Université de Bruxelles, 1987, page 484

Chapter 5
Article 227(3): Overseas Countries and Territories (OCTs)

Abstract This chapter provides an introduction and background to the original version of the third paragraph of Article 227 TEC 1957, dealing with OCTs. The aims and scope of Article 227 (3) are also examined.

5.1 Introduction and Background

The second general exception to the principle set out in Article 227(1) that the TEC applied to all Member States (including their territories) was the category of Member State jurisdictions referred to collectively as the Overseas Countries and Territories (OCTs). For the OCTs listed in Annex IV of the 1957 Treaty, a special regime was envisaged. This regime was set out in Part Four of the Treaty, specifically Articles 131 to 136 inclusive. The detailed rules and procedure for the OCTs were set out in an Implementing Agreement annexed to the Treaty which was agreed for an initial period of 5 years. One general consequence of this special regime was that that it excluded the application to the OCTs of all other EU provisions not provided for in Part Four of the Treaty, for example, the Internal Market and Common Commercial Policy.

The OCTs were therefore not intended to be part of the EU and, with the exception of Articles 131 to 136 and the Implementing Convention, were considered to be in the position of third countries *vis à vis* the Community. This original limited perspective on the scope of EU law applying to the OCTs has developed and altered considerably since the text was drafted.

F. Murray, *The European Union and Member State Territories: A New Legal Framework Under the EU Treaties*, DOI: 10.1007/978-90-6704-826-2_5,

5.2 Relevant Member States and Territories

It has already been noted above that at the timing of the signing of the TEC in 1957, the dependent territories having special relations with a Member State fell into two broad categories—those forming part of the Member State (namely the French DOMs and Algeria) and those having less close ties with a Member State. For territories falling into the latter category, the special OCT regime was devised. The original territories were:

French:

- French West Africa comprising Senegal, French Sudan, French Guinea, Ivory Coast, Dahomey, Mauritania, Niger and Upper Volta;
- French Equatorial Africa comprising Middle Congo, Ubangi-Shari, Chad and Gabon;
- Saint Pierre et Miquelon, the Archipelago of the Comores, Madagascar and dependencies, the French Somali Coast, New Caledonia and dependencies, French settlements in Oceania and French Southern and Antarctic Territories;

French/British:

- Autonomous Republic of Togo
- The trust territory of the Cameroons under French administration
- The British/French condominium of the New Hebrides

Belgian:

- The Belgian Congo and Rwanda-Urundi

Italian:

- The trust territory of Somaliland under Italian administration

Dutch:

- Netherlands New Guinea

Interestingly, as regards the Dutch territories, Article 227(3) applied originally only to the Netherlands New Guinea. A protocol to the 1957 Treaty provided that the Netherlands could ratify the TEC on behalf of the Kingdom in Europe and the Netherlands New Guinea only, excluding other parts of the Kingdom, specifically the Netherlands Antilles and Surinam.[1] This protocol was added by reason of the constitutional structure of the Netherlands resulting from the Charter of 1954.[2]

---

[1] Protocol relative to the application of the TEC to the non-European parties of the Kingdom of the Netherlands (Netherlands Antilles and Surinam), 1957.

[2] The Charter (*statuut*) of the Kingdom of the Netherlands (*Statuutvoor het koninkrijk der Nederlanden*) entered into force on 31 December 1954 and instituted a new legal order for the Kingdom of the Netherlands.

Article 27 of the Charter provided that the Netherlands Antilles and Surinam should be consulted in the preparation of international agreements affecting them. And Article 25 provided that they could not be bound to international economic and financial agreements without their consent. As it was considered in 1957 that the economic repercussions of joining the EU were unclear, the Dutch Government made use of the Protocol and originally ratified the Treaty only for the Kingdom in Europe and for New Guinea. A Declaration of Intent, agreed by the six Member States at the signature of the TEC provided that the Member States were ready, at the request of the Dutch Government, to enter into negotiations with a view to concluding conventions for the economic association of the Netherlands Antilles and Surinam with the EU.

Eventually, both territories became part of the current OCT regime. This came about at different times and by different methods. By a statutory act (*Rijkswet*) of 19 July 1962, the Netherlands ratified the TEC on behalf of Surinam which brought about its association from 1 September 1962.[3] A different procedure was adopted for the Netherlands Antilles due to the concerns raised by the trade in natural oil products refined in the Antilles, which accounted for virtually all of its exports. Finally, a Protocol to the TEC was agreed which provided for duty free imports into the Community, subject to a safeguard clause, administered by the Commission under the control of the Council and the final supervision of the European Court of Justice (ECJ). By a Convention of 13 November 1962,[4] the 6 Member States amended the Treaty by adding the Netherlands Antilles to those overseas countries and territories of Annex IV to which the provisions of Part Four of the Treaty apply. This Convention also added to the Treaty the special Protocol on imports into the EU of Antillean refined oil products. After ratification of the Convention by all Member States, this association entered into force on 1 October 1964.[5]

5.3 Aims and Scope of Article 227(3)

The original version of Article 299(3) (ex Article 227(3)) contained just one paragraph which provided simply that the countries and overseas territories listed in Annex IV (now Annex II) were the subject of a special association defined in Part Four of the Treaty (Articles 131–136). Thus, Article 227(3) merely acted as a

---

[3] The TEC was ratified for Surinam by the Kingdom statute of 19 July 1962, *Staatsblad 1962, no. 285*; see also Hillebrink 2008, 336.

[4] Convention amending the TEC with a view to making applicable to the Netherlands Antilles the special regime of association defined in Part IV of the TEC, concluded at Brussels, 13 November 1962 (entered into force 1 October 1964) Trb. 1963, no.11; JO No. 2414/64, 1 October 1964.

[5] For more information on the background to the negotiations regarding the association of the Netherlands Antilles and Surinam to the Community, see Brinkhorst 1972.

means of integrating Part Four with the Annex relating to it. The main purpose of Part Four was to address the then new situation where the EU customs union would replace the existing bilateral trade arrangements with the former colonies. The broad objective of the new association—as stated in Article 131—was to improve the social and economic development of these countries and territories and to establish economic relations between them and the Community. The remaining provisions (Articles 132–136) focused on progressively dismantling customs duties.

At the time of the signing of the TEC in 1957 the Member States also concluded for a five year period an Implementing Agreement according to the former Article 136(1), setting out the details of the OCT regime. The agreement was an integral part of the TEC. It consisted of 17 articles and two annexes setting out the terms and conditions of the OCT arrangement. In particular, it stated (in Article 1) the Member States' commitment to promoting the social and economic development of the OCTs listed in Annex IV (now II) to the Treaty, set out measures regarding the right of establishment and trade and provided for the setting up of a development fund (the EDF) to which the Member States would contribute the amounts agreed and set out in an annex (Annex A to the Agreement) over a five year period, as follows: (Table 5.1)

Table 5.1 Annex A of the OCT Implementation Agreement, 1957

Percentages Member State	1st year 10%	2nd year 12.5%	3rd year 16.5%	4th year 22.5%	5th year 38.5%	Total 100%
Belgium	7	8.75	11.55	15.75	26.95	70
Germany	20	25	33	45	77	200
France	20	25	33	45	77	200
Italy	4	5	6.60	9	15.40	40
Luxembourg	0.125	0.15625	0.20625	0.28125	0.48125	1.25
Netherlands	7	8.75	11.55	15.75	26.95	70

* *In millions of ECU (UEP)*

5.4 Part Four (Articles 131–136), TEC 1957

At the time of the signing of the 1957 TEC, the detailed provisions governing the OCTs were set out in Part Four of the Treaty (dealing with the Association of the Overseas Countries and Territories) and in the Implementing Agreement annexed to the Treaty. The specific provisions of Part Four (Articles 131–136) will now be examined.[6] While a detailed analysis of these provisions is not considered necessary to the overall aims of this book, nevertheless it is important and useful to

[6] See Annex IV Part Four (Articles 131–136) TEC 1957.

review these provisions in the context of later developments and their relevance for territories and the EU today.

Article 131 in paragraph one establishes the broad framework of the EU—OCT association, naming the relevant Member States having overseas territories—Belgium, France, Italy and the Netherlands and referring to the list of relevant territories set out in Annex IV (see list above). Paragraph two sets out the overall objective of the association, namely to promote the economic and social development of the countries and territories and to deepen the economic relations between them and also with the Community as a whole. In particular, the third paragraph states that the primary aim of the association is to further the interests and prosperity of the inhabitants of the OCTs.

An important point to note is that, as the OCTs lack the qualities of statehood under international law and are represented in international affairs by their respective Member States, Part Four of the Treaty and implementation decisions of the EU Council are addressed, not to the OCTs, but to their Member States and to the EU.[7] However, the ECJ has recognized the competence of the OCTs' courts to request the ECJ to give a preliminary ruling under Article 234.[8] Moreover, the ECJ and the Court of First Instance (CFI) have often interpreted and applied Articles 182–188 (formerly Articles 131–136) as well as the implementation decisions under Article 187.[9]

The promotion of the "*economic and social development of the countries and territories*" referred to in Article 131, second paragraph is a general principle of EU development policy not just to OCTs but also to ACPs. The additional goal of establishing "close economic relations between them and the Community as a whole" showed that the existing close relations between the OCTs and their respective mother countries were intended to be extended to all Member States in line with the principle of non-discrimination.

The remaining provisions of Part Four dealt with trade and customs duties.

Article 132 set out the broad substance of the association. These included a guarantee by Member States to apply to their trade with the countries and territories the same treatment as they accord one another. Likewise, each country or territory undertook to apply to its trade with Member States the same treatment as it applied to the Member State with which it had its special relations. Member States undertook to contribute to the investments required for the progressive development of these countries and territories.

---

[7] Zimmerman 2004.

[8] Joined Cases C-100/89 and 101/89, *Peter Kaefer and Andréa Procacci v. French State,* [1990] ECR I-4647; Case C-260/90 *Bernard Leplat v. Territory of French Polynesia* [1992] ECR I-643.

[9] Case C-430/92 *Kingdom of the Netherlands v. Commission* [1994] ECR I-5197; Case C-310/95 *Road Air BV v. Inspecteur der Invoerrechten en Accijnzen,* [1997] ECR I-2229; Joined Cases T-480/93 and T-483/93 *Antillean Rice Mills NV, Trading & Shipping Co. Ter Beek BV, European Rice Brokers AVV, Alesie Curaçao NV and Guyana Investments AVV v. Commission* [1995] ECR II-2305; Joined Cases T-332/00 and T-350/00 *Rica Foods (Free Zone) NV and Free Trade Foods NV v. Commission* [2002] ECR II-4755; Oliver 2002, 337.

Article 132 also provided that in relations between the Member States and the countries and territories the right of establishment of nationals and companies or firms should be regulated according to the relevant provisions on right of establishment set out in the Treaty, subject to any special provisions pursuant to Article 136. The details of the right of establishment broadly provided that a Member State should treat individuals and companies from OCTs linked to other Member States on a non-discriminatory basis and that the OCTs should exercise the same principle of non-discrimination in respect of nationals and companies from Member States. In certain circumstances, however, in order to promote or support local employment, the OCTs could, with the agreement of the European Commission, derogate from the general rules on establishment in order to protect sensitive areas of the economy.

Article 133 provided that customs duties on imports from the OCTs to the Member States, and from the Member States or from other OCTs to OCTs were prohibited. OCTs could, however, impose customs duties which met the needs of their development and industrialisation or produced revenue for their budgets provided such duties did not exceed the level of duties imposed on imports of products from the Member State with which each OCT had a special relation.

Article 134 provided that if the level of duties applicable by OCTs to third country imports was liable (when the provisions of Article 133(1) prohibition of customs duties on imports from OCTs to Member States were applied), to cause defections of trade which were detrimental to any Member State, that Member State could ask the Commission to propose to the other Member States the measures needed to remedy the situation.

Article 135 provided that, subject to provisions relating to public health, public security or public policy, the free movement within the Member States of workers from the OCTs and within the OCTs of workers from the Member States should be governed by agreements to be concluded subsequently with the unanimous approval of Member States.

Article 136 provided that for the first five years after the TEC came into force, the detailed rules governing the associations would be set out in an Implementing Convention annexed to the Treaty. Before this Convention was due to expire, this Article further provided that the Council would adopt provisions for a further period based on both the experienced acquired and the principles set out in the Treaty.

5.5 Implementing Convention

Article 136 of the 1957 Treaty provided that the detailed provisions governing the new EU/OCT association would be set out in an Implementing Convention to apply initially for a 5 year period.[10] The following is the text of and commentary

[10] See Annex V *infra*, Implementing Convention on the Association of Overseas Countries and Territories of the Community, 1957.

regarding the provisions of this Convention. The Convention consisted of 17 articles and 2 annexes.

Article 1 provided for the setting up of a Development Fund for the OCTs (which would later become the EDF applicable also to ACPs). The original Fund was initially established for the 5 year period of the Convention into which all 6 Member States would contribute the amounts agreed and set out in Annex A (see above).

Articles 2 to 7 dealt with the social and economic projects in the OCTs to be financed by the EU.

Article 2 required those authorities responsible for the OCTs, in agreement with the OCTs themselves, to submit to the European Commission for financing social and economic projects. Under Article 3 the Commission would draw up annually general programmes for allocation to the different types of funds made available in Annex B to the Convention. Such programmes would concern projects for financing relating specifically to certain social institutions (e.g. hospitals, teaching institutions) and to economic investments in the public interest. Article 4 provided for the determination by the EU Council each year of the amount of funds to be devoted to these projects. Article 5 required the Commission to determine how the funds for these projects would be specifically allocated. Article 6 provided that the Council would lay down rules for the collection and transfer of financial contributions, for budgeting and administration of the resources of the Development Fund. The allocation of votes per Member State concerning the application of the provisions set out in Articles 4 to 6, were laid down in Article 7.

Article 8 concerned the right of establishment. It provided for the gradual extension to individuals and companies of Member States other than the Member State with which the OCT in question had special relations of the right of establishment in that OCT.

Article 9 confirmed that the customs treatment to be applied to trade between Member States and the OCTs should be that provided for in Articles 133 and 134 of the Treaty (see above).

Article 10 provided for the elimination of quantitative restrictions in trade between Member States and the OCTs.

Articles 11 and 12 concerned import quotas—broadly the opening up of global quotas without discrimination to all Member States.

Article 13 permitted the restriction or prohibition of quantitative restrictions on trade between the Member States and OCTs on certain grounds including public morality, policy or security.

Article 14 concerned quotas for imports into the OCTs and into the Member States in the period following the expiration of the Convention and until provisions for the ensuing period had been adopted.

Article 15 introduced tariff quotas for certain sensitive products, namely imports from third countries of raw coffee into Italy and the Benelux countries and of bananas into the Federal Republic of Germany.

Finally, Article 16 provided that Articles 1–8 of the Convention should apply to Algeria and the French DOMs.

5.6 Conclusions

The main purpose of Part Four (Articles 131–136) of the 1957 TEC was to replace the former Member State/territory bilateral customs arrangements with EU ones and to address the economic and social development of these territories. The Implementing Convention, setting out the detailed provisions of this arrangement, was the forerunner to the later Council Decisions. Thus, Article 227(3) merely established the Treaty framework for the EU/OCTs relationship providing that the special arrangements set out in Part Four of the Treaty would apply to the OCTs listed in Annex IV of the Treaty. For all other purposes, the OCTs were to be treated as third countries.

Article 227(3) and Part Four provided the same legal framework for all the Member State territories listed in Annex IV. The arrangement provided for no flexibility as regards those (later) territories such as Greenland and Bermuda which might have preferred other arrangements with the EU. Nor did this framework contain any inbuilt mechanism to accommodate departing or new territories on the Annex IV list.

An important point to note is that Article 227(3) and Part Four were drafted for mainly African French developing territories, hence the underlying objective of the original EU provisions, namely to promote the economic and social development of these territories. This original objective and group of territories contrast with those present day territories to which the equivalent provision, Article 355(2) TFEU now applies, that is mainly comparatively wealthier, developed mostly Caribbean territories. See Part II for a more detailed review of these territories.

Although some account has been taken of this overall status change, nevertheless the texts of Article 355(2) TFEU and Part Four have changed little since the original text and the EU/OCT relationship still falls somewhat incongruously under the EU's development policy framework even though most of the OCTs are no longer developing countries.

References

Brinkhorst L J (1972) Special Relationships and the European Communities: Netherlands Antilles and Surinam, British Institute of Studies in International and Comparative Law, No.6

Oliver P (2002) Case Law Note, 39 Common Market Law Review (2002) 337 (Joined Cases T-332/00 and T-350/00, *Rica Foods (Free Zone) NV and Free Trade Foods NV v. Commission*, [2002] ECR II4755)

Hillebrink S (2008) The Right to Self-Determination and Post-Colonial Governance, Cambridge University Press, at Chapter 9, p 336

Zimmerman (2004) Vorbemerkungen, Articles 182 bis 188 in H. Von der Groeben and J. Schwarze (eds), Kommentar zum Vertrag über die Europäische Union und zur Gründung der Europäische Gemeinschaft

Chapter 6
Article 227(4): European Member State Territories for Whose External Relations a Member State is Responsible

Abstract This chapter provides an introduction and background to the original version of the fourth paragraph of Article 227 TEC 1957, dealing with European Member State territories for whose external relations a Member State is responsible. The aims and scope of Article 227(4) are also examined. The chapter ends with some general conclusions to Part I and in particular some key points regarding the background to Article 227 TEC and how this impacted the present day EU Treaties framework governing relations between the EU and Member State territories.

6.1 Introduction and Background

Article 227(4) provided that the Treaty should apply to "the European territories for whose external relations a Member State is responsible". Put simply, this provision meant that for all territories in Europe for whose external relations an EU Member State took charge, that territory would fall within the scope of the TEC and would therefore form part of the EU in the same manner as its own Member State and all Member States.

There has been some confusion as to the origin and scope of Article 299(4). It might have been considered that the provision applied to San Marino, Monaco, Andorra and other similar small jurisdictions having strong ties with a Member State, but, as these are in fact independent countries managing their own foreign affairs, Article 227 (4) was not created with them in mind. Neither was the provision obviously not intended for the UK and Danish European territories (e.g. Channel Islands, Faroe Islands) as neither the UK nor Denmark were original signatories to the 1957 Treaty.

F. Murray, *The European Union and Member State Territories: A New Legal Framework Under the EU Treaties*, DOI: 10.1007/978-90-6704-826-2_6,

6.2 Relevant Member States and Territories

In fact, at the time when the TEC was signed in 1957 there were no European territories falling within the ambit of Article 227(4) with the possible exception of West Berlin.

One might have assumed that the European micro-states—Monaco, San Marino, the Vatican and Andorra—because of their close associations with EU Member States, might qualify as "European territories for whose external relations a Member State is responsible" under paragraph (4). It is well-established, however, that these micro-states are not covered by this paragraph.[1] All of them are independent States, rather than 'territories', and in no case is an EU Member State responsible for their external relations. Although Monaco (like San Marino and Andorra) is part of the EU customs territory, the Principality retains the capacity to conclude international treaties. Likewise, San Marino, though part of the EC customs territory, is responsible for its own external relations. Regarding the Vatican, the Holy See is also responsible for its own diplomatic relations. In the case of Andorra, co-sovereignty is exercised jointly by the French President and by the bishop of the Spanish town of Urgel. In the case of the French President, it is in his personal capacity, rather than as a representative of the French State that he exercises co-sovereignty. Therefore, it is not France, the EU Member State which assumes this role.[2]

It is worth reiterating that Article 227(4) refers only to 'European' territories for whose external relations a Member States is responsible. It did not therefore apply to non-European territories, like the territories of French West Africa, the French DOMs or the Belgian Congo which, as we have noted above, were covered by Article 227 (2) and (3).

6.3 Aims and Scope of Article 227(4)

Paragraph (4) appears to have derived, in fact, from the equivalent provision (Article 79) of the ECSC Treaty, signed in Paris in 1951.[3] At that time, it was still not clear whether Germany or France was responsible for the Saar region and the wording of Article 79 ECSC reflects this. Article 79 ECSC provided:

---

[1] European Commission Legal Service JUR/CEE/638/62, 16 March 1962, *Legal Status of Monaco, San Marino and Andorra vis à vis the EC*; European Commission Legal Service JUR/413/74, 18 February 1974, *Territorial application of the agreements signed by the Community with EFTA countries and certain Mediterranean countries*; European Commission Legal Service JUR(78)D/01681, 17 May 1978, *Territories of Member States to which the EC competition rules apply.*

[2] European Commission Legal Service JUR(88)D/4014, 22 June 1988, *Application territoriale de la directive proposée fondée sur l'Article 235 concernant le droit vote municipale—notamment Monaco, Andorre, Gibraltar*; see also Murray 2006.

[3] European Commission Note Interne—Article 227, 18 June 1970 concerning the application of Community law to San Marino; European Commission Legal Service JUR: 1086/69; 15 May 1969 on the scope of application of TEC competition rules.

> This Treaty shall apply to the European territories of the High Contracting Parties. It shall also apply to European territories for whose external relations a signatory State is responsible; as regards the Saar, an exchange of letters between the Government of the Federal Republic of Germany and the Government of the French Republic is annexed to the Treaty.

In an exchange of letters between Germany and France, both Governments acknowledged that signing the ECSC Treaty did not imply recognition of the then present status of the Saar. Both parties further acknowledged that the final status of the Saar could only be finally settled by the Peace Treaty or similar Treaty.[4]

On 1 January 1957 (thus before the signing of the Treaty of Rome establishing the European Economic Community (EEC) which took place in March 1957), the Saar became a German Land,[5] thereby resolving the issue as to which country (Germany or France) had jurisdiction for its external relations. Therefore, Article 227 (4) of the EEC Treaty never applied to Saar. The result was that, at the time of the signing of the TEC, Article 227(4) was in fact redundant as there was no specific territory to which the provision applied.

In addition to the Saar, Article 227(4) might also have applied to West Berlin which in 1957 was under the joint sovereignty of France, Great Britain, the Soviet Union and the United States. Thus, EU law applied to West Berlin only until German reunification in 1990.

6.4 Conclusions

In conclusion, it is incongruent that the anomaly of Article 227(4) was not spotted at the time the 1957 Treaty was signed. The oversight was perhaps due to the short time span between the resolution of the status of the Saar region and the signing of the Treaty, a period of just two months. Or, perhaps it was felt that the provision should remain to cover possibly other European territories for whose external relations a Member State was responsible—as it was used later in relation to Gibraltar.

Nevertheless, the fact that subparagraph (4) at the outset did not apply to any Member State territories (with the possible exception of Berlin) created an imbalance from the beginning with subparagraph (1) which, by implication, was intended to apply to all Member State territories including "European territories for whose external relations a Member State is responsible".

---

[4] Exchange of Letters between the Government of the Federal Republic of Germany and the Government of the French Republic concerning the Saar, Treaty establishing the European Coal and Steel Community (ECSC), 1951.

[5] *Traité sur la Sarre du 29 octobre 1956; Gesetz uber die Eingliederung des Saarlandes vom 23 Juni 1956.*

6.5 General Conclusions to Part I

The objective of Article 227 was to set out in broad terms the territorial scope of the Treaty. Subparagraph (1) established the scope by reference to the Member States with no specific mention of its territories. One could infer therefore—despite the suggestion to the contrary made by the Commission in response to the status of French Clipperton Island (see later discussion on Clipperton Island in Part II)—that the Treaty was intended to apply to all Member State territories unless otherwise provided in specific terms. The very existence of subparagraphs (2) to (4) setting out the exceptions to subparagraph (1) would seem to support this inclusive interpretation. However, the implicit reference to all Member State territories in subparagraph (1) has never been confirmed.

The exceptions were made at the request of France for its two categories of territories: those forming an integral part of France, namely the DOMs and Algeria (subparagraph (2)), and those territories with less close ties to France. In addition to France, Belgium, Italy and the Netherlands also had territories falling into this category. Subparagraph (3) covering the OCT regime was created to address these countries. The specificity of both these subparagraphs for particular Member State territories with specific constitutional relations with their Member State at a particular time created a legal framework that was ill-suited to accommodating new future territories with different arrangements.

Finally, it has been noted that subparagraph (4) of Article 277 was probably redundant when the TEC was signed and did not apply to any specific territory until the UK—and Gibraltar—joined some 15 years later. Despite its ongoing application to Gibraltar, this book maintains that subparagraph (4) is still redundant as Gibraltar would automatically have been considered to be part of the EU by virtue of Article 227(1). Thus, subparagraph (4) was always and still is surplus to requirements.

In general, therefore, Article 227 was intended to apply in the broadest terms with some specific derogations for overseas territories. Subparagrah (4) made it clear that Member States' European territories were deemed also to be part of the EU.

Reference

Murray F (2006) Micro-states (Andorra, Monaco, San Marino and the Vatican City), in Blockmans S and Lazowski A (eds) The European Union and its Neighbours, The Hague, TMC Asser Press

Part II
Article 299 and Lisbon Treaty Amendments, Comparison with 1957

Chapter 7
General Introduction to Article 299 TEC

Abstract This chapter provides a general introduction to Article 299 TEC (just before the current Lisbon Treaty version entered into force). A comparison is made with the corresponding provisions of the original Article 227 TEC 1957, set against the different political and economic backdrop of the present day.

Box 7.1 Article 299 TEC

Article 299

1. *This Treaty shall apply to the Kingdom of Belgium, the Republic of Bulgaria, the Czech Republic, the Kingdom of Denmark, the Federal Republic of Germany, the Republic of Estonia, the Hellenic Republic, the Kingdom of Spain, the French Republic, Ireland, the Italian Republic, the Republic of Cyprus, the Republic of Latvia, the Republic of Lithuania, the Grand Duchy of Luxembourg, the Republic of Hungary, the Republic of Malta, the Kingdom of the Netherlands, the Republic of Austria, the Republic of Poland, the Portuguese Republic, Romania, the Republic of Slovenia, the Slovak Republic, the Republic of Finland, the Kingdom of Sweden and the United Kingdom of Great Britain and Northern Ireland.*[1]
2. *The provisions of this Treaty shall apply to the French overseas departments, the Azores, Madeira and the Canary Islands.*

However, taking account of the structural social and economic situation of the French overseas departments, the Azores, Madeira and the Canary

[1] As amended most recently by Article 17 of the Act of Accession of Bulgaria and Romania to the EU, OJ L157/209 21 June 2005.

F. Murray, *The European Union and Member State Territories: A New Legal Framework Under the EU Treaties*, DOI: 10.1007/978-90-6704-826-2_7,

Islands, which is compounded by their remoteness, insularity, small size, difficult topography and climate, economic dependence on a few products, the permanence and combination of which severely restrain their development, the Council, acting by a qualified majority on a proposal from the Commission and after consulting the European Parliament, shall adopt specific measures aimed, in particular, at laying down the conditions of application of the present Treaty to those regions, including common policies.

The Council shall, when adopting the relevant measures referred to in the second subparagraph, take into account areas such as customs and trade policies, fiscal policy, free zones, agriculture and fisheries policies, conditions for supply of raw materials and essential consumer goods, State aids and conditions of access to Structural Funds and to horizontal Community programmes.

The Council shall adopt the measures referred to in the second subparagraph taking into account the special characteristics and constraints of the Outermost Regions without undermining the integrity and the coherence of the Community legal order, including the internal market and common policies.

3. *The special arrangements for association set out in Part Four of this Treaty shall apply to the overseas countries and territories listed in Annex II to this Treaty.*

This Treaty shall not apply to those overseas countries and territories having special relations with the United Kingdom of Great Britain and Northern Ireland which are not included in the aforementioned list.

4. *The provisions of this Treaty shall apply to the European territories for whose external relations a Member State is responsible.*
5. *The provisions of this Treaty shall apply to the Åland Islands in accordance with the provisions set out in Protocol No. 2 to the Act concerning the conditions of accession of the Republic of Austria, the Republic of Finland and the Kingdom of Sweden.*
6. *Notwithstanding the preceding paragraphs:*

(a) *this Treaty shall not apply to the Faroe Islands;*

(b) *This Treaty shall not apply to the United Kingdom Sovereign Base Areas of Akrotiri and Dhekelia in Cyprus except to the extent necessary to ensure the implementation of the arrangements set out in the Protocol on the Sovereign Base Areas of the United Kingdom of Great Britain and Northern Ireland in Cyprus annexed to the Act concerning the conditions of accession of the Czech Republic, the Republic of Estonia, the Republic of Cyprus, the Republic of Latvia, the Republic of Lithuania, the Republic of Hungary, the Republic of Malta, the Republic of*

Poland, the Republic of Slovenia and the Slovak Republic to the European Union and in accordance with the terms of that Protocol[2]*;*

(c) *this Treaty shall apply to the Channel Islands and the Isle of Man only to the extent necessary to ensure the implementation of the arrangements for those islands set out in the Treaty concerning the accession of new Member States to the European Economic Community and to the European Atomic Energy Community signed on 22 January 1972.*

7.1 Introduction to Article 299 TEC

Part II of this publication will focus on the structure and content of Article 299 TEC as it existed at the end of 2009.[3] This first chapter will present a general overview of the main changes to Article 299 set against the present economic and political backdrop compared to that in 1957 when the original version of Article 299 (ex 227) was drafted. The ensuing chapters will examine the individual paragraphs of Article 299 and compare each with the original version, where applicable.

The major amendments to each paragraph will be examined including those introduced by the Lisbon Treaty.

In addition, each of the main territories or groups of territories concerned will be reviewed, specifically their geography, history, economy, Constitutional relations with their Member State, legal framework governing their relations with the EU. This territorial review will help us in Part III to judge the merits or otherwise of the present Treaties framework for these territories and help to define a new model provision which might act as a more adequate framework for Member State territories' relations with the EU in the light of the many changes since 1957.

7.2 Political and Economic Backdrop Today (Compared with 1957)

The political and economic backdrop to the TEC—and indeed to the present EU Treaties framework—has altered considerably since the founding of the TEC in 1957. The major changes included:

- the end of the cold war between east and west which, in addition to the two world wars, had been one of the driving forces behind the original Treaty
- an expanded Union from the original 6 to 27 States today with the ensuing greater variety and breadth of cultural and language differences

[2] As amended by the Cyprus Act of Accession, OJ L236, 23 September 2003.

[3] See Annex VI *infra*, Article 299 TEC 2009.

– a deepening union. Following completion of the single market in 1993 of people, goods, services and capital, the Treaty underwent a number of major amendments (e.g. Maastricht, Amsterdam, Lisbon) and Member States have focused their attention in broadening out the union to encompass other areas including the environment and security and defence.

These major changes in the overall political and economic landscape of today compared with 1957 are also reflected in the altered position of Member State territories. The process of decolonization started in the 1950s continued in subsequent decades so that today most of the original territories to which the original Article 227 applied have since gained independence and many of these now fall under the EU/ACP development framework. In addition, with accession of new Member States came new territories which demanded alternative solutions to the original Article 227 framework. As we shall note, the Article 227 was adapted and amended piecemeal to cater to these new territories.

7.3 Article 299 Compared with 1957 Original Version

The following are some general comparisons between the pre Lisbon Treaty Article 299 and the original version. A detailed comparison of each of the paragraphs of Article 299 and those of the 1957 version will be carried out in the ensuing chapters.

The first obvious difference between Article 299 compared with the 1957 version is in the number of paragraphs. In general, the Article refers to more Member States and to some of the same but also to many new territories. Whereas the original had just 4 paragraphs, the pre-Lisbon Treaty version had 6 paragraphs. Broadly, per paragraph the changes are as follows:

Article 299(1) refers to more Member States, now 27, with Bulgaria and Romania, compared to the original 6 Member States and to more territories.

Article 299(2) refers, in addition to the French DOMS, the Azores, Madeira and Canary Islands, now collectively known as the Outermost Regions for which the Community has developed a special policy regime. This compares with the 1957 versions which referred only to the DOMs and Algeria, the latter has since gained its independence and thus no longer falls within Article 299(2) or the corresponding provision under the Lisbon Treaty.

Unlike paragraph (2), the wording of Article 299(3) (and of Part Four of the Treaty to which Article 299(3) refers) has virtually remained unchanged from the original version as drafted, except for the additional subparagraph, added as the result of UK accession, which provides that the Treaty shall not apply to those UK OCTs not appearing in the list in Annex II. Obviously, as we shall see later, the list of territories and the relevant Member States has altered both as the result of the accession of new Member States, but also as certain territories gained their independence.

The one paragraph of Article 299 which has remained unchanged in its entirety as reflected in 1957 is Article 299(4). As noted, the provision in fact was redundant

Table 7.1 Relevant Member States today compared to 1957

1957 Member States		2011 Member States
Belgium		Belgium
Germany		Germany
France		France
Italy		Italy
Luxembourg		Luxembourg
Netherlands		Netherlands
	1972	
		UK
		Ireland
		Denmark
	1979	
		Greece
	1985	
		Spain
		Portugal
		1994
		Austria
		Finland
		Sweden
	2004	
		Czech Republic
		Estonia
		Cyprus
		Latvia
		Lithuania
		Hungary
		Malta
		Poland
		Slovenia
	2007	
		Bulgaria
		Romania

at the outset since no European territory fell within its ambit in 1957. Since then, Article 299(4) has been applied to just one territory—Gibraltar—and even in that case, the application was qualified.

To the original 4 paragraphs of Article 299, were added two more, both of which emerged as the result of the accession of new Member States: Article 299(5) applicable to the Finnish Aland Islands, and Article 299(6) concerning those European Member State territories to which the Treaty does not apply, namely the Danish Faroe Islands and the UK Sovereign Base Areas in Cyprus as well as the Crown Dependencies (The list of EU Member States today compared to 1957 shown in Table 7.1).

It is useful, not only to compare today's list of relevant territories with those of 1957, but also to include the original list of UK territories when it joined the

Table 7.2 Relevant territories today compared to 1957

1957 MS territories	1972 UK MS territories	2010[4] MS territories
		Article 299(1) - Ceuta and Melilla
Article 227(2) - French Overseas Departments (Guadeloupe, Martinique, French Guiana, Réunion) - French Algeria	**Article 227(2)** Not applicable	**Article 299(2) (Outermost Regions)** - French Overseas Departments Guadeloupe, Martinique, French Guiana, Réunion) - Portuguese Azores and Madeira - Spanish Canary Islands
Article 227(3) (OCTs) - French West Africa comprising Senegal, French Sudan, French Guinea, Ivory Coast, Dahomey, Mauritania, Niger and Upper Volta; - French Equatorial Africa comprising Middle Congo, Ubangi-Shari, Chad and Gabon; - Saint Pierre et Miquelon, the Archipelago of the Comores, Madagascar and dependencies, the French Somali Coast, New Caledonia and dependencies, French settlements in Oceania and French Southern and Antarctic Territories; - Autonomous Republic of Togo - The trust territory of the Cameroons under French administration - The Belgian Congo and Rwanda-Urundi - The trust territory of Somaliland under Italian administration - Netherlands New Guinea	**Article 227(3) (UK OCTs)** - The Bahamas - Bermuda - British Antarctic Territory - British Honduras - British Indian Ocean Territory - British Solomon Islands - British Virgin Islands - Brunei - Associated States in the Caribbean: Antigua, Dominica, Grenada, St Lucia, St Vincent, St Kitts-Nevis-Anguilla - Cayman Islands - Central and Southern Line Islands - Falkland Islands and Dependencies - Gilbert and Ellice Islands - Montserrat - Pitcairn - St Helena and - Dependencies - The Seychelles - Turks and Caicos Islands	**Article 299(3) (OCTs)** - Danish Greenland - French New Caledonia and Dependencies - French Polynesia - French Southern and Antarctic Territories - French Wallis and Futuna Islands, - French Mayotte, - French Saint Pierre and Miquelon - Dutch Aruba, - Dutch Antilles comprising Bonaire, Curaçao, Saba, Sint Eustatius, Sint Maarten - British Anguilla, - British Cayman Islands, - British Falkland Islands, - British South Georgia and the South Sandwich Islands, - British - Montserrat, - British Pitcairn,

[4] The list is by reference to the pre Lisbon Treaty Article 299 TEC framework. However, the only changes to the list of territories and Member States effected under the Lisbon Treaty were the specific mention of Saint Barthélemy and Saint Martin in the list of Outermost Regions

(continued)

Table 7.2 (continued)

1957 MS territories	1972 UK MS territories	2010[4] MS territories
		- British Saint Helena and Dependencies, - British Antarctic Territory, - British Indian Ocean Territory, - British Turks and Caicos Islands, - British Virgin Islands, - Bermuda
Article 227(4)	**Article 299(4)**	**Article 299(4)**
Redundant—no applicable territories	Gibraltar	Gibraltar
		Article 299(5)
		Finnish AlandIs lands
	Article 299(6)	**Article 299(6)**
	UK SBAs in Cyprus	Danish Faroe Islands
	UK Channel Islands and Isle of Man	UK SBAs in Cyprus
		UK Channel Islands and Isle of Man

Community in 1972 since the UK was not a member in 1957 and, like France, had several territories when it acceded to the EU, many of which have since gained independence (Table 7.2).

In summary, the territories to which Article 299 TEC and the current Lisbon Treaty framework applies today are:

I. Outermost Regions:

- French Overseas Departments (Guadeloupe, Martinique, French Guiana, Réunion, Saint Barthélemy, Saint Martin)
- Portuguese Azores and Madeira
- Spanish Canary Islands

II. Overseas Countries and Territories:

- Danish Greenland
- French New Caledonia and Dependencies, French Polynesia, French Southern and Antarctic Territories, Wallis and Futuna Islands, Mayotte, Saint Pierre and Miquelon
- Dutch Aruba, Netherlands Antilles comprising Bonaire, Curaçao, Saba, Sint Eustatius, Sint Maarten
- British Anguilla, Cayman Islands, Falkland Islands, South Georgia and the South Sandwich Islands, Montserrat, Pitcairn, Saint Helena and Dependencies, British Antarctic Territory, British Indian Ocean Territory, Turks and Caicos Islands, British Virgin Islands, Bermuda

III. Other territories:

- Spanish Ceuta and Melilla
- British Gibraltar
- Finnish Aland Islands
- Danish Faroe Islands
- British UK SBAs in Cyprus
- British Channel Islands and Isle of Man

7.4 Conclusions

From this initial overview of territories falling under the Article 299 and the Lisbon Treaty framework, it is immediately apparent that there is a sizeable change today both in the backdrop to the original version of Article 299, political, economic and social, and in the number and variety of territories falling within that framework.

Despite this new landscape, no attempt has been made to review and adapt the present EU Treaties provisions in order to create a dynamic, modern framework for relations between the EU and Member State territories of today.

Chapter 8
Article 299(1): Territorial Scope of the TEC (as Compared with 1957 Version)

Abstract This chapter provides an introduction to the first paragraph of Article 299 TEC, dealing with the territorial scope of the Treaty, just before entry into force of the corresponding Lisbon Treaty provision. The key developments since 1957 relevant to this paragraph are examined, including Member State accessions, main Treaty amendments including key amendments introduced by the Lisbon Treaty. The only relevant Member State territories falling under this provision are the Spanish enclaves of Ceuta and Melilla. An overview of these territories is given including their constitutional relationship with Spain and the legal framework governing relations between these territories and the EU.

8.1 Introduction (Comparison to 1957 Version)

There has been little change to the wording of Article 299(1) (repealed under the Lisbon Treaty and effectively replaced by Article 52(1) TEU) since the original 1957 version of the provision. The text still refers to the Member States and there is again no specific mention of territory. One may deduce therefore that that the same general intention of the drafters of the original version remains, namely that Article 299(1) provides that the Treaty applies to all Member States and their territories, save where otherwise provided. One notable development, however, from the original provision is the addition of many more Member States. As we will see in the following chapters this addition, along with new Member State territories requiring special treatment under the Treaty, has resulted in an interesting, if not entirely consistent, evolution of Article 299 in general.

F. Murray, *The European Union and Member State Territories: A New Legal Framework Under the EU Treaties*, DOI: 10.1007/978-90-6704-826-2_8,

8.2 Relevant Member States and Territories

Compared to 1957 when there were only 6 Member States and a small number of Member State territories, today, the equivalent provision, Article 52(1) TEU, refers to 27 Member States. In practice, however, the only territories (as defined in this thesis) that appear to be covered by this provision exclusively today are the Spanish enclaves of Ceuta and Melilla and possibly also the French Clipperton Island and Scattered Islands of the Indian Ocean. All the remaining Member State territories are subject to special conditions and derogations, whether they are part of the EU broadly or not, set out in Articles 349 (Outermost Regions) and 352 TFEU.

As Ceuta and Melilla are currently the only territories covered exclusively by Article 52(1),[1] it is worth reviewing at this point their EU Treaty framework and relations with the EU.

8.2.1 Ceuta and Melilla

Ceuta and Melilla are Spanish enclaves situated on the northern coast of Morocco. They have been part of Spain since the sixteenth and fifteenth centuries respectively. In 1995 Ceuta and Melilla became autonomous communities in Spain. As autonomous communities, Ceuta and Melilla are broadly responsible for their own health, education and infrastructure, whilst the Spanish central government retains overall competence in matters of international affairs, defence, monetary policy and other general matters.

Relations between Ceuta/Melilla and the EU are governed principally by Article 25 of the Spanish Act of Accession and by Protocol No. 2 of that Treaty. In general, these territories are part of the EU with some notable exceptions. Thus, Ceuta and Melilla are not part of the Community customs territory and EU provisions on free movement of goods, the Common Commercial Policy, EU fisheries and agricultural policies do not generally apply to these territories. Until 1991, the above Treaty provisions applied equally to the Canary Islands. In 1991, however, with the adoption of Regulation 1911/91, the Canary Islands agreed to become gradually incorporated into the EU.[2]

Geography: Ceuta is a city, military port and free port situated on a narrow isthmus which connects Mount Hacho to the mainland. The city covers an area of 20 square kilometres and has a population of approximately 75,000. Bordered by Morocco, the city is an enclave of Spain and is governed as part of Cadiz province in Spain.

Melilla, a town and also a military base, is situated on the eastern side of the Cap des Trois Fourches, a rocky peninsula that extends some 40 kilometres into

---

[1] With the possible exception of French Clipperton Island and the French Scattered Islands of the Indian Ocean (see in particular Section 10.5 *infra*).

[2] See further Chapter 9 *infra* on the Outermost Regions.

the Mediterranean Sea. Melilla covers an area of approximately 12 square kilometres and has a population of around 60,000. Melilla is administered by the Spanish province of Malaga.

Close to 80% of the residents of Ceuta and Melilla are Spanish, with much of the rest being Moroccan. Residents of Indian descent comprise about 1% of the population. Both Spanish and Moroccan are widely spoken, however, Spanish is the predominate language of business and government.

Economy: the status of Ceuta and Melilla as free ports and their economies are based almost entirely on trade and services, notably related to tourism.

History: Ceuta and Melilla have a long history. Both cities date their original establishment to the Phoenicians, the sailors and merchants of the ancient Mediterranean. Ceuta has been colonized in turn by the Carthaginians, the Greeks and the Romans. It gained independence under the Byzantine governor Count Julian. Due to its commercial importance in ivory, gold and slaves, Ceuta was the subject of continuous dispute until Portugal took it over in 1415. It came under Spanish rule in 1580. Since that time, except for a period from 1694 to 1720 when the Moors gained control, the enclave has remained a jurisdiction of Spain and was assigned to Spain under the Treaty of Lisbon in 1688.

Melilla's history is quite similar. It, too, was established by the Phoenicians and was subsequently ruled by the Carthaginians, Romans, Byzantines and various Berber dynasties until it was conquered by Spain in 1497. By the Treaty of August 1859, ratified in the Peace Treaty of 1860, Melilla officially became Spanish territory.

In 1956, when Spain handed over most of northern Morocco to the newly independent kingdom, it retained Ceuta, Melilla and some uninhabited islands off the Moroccan coast, including the Island of Perejil.

The government of Morocco has called for the integration of Ceuta and Melilla, along with uninhabited islands such as Isla Perejil, into its national territory, drawing comparisons with Spain's territorial claim to Gibraltar. The Spanish government and both Ceuta's and Melilla's autonomous governments and inhabitants reject these comparisons on the ground that both Ceuta and Melilla are integral parts of the Spanish state whereas Gibraltar, a British Overseas Territory, is not nor ever has been part of the UK. Morocco still lays claim to both Ceuta and Melilla and, consequently, these territories have been a continuing source of tension between Spain and Morocco.

8.2.1.1 Constitutional Relations with Spain

In 1995, the Spanish Government approved the Statutes of Autonomy for Ceuta and Melilla, thus replacing the cities' councils with legislatives assemblies similar to those of Spain's other autonomous communities. Ceuta is administered as part of the province of Cadiz which in turn is part of the autonomous region of Andalusia. Melilla is administered as part of the province of Malaga. The Statues of Autonomy delimit and define the competences of the institutions and the resources of both cities.

Ceuta and Melilla each have their own legislative Assembly, President and Council. The Assembly, the representative organ of the government has 25 directly elected members. The Assembly holds ordinary sessions at least once per month. Extraordinary sessions are held if either the President or at least a quarter of the Assembly decides to do so.

The President presides over the Assembly and the Council, directing and co-ordinating their activities. He is also mayor of the city and is elected by members of the Assembly and nominated by the King of Spain.

The Council is the executive and administrative arm of government. It oversees the policies of the region and implements the standards agreed by the Assembly regarding the executive of administrative services in the region.

The autonomous regions of Ceuta and Melilla have competences over a broad range of policies and matters including:

- The organization and functioning of their governments
- Promotion of economic development
- Local police
- Environmental protection
- Consumer protection
- Transport
- Culture
- Press and Media

For all matters not specifically allocated to Ceuta and Melilla under their Statutes of Autonomy, the Spanish Government has responsibility. These include defence, foreign affairs and economic and fiscal policy. In addition, each city has representatives in the Spanish Parliament.

8.2.1.2 Legal Framework Governing Relations Between Ceuta and Melilla and the EU

Relations between Ceuta and Melilla, on the one hand, and the EU, on the other, are governed principally by Article 25 of the Spanish Act of Accession and by Protocol No. 2 of that Treaty. In general, these territories are part of the EU with some notable exceptions. Thus, Ceuta and Melilla are not part of the Community customs territory and EU provisions on free movement of goods, the Common Commercial Policy, EU fisheries and agricultural policies do not generally apply to these territories. Until 1991, the above Treaty provisions applied equally to the Canary Islands. In 1991, however, with the adoption of Regulation 1911/91, the Canary Islands agreed to become gradually incorporated into the EU.[3]

---

[3] Council Regulation 1911/91 of 26 June 1991 on the application of the provisions of Community law to the Canary Islands, OJL171/1, 29 June 1991.

Article 25 of the Spanish Act of Accession[4] provides, in paragraph 1, that the Treaties and acts of the institutions of the European Communities shall apply to Ceuta and Melilla, subject to the derogations set out in paragraphs 2 and 3.

Paragraph 2 provides that the conditions governing the application to Ceuta and Melilla of Treaty provisions on free movement of goods, customs and the common commercial policy are set out in Protocol No. 2 to the Spanish Act of Accession. Protocol No. 2 broadly provides that, subject to certain exceptions, Ceuta and Melilla are excluded from the Treaty provisions on free movement of goods, customs and the common commercial policy (see below).

Paragraph 3 of Article 25 provides that, subject to Article 155 of the Spanish Act of Accession, the Treaty provisions regarding agriculture and fisheries do not apply to Ceuta and Melilla. Paragraph 3 goes on to provide, however, that certain provisions of a socio-structural nature within the field of agriculture may be applicable to Ceuta and Melilla.

Article 155 of the Spanish Act of Accession provides that, although the common fisheries policy does not apply to Ceuta and Melilla, the Council may adopt structural measures in favour of those territories and shall take account of their interests regarding negotiations on fisheries agreements with third countries and international conventions on fisheries.

Article 1 of Protocol No. 2 excludes Ceuta and Melilla from the Community's customs territory.[5] It thus provides that products originating in Ceuta and Melilla or imported there and re-exported to the Community are not deemed to fulfill the conditions in Articles 23 and 24 TEC (now Articles 28 and 29 TFEU) for goods to be in free circulation in the Community. Thus, Article 1 further provides that Community customs legislation for foreign trade applies to trade between the customs territory of the Community and Ceuta and Melilla. In effect, as regards trade with the Community, Ceuta and Melilla are therefore treated as third countries. Finally, Article confirms that the Community's common commercial policy, except where otherwise provided for in the Protocol, does not apply to Ceuta and Melilla.

Article 2 provides, subject to Articles 3 and 4 of the Protocol (dealing respectively with fishery and agricultural products), for exemption from customs duties in respect of products originating in Ceuta and Melilla. This exemption applied for such products entering Spain from January 1, 1986. As regards the import of these products into the rest of the Community, Article 2 provided for the progressive abolition of customs duties.

Articles 3 and 4 set out provisions regarding the free movement of specific fishery and agricultural products. They provide for exemption from customs duties for such products originating in Ceuta and Melilla when entering Spain and the rest of the Community, subject to certain conditions.

---

4 See Annex VII *infra*, Article 25 Spanish Act of Accession 1985 (Ceuta and Melilla).

5 See Annex VIII *infra* Protocol No. 2 Spanish Act of Accession 1985 (Ceuta and Melilla).

Article 5 contains safeguard provisions in cases where the import into the EU of products originating in Ceuta and Melilla may harm Community producers.

Article 6 provides for the progressive abolition of existing customs duties and charges having equivalent effect in Ceuta and Melilla in respect of products originating in the Community.

Article 7 provides that imports into Ceuta and Melilla from a third country must be accorded treatment no less favourable than that applied by the Community in its international commitments or preferential arrangements with that third country, provided that the same third country grants to imports from Ceuta and Melilla the same treatment as that which it grants to the Community. In concrete terms this means that imports into Ceuta and Melilla from third countries must be treated at least as favourably (in terms of customs duties, charges having equivalent effect and trade arrangements) as imports from that third country into the Community as long as that third country treats imports from Ceuta and Melilla the same treatment as it applies to imports from the Community. Article 7 adds that the trade arrangements applied to imports from third countries into Ceuta and Melilla may not be more favourable that those applied to imports into Ceuta and Melilla from the Community.

Article 8 provides that the trade arrangements applicable to goods between the Canary Islands, on the one hand, and Ceuta and Melilla, on the other, shall be at least as favourable as those applicable to Article 6.

Article 9 required the Commission to adopt, before March 1, 1986, the rules for the application of Protocol No. 2, in particular the rules of origin and those concerning, *inter alia*, the marketing and labeling of products.

For Ceuta and Melilla the main benefit of their relationship with the EU is economic. Both cities are treated as Phasing-out regions for the purposes of the EU Structural Funds. A phasing-out system is granted to those regions which would have been eligible for funding under the Convergence objective if the threshold of 75% of Gross Domestic Product (GDP) had been calculated for the EU at 15 and not at 25 Member States.

a) CEUTA: Under the current programme (which runs from 2007–2013), **Ceuta** receives EUR 72,5 million, of which EUR 54.911.762 comes from the European Regional Development Fund (ERDF) and EUR 17,6 million from the European Social Fund (ESF).[6]

b) MELILLA: Under the current programme (which runs from 2007–2013), **Melilla** receives EUR 66,9 million and EUR 14.275.607 from the ESF.[7]

---

[6] Source: European Commission DG Regional Policy.

[7] Ibid.

8.3 Article 299 (1): Developments Since 1957, Including Treaty Amendments

8.3.1 Clarification of the Aims and Scope of Article 299(1)

It was noted briefly in Part I that Article 299(1) defines the geographical scope of the Treaty by reference to the Member States. Thus, the determination of a territory's status under EU law is primarily by reference to its constitutional relationship with its Member State. This interpretation was later supported by the ECJ in *Hansen*.[8] It also explains why, for example, when Germany expanded in1990 to incorporate the five *Länder* of the former East Germany, no amendment of the TEC (including Article 299) was considered necessary.

It has been noted[9] that this broad general territorial application of the TEC was not by chance and that it is in line with the general spirit of the Treaty and its objective and that it carries specific legal implications: firstly, by its very general application, Article 299(1) recalls one of the fundamental principles of the Treaty, namely that Member States, as a general rule, are responsible for the application of the Treaty *vis à vis* the Community.[10] Secondly, the provision conforms to the nature of the TEC itself which is a framework treaty covering the broad spectrum of economic and social activities of the Member States, certain of which e.g. fisheries, commercial activities, the environment, can be regulated by general rules without reference to a specific territorial field of application.

Thus, it can be said that the scope of the Treaty established in Article 299(1) refers not simply to a strictly territorial principle, but is a more general principle concerning the field of application of Community law and the law of Member States.

8.3.2 Meaning of Territory

Aside from listing the 6 Member States of the Community, Article 227(1) did not define the meaning of territory. Subsequent commentary and case law have shed more light on the meaning of territory. It is useful here in Part II to reflect briefly on some of the main points of these early clarifications.

---

[8] Case 148/77 *H. Hansen jun & O.C. Balle GmbH & Co v. Hauptzollamt Flensburg* [1978] ECR 1787.

[9] For example, Megret 1987.

[10] Note for example Article 10 TEC (replaced in substance by Article 4, paragraph 3 TEU), which provides, *inter alia*, "Member States shall take all appropriate measures.....to ensure fulfilment of the obligations arising out of this Treaty or resulting from actions taken by the institutions of the Community...".

8.3.3 Application to Member State Territories

The EU Council of Ministers, in a 1979 speech by the then Director General of the Council's Legal Service, Mr. Jean-Louis Dewost, stated its view that Article 227(1) should be interpreted broadly to infer that the Treaty should be applied not only to the Member States themselves including their airspace, maritime waters and ground but also to "any place where the Member States exert, according to international law certain 'sovereign rights', however limited".[11] This interpretation, argued the Council, follows not only the letter of the same article (which refers to the States and not to their territories) but also the same nature of a framework treaty which potentially concerns all economic and social activities of States.

Despite this statement by the EU Council, the European Commission, in a response to a written question to the European Parliament in 1984 on the status *vis à vis* the EU of French Clipperton Island, seems to have taken a narrower view. Specifically, the Commission took the view that territories which were not explicitly listed as one of the territories under Article 227 (2) or (3) TEC fell outside the Treaty.[12]

Thus, there remains uncertainty as to the status of territories not specifically mentioned in the Treaty and by implication the intended scope of Article 299(1).

8.3.4 The Two Germanys

One early problem of interpretation, now resolved by German unification, was the application of the Treaty to the three former German territories—the Federal Republic (West Germany), the Democratic Republic (East Germany) and West Berlin. The Basic German Law (Constitution) applied to West Germany, not at all in East Germany and regarded West Berlin as the eleventh *Land* of West Germany. When the Treaty of Rome was concluded, West Germany attached a Declaration to the Final Act of the Rome Conference reserving the right to extend the Treaty to West Berlin at the time of ratification. Although the TEC did not apply to East Germany, West Germany regarded trade between the two Germanys as German internal trade. In view of this, a *Protocol on German Internal Trade and*

---

[11] Dewost 1979: Full text in French of phrase : « *L'article 227 par.1 du Traité et le droit dériveé, s'applique non seulement sur le territoire des Etats membres, avec ses prolongements aériens, maritimes (mer territoriale) et de sous-sol, mais en outre en tout lieu où les Etats exercent, selon le droit international, certains « droits souverains » même limités. Ceci résulte, non seulement de la lettre même de l'article (qui se réfère aux Etats e non a leurs territoires) mais également de la nature même d'un Traité-cadre qui concerne potentiellement l'ensemble des activités économiques et sociales des Etats.* »

[12] Written Question No 1007/84, OJ C62/34, 11 March 1985 by John Ford to the Commission: the status of Clipperton Island.

Connected Problems was appended to the TEC stating that trade between both Germanys should be considered as internal trade but permitted safeguard measures to prevent this trade disrupting the common market. The ECJ also made it clear that the Protocol did not have the result of making East Germany part of the Community but only that a special system applied to it as a territory which was not part of the Community.[13]

8.3.5 EU Customs Territory

Another issue that arose as a result of the absence of a precise definition of the territorial scope of the Treaty was the position of, on the one hand, certain Member State regions which are part of a the customs territory of a non-EU country and, on the other hand, a number of third countries which are part of the customs territory of a Member State. The first category includes the German enclave in Switzerland, Büsingen, which is part of the Swiss customs territory and the Commune of Campione d'Italia, situated on the shore of Lago di Lugano completely surrounded by Swiss territory. The second category includes Monaco which is part of the French customs territory and the Republic of San Marino which is part of the part of Italy's customs territory.

The position of Monaco, San Marino and other third countries which are similarly part of an EU Member State customs territory, is discussed below—see Article 227(4). Generally speaking, those territories in the first category are part of the territorial scope of the Treaty as defined in Article 299(1), whereas those territories in the second category are not part of the EU. Council Regulation 2913/92 establishing the Community Customs Code provides a complete list of areas in the EU customs territory, as set out in the following chart (Table 8.1).

Regulation 2913/92 further clarifies that, also included in the EU customs territory are:

- the territorial sea of the coastal Member States and their internal waters
- the airspace of each Member State[14]

except for the territorial waters, the inland maritime waters and the airspace of those territories which are not part of the customs territory of the Community as listed above.

---

13 Case 14/74 *Norddeutsche Vieh- und Fleisch Kontor GmbH v. Hauptzollamt Hamburg-Jonas*, [1974] ECR 899.

14 Council Regulation 2913/92 of 12 October 1992 (as amended) establishing the Community Customs Code, OL L302/1, 19 October 1992. See also in general, European Court of Auditors, Special Report No 2/93 on the customs territory of the Community and related trading arrangements accompanied by the replies of the Commission, OJ C 47/1, 27 December 1993.

Table 8.1 EU Customs Territory

EU Customs Territory	
EU	Non-EU
Belgium	Principality of Monaco
Bulgaria	UK Sovereign Base Areas of Akrotiri and Dhekelia, in Cyprus
Czech Republic	The UK Channel Islands and the Isle of Man
Denmark, except the Faroe Islands and Greenland	
Germany, except the Island of Heligoland and the territory of Buesingen	
Estonia	
Ireland	
Greece	
Spain, except Ceuta and Melilla	
France, except New Caledonia, Mayotte, Saint-Pierre and Miquelon, Wallis and Futuna Islands, French Polynesia and French Southern and Antarctic Territories	
Italy, except the municipalities of Livigno and Campione d'Italia and the national waters of Lake Lugano which are between the bank and the political frontier of the area between Ponte Tresa and Porto Ceresio	
Cyprus (pending a settlement to the Cyprus problem, the application of the Community 'acquis' is suspended in those areas in which the Government of the Republic of Cyprus does not exercise effective control),	
Latvia	
Lithuania	
Luxembourg	
Hungary	
Malta	
the Netherlands in Europe	
Austria	
Poland	
Portugal,	
Romania	
Slovenia	
Slovak Republic	
Sweden	
the UK of Great Britain and Northern Ireland, except Gibraltar	

Source: European Commission Directorate General for Taxation and Customs website

Unlike Monaco, which is fully part of the EU customs territory through its relationship with France, Andorra and San Marino are not part of the EU customs territory but have a customs union with the EU.

In summary, the meaning of territory in Article 299 (1) refers to:

- the landmass of each of the 27 Member States
- the territories over which they have jurisdiction, both European and overseas
- the Continental Shelf and marine areas over which Member States exercise jurisdiction (or where there is no conflict with the jurisdiction of another Member State)
- the airspace of each Member State.

8.3.6 Application of Second and Third Pillars to Article 299

An important question to note at the outset in Part II is whether and if so to what extent the second and third pillars (respectively dealing with the Common Foreign Security Policy and with Police and Judicial Cooperation in Criminal Matters), introduced by the Maastricht Treaty in 1992 applied (pre-Lisbon Treaty) to Article 299 and specifically to Member State territories. Prior to entry into force of the Maastricht Treaty there was just one pillar, the TEC encompassing Article 299 and applying to Member State and their territories. With the Maastricht Treaty there came the original TEC (first pillar) and the two new pillars. The EU Treaty was silent on the question of the territorial scope, except for Declaration 25 of the Maastricht Treaty. The Declaration provides that where there is a divergence between the interests of the EU and those of the territories, a Member State may, in exceptional circumstances, take action in the interests of its territories.[15] However, the Declaration was not legally binding and so did not carry definite legal weight.[16]

The question as to the application or otherwise of the second and third pillars to Article 299 and Member State territories had been the subject of some debate but was never fully resolved.[17] Unlike the EC and Euratom Treaties, the EU Treaty did not contain any specific provision on territorial scope. Some commentators suggested therefore that the territorial scope of the EU Treaty should thus be broader than the EC and Euratom Treaties, covering all the territories of the Member States in their entirety.[18] Others argued that the EU Treaty assumes the territorial scope of the TEC.[19]

---

[15] Declaration 25 on the representation of the interests of the overseas countries and territories referred to in Article 227(3) and (5)(a) and (b) of the Treaty establishing the European Community appended to the Final Act of the Maastricht Treaty, 7 February 1992, OJ C191/103, 29 July 1992.

[16] For an analysis of Declaration 25, see Karagiannis 1998.

[17] For example, Dewost 1979; Rigaux 1995; Ziller 2007; Kochenov 2008–9, pp 195–288.

[18] For example Karagiannis 1998.

[19] For example Ziller 2007.

Various arguments have been put forward to support both of these positions. For example, Kochenov argued that issues covered by the second and third pillars were not geographically limited under the EU Treaty.[20] He further expounded that as the special statuses of territories (specifically the OCTs and the Outermost Regions) are not recognized under the EU Treaty, then he suggested there cannot be a distinction drawn between territories having a special status under the TEC and those that do not, in respect of the application of the EU Treaty. Other commentators, like Ziller, argued that the EU Treaty should apply to the entire territory of Member States as long as nothing else was specified.

However, whatever the arguments on either side, they do not have direct implications for this thesis, specifically for an analysis of Article 299 TEC as a legal framework for relations between the EU (in the generic sense of the term) and Member State territories. With the entry into force of the Lisbon Treaty, the pillar structure has disappeared and the new Treaties provisions clarify the general principle that the EU Treaties (incorporating the present three pillar structure) applies to all Member States (and their territories) with the current derogations and exceptions continuing.

Significantly and in particular for the prior debate on the application of the second and third pillars to the EU Member State territories, the Lisbon Treaty clarifies broadly that for those territories forming part of the EU, for example, the Outermost Regions, the EU Treaties (ie all three pillars) apply, whilst in relation to those territories outside the EU, such as the OCTs, only the TEC (ie the first pillar provisions specifically provided for in what was previously Article 299(3) and Part Four) will apply.

8.3.7 Member State Accessions

The scope of Article 299(1) expanded with the accessions of new Member States. When the Treaty of Rome was signed in Rome in 1957, the precursor to Article 299(1)—Article 227(1)—provided that the Treaty applied to the original 6 signatory Member States, namely Belgium, Germany, France, Italy, Luxembourg and the Netherlands. This initial list of 6 countries was extended with the accession of new Member States as follows:

- 1972 with the accession of Denmark, the UK and Ireland,
- 1979 with the accession of Greece
- 1985 to 12 Member States upon the accession of Spain and Portugal
- 1994 to 15 Member States when Austria, Finland and Sweden joined the Community

[20] For example Kochenov 2008-9, pp 195–288.

- 2005 to 25 Member States with the accession of the following 10 new countries: Cyprus, Malta, Estonia, Hungary, Lativa, Lithuania, Poland, the Czech Republic, Slovakia and Slovenia
- 2007 to Bulgaria and Romania.

8.3.7.1 1972: UK Accession (Hong Kong)

Hong Kong was a crown colony (later a dependent territory) when the UK joined the EU. It has been a special administrative region of the People's Republic of China since July 1997. EU law did not apply, and since it was not under British jurisdiction, Euratom did not apply either (see also commentary on Article 299(3) below).

8.3.7.2 1972–1984: Danish Accession and Greenland's 'Segregation' From the Community

At the time of Denmark's accession to the EU in 1972, Greenland, as part of Denmark, fell within the territory of the Community and therefore under Article 299(1). Protocol No. 4 of the Danish Action of Accession, however, permitted certain restrictions on the right of establishment and charged the Community institutions with finding, within the framework of the common market for fisheries, adequate solutions to the specific problems of Greenland. Protocol No. 4 lapsed when, with the signing of the 1984 Treaty,[21] Greenland ceased to be a part of the Community and instead became one of the OCTs. Greenland's segregation from the Community required an amendment to the TEC since Greenland remained part of Denmark's territory. Thus, Article 299(1) made any solution other than an amendment to the Treaty impossible. (See further commentary on Article 299 (3) below).

8.3.7.3 1985: Accession of Portugal (East Timor and Macau, Azores and Madeira)

Until 1975, East Timor was a Portuguese colony. Despite occupation of the territory by Indonesia since 1975, East Timor was considered a non-self-governing-territory under Portuguese administration by the United Nations when Portugal became an EU member in 1986. Finally, in 1999, Indonesia and Portugal reached agreement under the auspices of the United Nations to settle the conflict over East Timor. None of the EU laws were in force during its period under Portuguese administration, which formally ceased on 20 May 2002 when Portugal recognised East Timor's independence.

---

[21] Treaty amending with regard to Greenland, the Treaties establishing the European Communities OJ L29 1 February 1985.

Macau was an overseas province of Portugal until 1976 when its status was changed to a *special territory*. It has been a special administrative region of the People's Republic of China since 1999. EU law did not apply and it had its own currency. Residents who had Portuguese citizenship could vote when they were in Portugal.

Initially, when Portugal acceded to the EU the Azores and Madeira, the EU had not yet developed the concept of Outermost Region although the economic and social backwardness of these Portuguese territories was acknowledged and provided for in the Accession Treaty. These territories were therefore deemed to be part of the EU by virtue of Article 299(1), rather than by specific reference in Article 299(2).

8.3.7.4 1985: Accession of Spain (Ceuta and Melilla and Canary Islands)

As with the Portuguese territories of Azores and Madeira, so also the Spanish territories of Ceuta and Melilla and the Canary Islands were deemed to be part of the EU by virtue of Article 299(1). Later when the Canary Islands became one of the Outermost Regions, Ceuta and Melilla were not included as Outermost Regions so remained part of the EU by virtue of Article 299(1).

8.3.8 2007: Lisbon Treaty Amendments to Article 299 in General

As outlined in the "General introduction" at the beginning of this paper, it is instructive to review the Lisbon Treaty amendments to Article 299 to see whether and if so to what degree an attempt has been made to update and reform Article 299.

Before looking at the proposed Lisbon Treaty[22] amendments to Article 299(1) specifically, it is worth summarising at this stage the overall changes introduced by this Treaty to Article 299. As the table below outlines, the Lisbon Treaty amended the EU's two core treaties, the Treaty on European Union and the Treaty establishing the European Community. The former contains the broad essential principles of the EU and remains the TEU; the latter contains the operational detailed part of the Treaty and is renamed the Treaty on the Functioning of the European Union (TFEU).

In general, the Lisbon Treaty does not make any substantive changes to Article 299. Rather, the suggested changes are to structure and wording and also to take account of certain developments since the last major Treaty amendments, for example, the accession of new Member States. Unlike the TCE which did attempt to consolidate certain texts, notably the various Accession Treaty protocols and

---

[22] Treaty of Lisbon amending the Treaty on European Union and the Treaty establishing the European Community, OJ C306 17 December 2007.

Table 8.2 Article 299 TEC and Lisbon Treaty provisions: summary equivalence table:

Numbering of the Treaty on European Community (TEC)	New numbering of the Treaty on European Union (TEU) and Treaty on the Functioning of the European Union (TFEU)
Article 299 (1)	Article 52 TEU (1) and (2)
Article 299 (2), second, third and fourth subparagraphs	Article 349 TFEU
Article 299(2), first subparagraph and Articles (3)–(6)	Article 355 TFEU

declarations concerning certain of the territories, the Lisbon Treaty makes no such changes. All protocols and declarations forming part of the previous Treaties, including Accession Treaties remain unchanged under the Lisbon Treaty.

The main changes to Article 299 are as follows:

Article 299 is split up into three broad parts: Article 299 (1) is deleted and is in effect replaced by Article 52, TEU. Article 52 sets out the territorial scope of the Treaty to Member States and is included into that part of the Treaty dealing with the Treaty on the European Union (TEU) which broadly covers the main principles of the Treaty.

Article 299(2), first subparagraph and Article 299(3) to (6) became Article 355 TFEU. The new Article 355 replaces the broad substance of Article 299 as the Treaty framework defining the relations between the EU and Member State territories.

The remaining subparagraphs of Article 299(2) are renumbered into a new Article 349 dealing specifically with the Outermost Regions. Article 349 is also set out in the TFEU.

The reason for the splitting up of Article 299 into these three parts was, in the minds of the Member States drafting the Lisbon Treaty, to create a more logical structure.[23] Firstly, Article 299 (renumbered Article 355) remains part of what was the EC Treaties and is called the TFEU. It continues to set out the broader territorial scope of the Treaty, particular in relation to Member State *territories*. However, the drafters of the Lisbon Treaty considered it made sense to set out the broad territorial scope of the Treaty as it applies to *Member States* (previously in Article 299(1)) in a new Article 52 and to create this new Article in what is currently the TEU which contains the broad general principles of the Treaty. Finally, given the special regime that has developed for Outermost Regions and the fact that these are fully part of the EU, the drafters considered it clearer to set out the more detailed provisions of Article 299(2) on these Regions in a new separate Article 349 TFEU.[24]

The following table illustrates both the Article 299 TEC provisions and the new corresponding Lisbon Treaty provisions (Tables 8.2 and 8.3).

---

[23] Interview by author with EU Council Legal Service.

[24] Ibid.

Table 8.3 Article 299 TEC and Lisbon Treaty provisions: full text equivalence table:

Numbering of the Treaty on European Community	New numbering of the Treaty on European Union
Article 299	Article 52 (1) and (2)
1. This Treaty shall apply to the Kingdom of Belgium, the Republic of Bulgaria, the Czech Republic, the Kingdom of Denmark, the Federal Republic of Germany, the Republic of Estonia, the Hellenic Republic, the Kingdom of Spain, the French Republic, Ireland, the Italian Republic, the Republic of Cyprus, the Republic of Latvia, the Republic of Lithuania, the Grand Duchy of Luxembourg, the Republic of Hungary, the Republic of Malta, the Kingdom of the Netherlands, the Republic of Austria, the Republic of Poland, the Portuguese Republic, Romania, the Republic of Slovenia, the Slovak Republic, the Republic of Finland, the Kingdom of Sweden and the United Kingdom of Great Britain and Northern Ireland.[25]	1. The Treaties shall apply to the Kingdom of Belgium, Republic of Bulgaria, the Czech Republic, the Kingdom of Denmark, the Federal Republic of Germany, the Republic of Estonia, the Hellenic Republic, the Kingdom of Spain, the French Republic, Ireland, the Italian Republic, the Republic of Cyprus, the Republic of Latvia, the Republic of Lithuania, the Grand Duchy of Luxembourg, the Republic of Hungary, the Republic of Malta, the Kingdom of the Netherlands, the Republic of Austria, the Republic of Poland, the Portuguese Republic, Romania, the Republic of Slovenia, the Slovak Republic, the Republic of Finland, the Kingdom of Sweden and the United Kingdom of Great Britain and Northern Ireland.
	2. The territorial scope of the Treaties is specified in Article 355 of the Treaty on the Functioning of the European Union.
	New numbering of the Treaty on the Functioning of the European Union (Lisbon Treaty numbering in brackets)
Article 299 (2), second, third and fourth subparagraphs	Article 349
2. However, taking account of the structural social and economic situation of the French overseas departments, the Azores, Madeira and the Canary Islands, which is compounded by their remoteness, insularity, small size, difficult topography and climate, economic dependence on a few products, the permanence and combination of which severely restrain their development, the Council, acting by a qualified majority on a proposal from the Commission and after consulting the European Parliament, shall adopt specific measures aimed, in particular, at laying down the conditions of application of the present Treaty to those regions, including common policies.	Taking account of the structural social and economic situation of Guadeloupe, French Guiana, Martinique, Réunion, Saint-Barthélemy, Saint-Martin, the Azores, Madeira and the Canary Islands, which is compounded by their remoteness, insularity, small size, difficult topography and climate, economic dependence on a few products, the permanence and combination of which severely restrain their development, the Council, acting by a qualified majority on a proposal from the Commission and after consulting the European Parliament, shall adopt specific measures aimed, in particular, at laying down the conditions of application of the present Treaty to those regions, including common policies. Where the specific measures in question are adopted by the Council in accordance with a special legislative procedure, it shall also act on a proposal from the Commission and after consulting the European Parliament.

(continued)

[25] As amended by Article 17, Act of Accession of Bulgaria and Romania to the EU, OJ L157/209 21 June 2005.

Table 8.3 (continued)

Numbering of the Treaty on European Community	New numbering of the Treaty on European Union
The Council shall, when adopting the relevant measures referred to in the second subparagraph, take into account areas such as customs and trade policies, fiscal policy, free zones, agriculture and fisheries policies, conditions for supply of raw materials and essential consumer goods, State aids and conditions of access to Structural Funds and to horizontal Community programmes.	The measures referred to in the first paragraph concern in particular areas such as customs and trade policies, fiscal policy, free zones, agriculture and fisheries policies, conditions for supply of raw materials and essential consumer goods, State aids and conditions of access to structural funds and to horizontal Union programmes.
The Council shall adopt the measures referred to in the second subparagraph taking into account the special characteristics and constraints of the Outermost Regions without undermining the integrity and the coherence of the Community legal order, including the internal market and common policies.	The Council shall adopt the measures referred to in the first subparagraph taking into account the special characteristics and constraints of the Outermost Regions without undermining the integrity and the coherence of the Union legal order, including the internal market and common policies.
Article 299(2), first subparagraph and Articles (3)–(6)	Article 355 (1)–(6)
	In addition to the provisions of Article 52 of the Treaty on European Union relating to the territorial scope of the Treaties, the following provisions shall apply:
2. The provisions of this Treaty shall apply to the French overseas departments, the Azores, Madeira and the Canary Islands.	1. The provisions of the Treaties shall apply to Guadeloupe, French Guiana, Martinique, Réunion, Saint-Barthélemy, Saint-Martin, the Azores, Madeira and the Canary Islands in accordance with Article 349.
3. The special arrangements for association set out in Part Four of this Treaty shall apply to the overseas countries and territories listed in Annex II to this Treaty.	2. The special arrangements for association set out in part four of this Treaty shall apply to the overseas countries and territories listed in Annex II to the Treaties.
This Treaty shall not apply to those overseas countries and territories having special relations with the United Kingdom of Great Britain and Northern Ireland which are not included in the aforementioned list.	This Treaty shall not apply to those overseas countries and territories having special relations with the United Kingdom of Great Britain and Northern Ireland which are not included in the aforementioned list.
4. The provisions of this Treaty shall apply to the European territories for whose external relations a Member State is responsible.	3. The provisions of the Treaties shall apply to the European territories for whose external relations a Member State is responsible.
5. The provisions of this Treaty shall apply to the Åland Islands in accordance with the provisions set out in Protocol No. 2 to the Act concerning the conditions of accession of the Republic of Austria, the Republic of Finland and the Kingdom of Sweden.	4. The provisions of the Treaties shall apply to the Åland Islands in accordance with the provisions set out in Protocol 2 to the Act concerning the conditions of accession of the Republic of Austria, the Republic of Finland and the Kingdom of Sweden.

(continued)

Table 8.3 (continued)

Numbering of the Treaty on European Community	New numbering of the Treaty on European Union
6. Notwithstanding the preceding paragraphs: (a) this Treaty shall not apply to the Faroe Islands; (b) This Treaty shall not apply to the United Kingdom Sovereign Base Areas of Akrotiri and Dhekelia in Cyprus except to the extent necessary to ensure the implementation of the arrangements set out in the Protocol on the Sovereign Base Areas of the United Kingdom of Great Britain and Northern Ireland in Cyprus annexed to the Act concerning the conditions of accession of the Czech Republic, the Republic of Estonia, the Republic of Cyprus, the Republic of Latvia, the Republic of Lithuania, the Republic of Hungary, the Republic of Malta, the Republic of Poland, the Republic of Slovenia and the Slovak Republic to the European Union and in accordance with the terms of that Protocol[26]; (c) this Treaty shall apply to the Channel Islands and the Isle of Man only to the extent necessary to ensure the implementation of the arrangements for those islands set out in the Treaty concerning the accession of new Member States to the European Economic Community and to the European Atomic Energy Community signed on 22 January 1972	5. Notwithstanding Article 52 of the Treaty on European Union and paragraphs 1 to 4 of this Article: (a) the Treaties shall not apply to the Faroe Islands; (b) The Treaties shall not apply to the United Kingdom Sovereign Base Areas of Akrotiri and Dhekelia in Cyprus except to the extent necessary to ensure the implementation of the arrangements set out in the Protocol on the Sovereign Base Areas of the United Kingdom of Great Britain and Northern Ireland in Cyprus annexed to the Act concerning the conditions of accession of the Czech Republic, the Republic of Estonia, the Republic of Cyprus, the Republic of Latvia, the Republic of Lithuania, the Republic of Hungary, the Republic of Malta, the Republic of Poland, the Republic of Slovenia and the Slovak Republic to the European Union and in accordance with the terms of that Protocol; (c) the Treaties shall apply to the Channel Islands and the Isle of Man only to the extent necessary to ensure the implementation of the arrangements for those islands set out in the Treaty concerning the accession of new Member States to the European Economic Community and to the European Atomic Energy Community signed on 22 January 1972 6. The European Council may, on the initiative of the Member State concerned, adopt a decision amending the status, with regard to the Union, of a Danish, French or Netherlands country or territory referred to in paragraphs 1 and 2. The European Council shall act unanimously after consulting the Commission.

8.3.9 2007: Lisbon Treaty Amendments to Article 299 (1) Specifically

The Lisbon Treaty repeals Article 299(1), removing it from the Article 299 structure and indeed from the TEC. Article 299(1) is replaced in substance by Article 52 which is set out in the TEU dealing with the broad general principles of the EU. Reference is made to all 27 Member States.

In addition to the first paragraph dealing with the application of the Treaty to Member States, the Lisbon Treaty inserts a new second paragraph. This paragraph

[26] As amended by the Cyprus Act of Accession, OJ L236, 23 September 2003.

refers to Article 355 which sets out—as Article 299 purported to do—the territorial scope of the Treaty, particularly as regards territories.

On the one hand, one can understand the logic behind the splitting up of Article 299 in three parts: the first as part of the overarching principles setting out the territorial scope as regards the Member States; the second dealing separately with the position of the Outermost Regions as they are not only fully part of the EU but have a specific relationship (new Article 349); the third part (to which the first and second parts refer) setting out the broad framework of relations between the EU and in particular Member State territories. However, the Article 299 split does result in a lack of cohesion and indeed some confusion, both by the fact that part of the Article is moved to the TEU principles and the rest remain in the TFEU, and also because the territorial scope of the Treaty is in effect repeated both in Article 52 referring mainly to Member States and in Article 355 dealing mainly with territories.

Finally, the Lisbon Treaty does not make any changes to the TEC provisions in respect of Ceuta and Melilla.

8.4 Conclusions

Compared to 1957 when Article 299(1) TEC was drafted, today there are many more Member States and territories to which the corresponding provisions under the Lisbon Treaty apply. As with Article 299 in general, regarding specifically subparagraph (1), the only change has been to add the new Member States. Thus, from an original 6 Member States in 1957, the current EU Treaties framework refers to 27 Member States. Implicitly Member State territories are still covered by Article 52(1) TEU (ex Article 299(1) TEC). In reality, since 1957, the only territories that have appeared to be deemed part of the Treaty by virtue of this subparagraph are Greenland (which later opted for home rule and became an OCT), for a time Azores, Madeira and the Canary Islands, and currently only Ceuta and Melilla. All other relevant Member State territories that might have fallen under subparagraph (1) negotiated special arrangements that are covered elsewhere in the EU Treaties.

The lack of specific reference in Article 52(1) (ex Article 299(1) TEC) or subsequent subparagraphs to either Greenland or Ceuta and Melilla results in a lack of clarity and transparency as regards the status of these territories, including *vis à vis* other Member State territories mentioned in other parts of the EU Treaties.

Regarding Ceuta and Melilla in particular, their relationship *vis à vis* the EU was originally clearly aligned with the Canary Islands but when the latter joined the CCT and became one of the Outermost Regions, there was no similar review of Ceuta and Melilla's relationship to the EU under Article 299 or the Lisbon Treaty equivalent provisions. This created yet further inconsistency between territories, which despite their similar relations with their Member State (Spain), had different relations and treatment under the EU Treaties framework.

References

Dewost J L (1979) L'Application Territoriale du Droit Communautaire: disparition et resurgence de la notion de frontière, Société Française pour le Droit International, Colloque de Poitiers

Karagiannis S (1998) A propos du règlement des conflits d'intérêts entre les territoires dépendants d'Etats members et les Communautés européennes 75 Revue du Droit Internationale et de Droit Comparé at 340

Kochenov D (2008–9) Substantive and Procedural issues in the application of European law in the overseas possessions of European Union Member States, 17 Michigan State Journal of International Law 2, pp 195–288

Megret J (1987) Le Droit de la Communauté Economique Européene, Editions de L'Université de Bruxelles, 1987, page 484

Rigaux A (1995) Territoire communautaire: Rép. Communautaire, Dalloz

Ziller J (2007) The European Union and the Territorial Scope of the European Territories, 38 Vict. U. Wellington L. Rev 51

Chapter 9
Article 299(2): The Outermost Regions

Abstract This chapter provides an introduction to the second paragraph of Article 299 TEC, dealing with the Outermost Regions, just before entry into force of the corresponding Lisbon Treaty provision. The key developments since 1957 relevant to this paragraph are examined, including Member State accessions, relevant legislation and case law of the European courts, main Treaty amendments including key amendments introduced by the Lisbon Treaty. An overview of the Outermost Regions is provided including their constitutional relationships with their mother countries and the legal framework governing relations between these territories and the EU.

9.1 Introduction (Comparison with 1957 Version)

Unlike Article 299(1), which changed little in content from the original 1957 provision, the content and focus of Article 299(2) (Article 349 and 355(1) TFEU) altered considerably with time.

Firstly, whereas the original version of Article 299(2) applied only to the French DOMs and Algeria, the current provision applies (with the exception of Algeria) also to the Portuguese Azores and Madeira and to the Spanish Canary Islands.

Secondly, whereas the original provision makes a general reference to the economic and social development of these regions, the current provision much more specifically lists the particular physical, economic and social constraints and drawbacks experienced by these regions which justify their special treatment in order to aid their economic and social development.

Thirdly, the original provision limits the application of the Treaty to the regions to certain provisions e.g. free movement of goods, services, competition, the

F. Murray, *The European Union and Member State Territories: A New Legal Framework Under the EU Treaties*, DOI: 10.1007/978-90-6704-826-2_9,

institutions, providing that the applicability of other EU Treaty provisions will be decided within two years of the entry into force of the EU Treaty. The present text, on the other hand, provides for the general application to these regions of the EU Treaties in their entirety, taking into account their economic and social handicaps, and goes on to highlight in particular certain provisions such as customs and trade policies, fiscal policy and State aids.

Finally, unlike the original 1957 text, the current provision adds that the Council will adopt special measures provided for in the second subparagraph "without undermining the integrity and the coherence of the Community legal order, including the internal market and common policies". The final paragraph of the 1957 version merely stated that the Community institutions would, within the framework of the Treaty procedures, including Article 226 (permitting a Member State—during the transitional period—to take protective measures in order to address difficulties in the economy) take care to ensure that the economic and social development of these regions was made possible.

9.2 Applicable Member States and Territories: Present Day

The first exception to the general principle that the Treaties apply to all Member States is the so-called Outermost—or Ultra-Peripheral—Regions. The first paragraph of Article 299(2) named these regions[1] as:

French:

- the French DOMs (namely, Guadeloupe, Martinique, French Guiana, Réunion, Saint Barthélemy and Saint Martin),

Portuguese:

- the Azores and Madeira and

Spanish:

- the Canary Islands. Once again Article 299(2) like paragraph (1) before it begins by stating that the general rule that the Treaty applies to these regions. Therefore, these regions are deemed to be part of the EU.

[1] Worth noting here is the unique position of St Pierre et Miquelon. Originally a French Overseas Territory (TOM), St Pierre et Miquelon became a DOM in July 1976. Although the TEC (specifically Annex IV *infra*, listing the OCTs) was never amended to reflect this change, St Pierre et Miquelon was treated as a DOM and the specific EU regime for DOMS was applied to it. However, 9 years later, in July 1985, St Pierre et Miquelon once again became a TOM and has remained so ever since.

9.3 General Characteristics of Outermost Regions

The Outermost Regions—like other regions in the EU e.g. Brittany in France or Cornwall in the UK—are an integral part of the Community. However, unlike other regions, they suffer from a number of constraints which hinder their economic development. EU policy on the Outermost Regions is designed to assist these regions to reach the same level of development as other regions in the EU. Article 299(2) lists those physical, social, economic and geographical characteristics which distinguish the Outermost Regions from other regions of the EU. Article 299(2) goes onto to elaborate that the combination and permanence of all of these characteristics severely restrain their development. These characteristics are:

- remoteness: distance from mainland Europe, often proximity to less-developed non-member countries
- insularity: 6 of the 7 Outermost Regions are islands, while French Guiana in an enclave in the Amazon forest
- small size: making heavy investments unprofitable and does not permit economies of scale
- difficult topography and climate: often volcanic and mountainous terrain and tropical climate
- high population density: all except French Guiana have a high population density
- economic dependence on a few products and heavy reliance on imports.

In addition to the above, the GDP of the Outermost Regions tends to be lower than the EU average and most of these regions have a high rate of unemployment. The following chart, prepared by the European Commission summarises these characteristics (Table 9.1):

Table 9.1 Overview of GPD in the Outermost Regions

	Location	Capital	Surface area (km^2)	Population	Per capita GDP (EU = 100)
Azores	Atlantic	Ponta Delgada	2,333	237,900	66.7
Canaries	Atlantic	Las Palmas	7,447	1,715,700	93.7
Guadeloupe	Caribbean	Pointe-à-Pitre	1,710	425,700	70.6
French Guiana	South America	Cayenne	84,000	161,100	50.5
Madeira	Atlantic	Funchal	795	244,800	94.9
Martinique	Caribbean	Fort-de-France	1,080	383,300	75.6
Réunion	Indian Ocean	Saint-Denis	2,510	715,900	61.6
Saint-Barthélemy	Caribbean	Gustavia	25	8,300	111
Saint-Martin	Caribbean	Marigot	53	35,000	61.9

Source: 2006 European Commission, DG REGIO

9.4 Overview of the Outermost Regions

As mentioned, there are nine Outermost Regions—the French Guadeloupe, Martinique, French Guiana, Réunion, Saint Barthéelemy and Saint Martin), the autonomous Spanish Community of the Canary Islands and the Portuguese autonomous regions of the Azores and Madeira. Unlike the OCTs, these regions are an inherent part of the EU. As a broad principle, therefore, all provisions of the TEC apply to the Outermost Regions by virtue of Article 299(2) (Article 355(1) TFEU). These regions are therefore as much a part of the EU as other EU regions, for example, Brittany or Tuscany.

These most remote regions enable the EU to have a very widely spread maritime territory, but also an even more diverse economy, by supplying, for example, agricultural produce such as rum, cane sugar, bananas and other exotic fruits and vegetables to meet a demand among European consumers. These remote regions are also rich in opportunities that can help foster relations between neighbouring countries and Europe, while also offering attractive sites for certain research and high technology activities, such as the Astrophysics Institute in the Canary Islands, the European Space Agency in French Guiana and the Department of Oceanography and Fishing at the University of the Azores.

However, their insularity, tropical climate, often volcanic rock and mountainous terrain, distance from mainland Europe and proximity to less developed third countries are all obstacles to the development of these regions. Also, despite a relatively high population density—with the exception of French Guiana—they are of relatively modest demographic, economic and territorial importance in relation to the EU as a whole.

Their difficulty in achieving economies of scale and generating profits from major investments, coupled with low wages and often very high unemployment (especially among young people), make these regions among the poorest in the Union.

Before the Amsterdam Treaty, the old version of Article 299(2) (Article 227(2)) only applied to the French DOMs which merely stated that the Community institutions would provide for the economic and social development of these regions. It was in the late eighties that the idea was first aired of giving the European Community instruments designed specifically for these remote or Outermost Regions. Major changes were subsequently made to the type of Structural Fund assistance available to them, and they were earmarked for a substantial part of the Community budget. Specifically, in 1989, following a detailed study of the DOMs' issues in relation to the completion of the Single Market, the Council adopted the so-called "POSEI" (programmes of options specific to their remote and insular nature), first, for the DOMs (POSEIDOM) and later for the Canary Islands (POSEICAN) and the Azores and Madeira (POSEIMA).

At the same time, the notion of "economic and social cohesion" appeared. This adopted and deepened the concept and field of action of Community regional policy in respect to these remote regions, increasing the resources available and becoming a Community and then Union "objective" rather than a simple "Community policy". In 1997, the Amsterdam Treaty introduced a specific legal basis (Article 299(2)) for the adoption of measures to assist the economic and social development of the Outermost Regions, in recognition of their "special characteristics and constraints". In concrete terms, this means that the EU recognises the specificity of the most remote regions and the need to adapt Community policy to allow for their characteristics and circumstances.

The Outermost Regions of the EU benefited from the Objective 1 programmes co financed by the EU Member States during the years 1989–1993 and 1994–1999. In the 2000–2006 period, they were allocated EUR 7.671 billion under the Structural Funds. The programmes developed specifically for these most remote regions—POSEIDOM for the French Overseas Departments (1989), POSEICAN for the Canary Islands (1991) and POSEIMA for the Azores and Madeira (1991)—are the main channels for Community policy in this field. These concentrate their efforts on improving infrastructures, promoting productive sectors which generate jobs and human resources development. There are also many other initiatives which take account of the handicaps of these regions (distance, insularity, reduced competitiveness). Total EU funding for 2007–13 for the outermost regions—EUR7.84bn, chiefly from the European regional development fund (EUR4.5bn) and the European social fund (EUR1.3bn) but also the agricultural fund for rural development and the fisheries fund.

In addition to funding programmes, the EU takes account of the regions' special needs in initiatives on competition, agriculture, research, trade and transport.

9.4.1 Constitutional Relations with their Member States

9.4.1.1 The DOMS, TOMs and France

It is useful at the outset to distinguish between the various French territories and their respective relations with France. The French Overseas Departments and Territories (respectively, *départements d'outre-mer* and *territoires d'outre-mer* or *DOM-TOM*) consist broadly of French -administered territories outside of Europe. These territories have varying legal status and different levels of autonomy, although all have representation in the French Parliament (except those with no permanent inhabitants), and the right to vote in elections to the European Parliament. The total population of these territories is just over 2.5 million.

From a legal and administrative standpoint, departments are very different from territories: according to the French Constitution, French laws and regulations generally apply (civil code, penal code, administrative law, social laws, tax laws et cetera), in departments as in the mainland. The law, however, contains a number of modifications in respect of the DOMs which aim to take account of the particular economic and social difficulties of these regions. Thus, the French DOMs, with certain modifications, have the same tax and customs system, the same system of health, of social protection, the same administration and bodies charged with managing public services. Even where there are modifications (for example, in taxes and social security), these are always provided by reference to French law. In territories, the principle is the opposite: territories are governed by autonomy statutes that allow them to make their own laws, except for some specific areas (like defense, international relations, international trade and currency, courts and administrative law), as provided in the autonomy statute, that are reserved to the central government and its local appointee.

Each inhabited French territory, metropolitan or overseas, is represented in both the French National Assembly and the French Senate (which make up the French Parliament). The overseas departments and territories are governed by local elected assemblies and by the French Parliament and French Government (where a cabinet member, the Minister of Overseas France, is in charge of issues related to the overseas departments and territories).

The French DOMs consist of Guadeloupe, Martinique, French Guiana and Réunion are part of France and therefore part of the EU. Since 1982, following the French government's policy of decentralisation, the DOMs have elected regional councils with powers similar to those of the regions of metropolitan France. As a result of a constitutional revision which occurred in 2003, these regions are now to be called overseas regions; indeed the new wording of the Constitution gave no precedence to the phrase overseas department or overseas region, though the latter is still virtually unused in general parlance.

The French TOMs consist essentially of the overseas collectivities (a relatively new category created by constitutional reform in March 2003). They are French Polynesia, Mayotte, St Pierre et Miquelon and Wallis and Futuna. Saint Pierre and Miquelon became an overseas department in 1976, but its status changed to that of an Overseas collectivity in 1985. In 2003 Saint Martin and Saint Barthélemy voted in favour of secession from Guadeloupe in order to form separate overseas collectivities of France. In February 2007, the French Parliament passed a bill granting TOM (overseas collectivity) status to both Saint Barthélemy and neighbouring Saint Martin. They remain part of the EU and following entry into force of the Lisbon Treaty, they became officially Outermost Regions.

New Caledonia has a unique status and is not even a territorial collectivity, unlike all other French subdivisions. As a result of the 1998 Nouméa, New Caledonians will vote on an independence referendum scheduled between 2014 and 2019. This referendum will determine whether the territory remains a part of the French Republic as an overseas collectivity, or whether it will become an independent nation. The accords also specify a gradual devolution of powers to the local New Caledonian assembly. The French Southern and Antarctic Lands have been an overseas territory of France since 1956. According to new French law 2007-224 of February 21, 2007 the Scattered Islands in the Indian Ocean are also an overseas territory. Finally, the uninhabited island of Clipperton is French state private property.

Regarding their status in the EU, the French DOMs are Outermost Regions, Despite their recent status change to TOMs (which are traditionally OCTs under the EU), St Barthélemy and St Martin are also Outermost Regions. They elect a Member of the European Parliament and use the euro as their currency. However, they are outside the Schengen area and the VAT area.

With the exception of St Barthélemy and St Martin and the French Scattered Islands of the Indian Ocean and Clipperton Island (whose status under EU law is in question) the remaining French overseas collectivities and New Caledonia are part of the EU/OCTs association. Mayotte and Saint-Pierre and Miquelon are both part of the Euro zone,[2] while New Caledonia, French Polynesia and Wallis and Futuna use the Franc Pacifique, a currency which is tied to the Euro. Natives of the collectivities are European citizens owing to their French citizenship and elections to the European Parliament are held in the collectivities.

9.4.1.2 The Canary Islands and Spain

The Canary Islands form one of the seventeen Autonomous Spanish Communities established by the 1978 Spanish Constitution. The Constitution expressly refers to the particular remoteness and isolation of the Canaries as the traditional basis for their specific economic and fiscal treatment. The Statute of Autonomy of the Canaries, which was approved in August 1982 and amended in 1996,[3] gives the Islands the power to establish an internal administration system which complies with the constitutional principles and basic standards of the Spanish State. The State has exclusive competence for defence, foreign affairs and coinage.

The Canaries' administrative authorities consist of a Community Government and Parliament for the archipelago as a whole, a local government authority ("Cabildo") for each island in the archipelago, and municipal authorities. The *Cabildos* represent the Community Government in their respective islands, which they administer under powers attributed to them by the Community Parliament. The Community or the *Cabildos* may also delegate powers to the municipal authorities. The Islands have 13 seats in the Spanish Senate. Of these, 11 seats are directly elected, 3 for Gran Canaria, 3 for Tenerife, 1 for each other island; 2 seats are indirectly elected by the regional Autonomous Government.

Spain has always recognized the specific situation of the Canary Islands in terms of the geography, remoteness from Spain, isolation, climate and poor natural resources. Law 30/72 of 22 July 1972 on the Economic and Fiscal Regime (EFR) of the Canary Islands defines a number of exemptions from the various tax systems

---

[2] By virtue of Council Decision 1999/95/EC of 31 December 1998 concerning the monetary arrangements in the French territorial communities of St Pierre et Miquelon and Mayotte, OJ L30/29 4 February 1999.

[3] Statute of the Autonomy of the Canary Islands, Basic Law 10/1982, 10 August 1982, amended by Basic law 4/1996, 10 December 1996.

which make up Spain's fiscal regime. It also prohibits all types of monopoly on goods and services. As a result of Spain's accession to the EU, the EFR has had to be amended many times.

9.4.1.3 Azores, Madeira and Portugal

The Azores comprise nine volcanic islands situated in the middle of the North Atlantic Ocean, around 1,500 km west of Lisbon and 3,900 km east of the east coast of North America. Its main industries are agriculture, dairy farming, minor livestock and tourism. Madeira is an archipelago that lies around 400 km north of Tenerife, the Canary Islands. Its principle industries are wine, flowers, and tourism. Together, the Azores and Madeira form the only two autonomous regions of Portugal. As such, under the Portuguese Constitution, each autonomous region has its own political and administrative statute and has its own Government. The branches of Government are the Regional Executive (*Governo Regional*), and the Legislative Parliament (*Assembleia Legislativa*).

The Azores and Madeira have been granted broad legislative, political and administrative powers under the Portuguese Constitution of 1976. In particular, the Portuguese Constitution contains a "specific interest" clause according to which the Islands have autonomy over areas of specific interest to them. These areas of specific interest include culture, the environment, agriculture, mineral and similar resources, housing, infrastructure, commercial and industrial development, health, education, sports and tourism. The regions also have certain powers in the area of taxation, for example, the right to use the taxes collected in the regions as well as increased powers as to the rates of taxation to be applied locally.

As to those powers retained by the Portuguese Government, these include defence and foreign affairs. In addition, the Islands may not legislate in areas within the exclusive jurisdiction of "sovereign bodies", namely, the Portuguese Parliament. Areas within the Parliament's exclusive jurisdiction include the power to ratify treaties, to regulate elections, parties and associations and referenda, to define crimes, the monetary system, essential rights and freedoms as well as outlining the basic principles in various areas such as environmental protection and social security. In all of these areas, however, the Islands have a right to be consulted on matters which directly concern them. Also, in certain circumstances, the Islands have the right to participate and to be represented in the negotiation of international treaties of direct concern to them. Finally, it is also worth noting that the Portuguese Government alone is responsible for ensuring the implementation of EU legislation in the Islands. This is because the Government is liable for non-implementation of EU Directives in Madeira and the Azores.

9.5 Article 299(2): Developments Since 1957, Including Treaty Amendments

9.5.1 Member State Accessions

9.5.1.1 1972: Accessions of Denmark, UK and Ireland

The accessions of Denmark, the UK and Ireland in 1972 with their several territories might have been expected to add to the list of Outermost Regions to which the TEC applied. None of the territories of these new Member States, however—with the exception of Gibraltar and Greenland—wished to become part of the Community. Special provision was made for Gibraltar (see chapter on Article 299(4)) and for the other UK and Danish territories.[4]

9.5.1.2 1985: Accessions of Spain and Portugal

The accessions of Portugal and Spain to the Community involved addressing the special position of their Member State territories, specifically:

- the Portuguese Azores and Madeira
- the Spanish Canary Islands and Ceuta and Melilla

As regards the Portuguese territories, a Joint Declaration was appended to the Portuguese Accession Act concerning the economic and social development of the autonomous regions of the Azores and Madeira.[5] The Declaration was a forerunner of the later Article 299 (2) introduced by the Amsterdam Treaty.

In summary the Joint Declaration provided for the economic and social development of the Azores and Madeira by the EU to overcome their physical handicaps and economic backwardness, a process which the Portuguese Government was pursuing prior to accession.

At the time of Spain's accession to the EU, the Canary Islands and the Spanish enclaves in Africa of Ceuta and Melilla opted for a slightly different status to the Portuguese Azores and Madeira. Thus, instead of becoming fully part of the EU, subject to special provision being made for their economic and social disadvantages, the Canary Islands and Ceuta and Melilla were excluded from Common Customs Tariff and from the application of the Common Commercial Policy (CCP). This was achieved by Article 25 and Protocol No. 2 to the Spanish Act of Accession to the EU. The main reason for the Canary Islands' exclusion from the

[4] See further Chap. 11 on Article 299(4) in respect of Gibraltar, Chap. 10 on Article 299 (3) regarding the UK territories which became OCTs and Chap. 13 on Article 299 (6) regarding the Channel Islands, Isle of Man and the Faroe Islands.

[5] See Annex IX *infra*, Joint Declaration on the Azores and Madeira, Portuguese Act of Accession (1985).

CCT was that they were already outside the Spanish customs territory and wished to remain so. Also, the Islands were subject to tariff quotas by Spain in relation to agricultural and fisheries products.

In 1989, Spain was approaching the end of its transitional period prior to becoming a full member of the EU. The Canary Islands, not wishing to be subjected to tariff quotas by both Spain and all EU Member States upon full Spanish accession, decided that economically it would be more advantageous for the Islands to become part of the CCT. Therefore, following a request from Spain, the Council agreed that the Canary Islands should become gradually incorporated into the customs territory of the Community, accompanied by appropriate measures to take account of the remoteness and insularity of the Islands. Protocol No. 2 of the Spanish Act of Accession, therefore, no longer applies to the Canary Islands.

Regarding the accessions of the Portuguese Azores and Madeira and the Spanish Canary Islands and Ceuta and Melilla, it is also important to note here that one of the reasons for the Joint Declaration in regard to the Portuguese territories and Article 25 and Protocol No. 2 of the respective Acts of Accession of their Member States was precisely because none of these territories qualified as 'European' and therefore for automatic inclusion within the EU as provided for under Article 299 (4)—see below.

None of the other accessions—whether of Greece in 1979, Austria, Finland and Sweden in 1994 or the 12 new Member States which joined in 2005 and 2007—had regions or territories that fulfilled the characteristics of and might therefore qualify as Outermost Regions.

9.5.2 1960s and 1970s: Early Developments and Interpretation of Article 227(2)

It will be recalled that the original version of Article 299(2) provided for the immediate application of the core EC principles and, in the second paragraph, provided that the Council would decide within a two year transitional period the conditions under which other provisions of the Treaty would apply.

Concerning the two year period referred to in the original version of Article 299(2), second paragraph, the Council adopted a number of measures. These included the Council Directives on the right of establishment of 23 November 1959 (which, however, did not refer to Article 227) and by a Decision on the applicability of the Treaty rules on the movement of capital, adopted in 1960. Later, additional decisions (and in certain cases regulations) were adopted, making other specific Treaty rules or Community secondary legislation applicable to the French DOMs including the rules concerning the free movement of workers, the European Social Fund and the European Regional Development Fund.

The question then arose as to the legal effect of the two year expiration date. In particular, what was the effect of those Community law provisions regarding which the Council had not adopted before the 31 December 1959 decisions concerning their application to the DOMs and Algeria? The prevailing opinion, based on a literal reading of Treaty was that in the absence of Council decisions, other Community law provisions did not apply to these regions.

The status of these provisions *vis à vis* the French DOMs and Algeria was further clarified by the ECJ in a number of cases.[6] Finally, the application to the DOMs (and Algeria) of other provisions of the Treaty was settled in the *Hansen*[7] judgment of 10 October 1977. In its judgment, the Court reiterated the fact that the status of the DOMs within the EU was defined by reference to the French Constitution under which the DOMs are an integral part of France. However, in order to make allowances for the specific geographic, economic and social situation of these departments, the Court said that Article 227(2) permitted the Treaty to be applied in stages and, in addition, it made available the widest powers for the adoption of special provisions commensurate with the specific requirements of the DOMs. Thus, Article 227 precisely stated certain chapters and articles which were to apply as soon as the Treaty entered into force, while at the same time reserving a period of 2 years within which the Council could determine special conditions under which other groups of provisions were to apply. Therefore, the Court concluded, after the expiry of that period, the provision of the Treaty and of secondary legislation must apply automatically to the DOMs in as much as they are an integral part of France, it being understood however, that it always remained possible subsequently to adopt specific measures in order to meet the needs of those territories.

In summary, the clarification in *Hansen* confirmed that primary and secondary Community law applied in full to the DOMS (Algeria having by then gained its independence), except where the Council unanimously decided otherwise. The Council could either exclude these territories from the application of Community law or adapt their position *vis à vis* the Treaty or secondary Community legislation provided that the objective needs of the DOMS required such a decision.

9.5.3 1980s: The POSEI Programmes

It is notable that subsequent interpretation of Hansen no difference was made between the core provisions listed in the main body of Article 227(2) and other provisions of the Treaty. It was considered that all of them could be adapted.

---

[6] See Case 148/77 *H. Hansen jun & O.C. Balle GmbH & Co v. Hauptzollamt Flensburg* [1978] ECR 1787 discussing in particular the tax provisions of the Treaty; remarks of Advocate General Reischl in Case 54-60/76 *Compagnie Industrielle et Agricole du Comté de Loheac v. Council and Commission* [1977] ECR 645; also Case 91/78 *Hansen GmbH & Co v. Hauptzollamt Flensburg* [1979] ECR 935, ruling that the provisions of Article 37 TEC on commercial monopolies applied to these territories by virtue of a Council Decision.

[7] Ibid.

On the basis of the Hansen judgment, the European Commission proceeded in the late 1980s to prepare and adopt the so-called 'POSEI' programmes of specific measures adapted to the particular needs of first the DOMs and then to the other Outermost Regions—the Canary Islands and the Azores and Madeira.

In 1987, the Commission carried out an in-depth study of the DOMs' problems connected with the completion of the Single Market in 1993. In particular, it was acknowledged that whilst the Outermost Regions were an integral part of the Community and therefore would have to take on board EU Single Market legislation, it was necessary to step up Community support to promote their economic and social development in order to facilitate the integration of their economies in the Single Market. In other words, the need to implement the Single Market legislation in the Outermost Regions had to be balanced with the reality of helping these more backward EU regions to catch up with the average Community economic and social level. The idea thus emerged of creating specific Community instruments for these remote or 'outermost' regions.

This recognition led, in 1989, to the adoption of "programmes of options specific to their remote and insular nature" in relation to the DOMs (POSEIDOM programme[8]), to the Canary Islands (POSEICAN in 1991[9]) and to the Azores and Madeira (POSEIMA in 1991[10]).

EU policy towards the Outermost Regions under the POSEI programmes consists of two types:

1. Work under EU financial instruments (principally the Structural Funds);
2. Adaptation of the EU's common policies to deal with the specific problems of these regions.

Initially, the main focus of the POSEI programmes was to support traditional production in agriculture and fisheries. Over the years, however, and especially since the Amsterdam Treaty included a specific legal basis in Article 299(2) for Outermost Regions (see below), this focus has broadened to take account of the Outermost Regions in all Community policies.

9.5.4 1993: Maastricht Treaty

The Maastricht Treaty, which entered into force in November 1993, effected a number of changes to Article 299(2) and for the Outermost Regions. First, as

---

[8] Council Decision 89/687/EEC of 22 December 1989 establishing a programme of options specific to the remote and insular nature of the French overseas departments (POSEIDOM), OJ L399/39, 30 December 1989.

[9] Council Decision 91/314/EEC of 26 June 1991 setting up a programme of options specific to the remote and insular nature of the Canary Islands (POSEICAN), OJ L171/5, 29 June 1991.

[10] Council Decision 91/315/EEC of 26 June 1991 setting up a programme of options specific to the remote and insular nature of Madeira and the Azores (POSEIMA), OJL 171/10, 29 June 1991.

mentioned above, the Maastricht Treaty amended Article 299(2) (*ex Article 227(2)*) to apply only to the French DOMs—and no longer Algeria. Second, for the first time, the Treaty—in a Declaration annexed to the Treaty—acknowledged the special position of Outermost Regions in the Community.[11] This therefore represented a first step in the Treaty recognition of the outermost region status. Specifically, the Declaration did three things:

- first, it included specifically within the group of Outermost Regions the Portuguese Azores and Madeira and the Spanish Canary Islands, in addition to the French DOMs,[12]
- second, it recognized that all of these regions suffered structural backwardness (remoteness, island status, small size, difficult topography and climate, economic dependence of a few products), all of which resulted in restraining their economic and social development,
- third, the Declaration, while acknowledging that Community law fully applies to these regions, provided that specific measures could be adopted in order to assist their economic and social development with the aim of bringing them up to the average economic and social level of the Community.

9.5.5 1990s: Legros, Lancry Judgments

As noted above, in applying the *Hansen* judgment, no distinction was made, whether by the EU institutions or others, between the core principles enumerated in the original version of Article 299(2) and other provisions of the Treaty. Any of these could be adapted in order to enable the "economic and social development" of these regions. However, in two judgments of the ECJ in the early 1990s, the ECJ adopted a more restrictive interpretation of Hansen. In particular, the Court took the view that the adaptations to Community law in respect of the Outermost Regions could only apply to provisions 'other than' the core provisions set out in Article 227(2). Thus, in *Legros*,[13] concerning the dock dues, a tax regime specific to the DOMS, the Court considered that the exemptive power of the Council was to be limited to the provisions not listed in Article 227(2). This view was confirmed in the later case of *Lancry*,[14] which invalidated that part of the December

[11] Declaration on the Outermost Regions, Maastricht Treaty, OJ C 191, 29 July 1992, see Annex X *infra*.

[12] Only the French DOMs however were specifically mentioned in the body of Article 299(2) itself. The Azores, Madeira and the Canary Islands were included in Article 299(2) following amendment under the Amsterdam Treaty.

[13] Case C-163/90 *Administration des Douanes et Droits Indirects v. Léopold* Legros *and Others.* [1992] ECR I-4685.

[14] Case C-363/93 *Rene Lancry SA v. Direction Generale des Douanes* [1994] ECR I-3978.

1989 decision on dock dues which had permitted France to maintain a derogatory taxation regime in the DOM until December 1992.

9.5.6 1997: Amsterdam Treaty

The uncertainty created by the *Legros* and *Lancry* judgments together with concerted lobbying by political representatives of the Outermost Regions, led to substantive changes to Article 299(2) in the Amsterdam Treaty. In particular, the new wording of Article 299(2) sought to reaffirm the *Hansen* principles.

As part of the consolidation process of Community law achieved by the 1997 Amsterdam Treaty, the former Article 227 dealing with the territorial scope of the TEC became Article 299. More specifically, the Amsterdam Treaty introduced for the first time a specific legal basis (Article 299(2)) for the Outermost Regions. This development proceeded from a realisation that the specific EU ('POSEI') programmes intended to enable these regions to catch up with other EU regions were inadequate to the task.

Article 299(2) introduced a number of important changes regarding Outermost Regions:

- first, Article 299(2) referred, not only (as previously) to the DOMs, but also to the Azores, Madeira and the Canary Islands,
- second, Article 299(2) recognised for the first time the particular handicaps of these regions, for example, their remoteness, insularity, small size, difficult terrain and climate and which collectively hinder the economic and social development of the Outermost Regions. On the basis of these disadvantages, Article 299(2) provided that the Council should adopt specific measures setting out the conditions for application to the Outermost Regions of the Treaty and its common policies, including—but not limited to—customs and trade policies, fiscal policy, free zones and agriculture and fisheries policies. In addition, unlike the former Article 227(2), Article 299(2) provided that specific measures for Outermost Regions would be taken by Council acting by qualified majority rather than (as before) by unanimity,
- third, Article 299(2) provides that the special Council measures adopted under the previous paragraph must not undermine the integrity and coherence of the Community legal order, including the internal market and common policies.

Thus, the new Article 299(2) no longer listed Community policies which automatically apply to the Outermost Regions. Rather, the new provision allowed for the adaptation of any Community measure (whether in the form of Directives, Regulations or Decisions). At the same time it added a safeguard, namely that such adaptations must not "undermine the integrity and coherence of the Community legal order."

It is noteworthy also that, under the new framework the Council may adopt specific measures by qualified majority rather than, as before, by unanimity. However, there is consultation only of the Parliament. Thus, the co-decision procedure does not apply even though the derogations may relate to measures which themselves were adapted under the co-decision procedure, thus denying Parliament the right of veto. There are two reasons for this: firstly, it was felt that it would be more difficult to convince Members of the European Parliament of the need for derogations in the Outermost Regions, particularly since only a small number of Member States have Outermost Regions. Secondly, it could be argued that the powers of the Council were more executive rather than legal, hence it was not necessary to use the co-decision procedure.[15]

9.5.7 2000: Post Amsterdam Treaty

Since the Amsterdam European Council included a provision in the Treaty (Article 299(2)) specifically devoted to the Outermost Regions, the broadening out of EU policies beyond the traditional ones of agriculture and fisheries and gradually increased. This process has been emphasized and supported by various documents adopted since 2000 by the European Commission, other EU institutions and Member States concerned.[16] Two Commission reports in March 2000 and December 2002[17] assessed the range of measures adopted for the Outermost Regions and the prospects for their greater convergence and integration.

In May 2004, the European Commission adopted a Communication on 'A stronger partnership for the Outermost Regions'.[18] The proposed strategy also took account of the reform of the EU cohesion policy for 2007–2013. Despite progress in integrating the Outermost Regions with the rest of the EU, the Commission's 2004 Communication identified a number of shortcomings. These included:

- first, a significant difference in the development strategies devised for the various Outermost Regions,

[15] See Ziller 2006.

[16] Most notably, Communication from the Commission: *Strategy for the Outermost Regions: Achievements and Future Prospects*, COM (2007) 507 final, 12 September 2007 and Annex SEC (2007) 1112, 12 September 2007; European Parliament resolution of 28 September 2005 on a stronger partnership for the outermost regions–A60246/2005; Report by the Presidents of the Outermost Regions on the Commission Communication *A stronger partnership for the Outermost Regions*, sent to the European Commission on 17 June 2004; Communication from the Commission: A stronger partnership for the outermost regions COM(2004) 343, 26 May 2004, and Annex SEC (2004) 1030, 6 August 2004; Commission report on measures to implement Article 299(2): the Outermost Regions of the European Union, COM (2000) 147, 14 March 2000.

[17] Ibid. COM (2000) 147 final of 14 March 2000 and COM (2002) 723 final of 19 December 2002.

[18] COM (2004) 343 final, 26 May 2004 and SEC (2004) 1030, *supra* footnote 16.

- second, the fact that some Community policies did not take adequate account of the special features of these regions and that instruments are ill-suited to the Outermost Regions having been devised for the EU as a whole, for example, transport, the environment and the internal market,
- third, in terms of aid and compensation measures, the overemphasis on certain sectors like agriculture and fisheries and a lack of uniformity in the guidelines for aid i.e. most EU aid helps reduce the impact of isolation by lowering costs of transport between mainland Europe and the Outermost Regions, but not in the other direction,
- fourth, absence of a consolidated methodology allowing a more precise evaluation of the handicaps and economic policy.

The Communication went on to highlight 3 priorities for future EU strategy on the Outermost Regions which attempted to address these issues, namely:

- first, stepping up cohesion to benefit the Outermost Regions,
- second, improving the competitiveness of the Outermost Regions,
- third, promoting effective integration into the regional environment.

As regards Cohesion Policy reform, the 2004 Communication highlighted 2 main ways of addressing these priorities:

- first, additional allocation of EU funds to compensate for handicaps and constraints of the Outermost Regions which engender extra production costs, to be financed by the ERDF,
- second, a wider neighbourhood action plan aimed at facilitating cooperation with the neighbouring countries, thus increasing economic, social and cultural links, trade in goods and services and movement of people. As part of this plan, the Outermost Regions would be included in the Economic Partnership Agreements (EPA) between the EU and ACP countries within the general context of the Cotonou Agreement. The Outermost Regions would also be included in the EU's preferential agreements with other non-member countries.

Finally, in addition to the Cohesion Policy, the Commission's 2004 Communication emphasized that other Community policies could also help the development strategy of the Outermost Regions, specifically actions related to competitiveness and growth (e.g. developing human resources, increasing competition in the public services) and constraints on the Outermost Regions (e.g. recommendations included using existing instruments in air and sea transport to improve links between the Outermost Regions and with mainland Europe).

In September 2007, the European Commission adopted a Communication entitled "Strategy for the Outermost Regions: Achievements and Future Prospects".[19] Thedocument takes stock of the action taken since the previous Communication of 2004 and proposes new measures to secure the future of these regions.

[19] COM (2007) 507 final, 12 September 2007, *supra* footnote 16.

The Communication:

- assessed the implementation of the strategy since 2004, giving a detailed description in a working document attached to the Communication,[20]
- put forward short-term measures for fully implementing the 2004 strategy,
- launched a debate on the long-term implications, referring to main themes which are sensitive issues for the Outermost Regions: climate change, demographic change and migration management, agriculture, and EU maritime policy.

As regards progress since the 2004 Communication, the 2007 paper reported that all of the key instruments for the economic and social development of these regions had been redefined and revised. Examples include the revised cohesion policy comprising a special financial allocation to offset the additional costs linked to the handicaps defined in Article 299(2) of the Treaty and specific provisions in favour of the Outermost Regions in the context of the reform of the sugar and banana market organisations. Improved accessibility, stronger competitiveness and better regional integration remain relevant issues and an appropriate response to the development priorities of these regions.

Some of the initiatives put forward in 2004 are still at the development stage, however, particularly the efforts to incorporate the Outermost Regions in the European Research Area, and adapt Services of General Economic Interest to the needs of local markets. Thus, the Communication proposed new measures to secure the future of these regions.

Specifically, the Communication focused on:

(1) Reducing the accessibility deficit and the effects of other constraints specific to the Outermost Regions. For example by:

- exploiting the opportunities offered by the use of the specific allocation to offset the additional costs of transport and new information and communication technologies,
- continuing the effort to fill the broadband gap, particularly via ERDF Ops,
- exploiting the opportunities offered by implementing the Trans European Networks-Transport (TEN-T),Trans European Networks-Energy (TEN-E) and Marco Polo II programmes,
- assessing the specific needs of the Outermost Regions when the POSEI programme implementation report is drawn up.

(2) Making the Outermost Regions more competitive

In particular, strengthening the competitiveness of the Outermost Regions through the financial instruments such as:

[20] Commission Working Document, SEC (2007) 1112, 12 September 2007, *supra* footnote 16.

- Cohesion policy: using the OPs for the 2007–2013 period for both the ERDF and the ESF, the "Regions for Economic Change"[21] initiative, and technical assistance at the initiative of the Commission to help to make the ORs more competitive in terms of the Lisbon strategy for growth and employment and the Community Strategic Guidelines,
- Framework programmes: including for example the 7th FPRTD, the Framework Programme on Innovation and Competitiveness and the Lifelong Learning,
- Services of general economic interest: in relation to the operation of services of general economic interest in these regions, the Commission will continue to take account of regional specificities as well as of a detailed analysis of the relevant market.

(3) Strengthening the Wider Neighbourhood Action Plan

Dialogue between the regions and their neighbouring countries, particularly the ACP countries and the OCTs associated with the EU is the tool for pushing this process forward. Potential measures for pursuing this priority, identified by the 2007 Communication include:

- recognising the special nature of the Outermost Regions in EPAs,
- coordination of financial instruments: on the basis of the dialogue with the ACP and the OCTs under the programme for the 10th EDF, each partner is called on to implement the specific possibilities and practicalities of a concerted EDF and ERDF programming with parallel co-financing arrangements, with a view to cooperation schemes at national and regional level,
- strengthening sea connections between Outermost Regions and neighbouring non-member countries: in the same way that the accessibility of the Outermost Regions has been improved via air transport, a similar approach in called for in the area of maritime transport, specifically by authorising State aid for launching transport services between these regions and neighbouring non-member countries.

In addition to the above measures, the Commission launched in September 2007 a consultation with its partners in order to consider the future of the European strategy for the Outermost Regions. To this end it identified at least four issues for discussion with serious implications for the Outermost Regions both now and in years to come notably:

- first, the challenge of climate change,
- second, the implications of demographic change and migration,
- third, agriculture in the Outermost Regions,
- four, the role of the Outermost Regions in EU maritime policy.

[21] http://ec.europa.eu/regional_policy/cooperation/interregional/ecochange/index_en.cfm.

9.5.8 2007: Lisbon Treaty Amendments to Article 299(2)

Regarding the Outermost Regions, the Lisbon Treaty splits Article 299(2). Thus, Article 299(2) second, third and fourth paragraphs are inserted into a separate new Article 349. The remaining part of Article 299(2), first subparagraph is set out in Article 355 (1).

The reason for the split was that since the first subparagraph merely states the fact of the Treaty applying to the Outermost Regions, it was felt it would be cleaner if only this provision remained with Article 355 (which contains most of what was formerly Article 299 and remains a framework provision for relations between the EU and in particular Member State territories).[22] The remaining provisions of Article 299(2), setting out the more detailed arrangements for the Outermost Regions were taken out and placed in a new Article 349. This was again felt by the drafters of the Treaty to be cleaner and more logical.

In addition to these structural changes and at the request of France, two more territories were added to the list of French DOMs, namely Saint-Barthélemy, Saint-Martin. These latter territories were added to reflect the greater autonomy now accorded them by France, similar to that given to the other French DOMs.

Both Article 349 and 355 are set out under the "General and Final Provisions" of the Lisbon Treaty dealing with the TFEU (formerly the TEC).

In addition to the above provisions, a new paragraph has been added to the existing Article 299 framework, namely Article 355(6), which also has implications for the Outermost Region framework.

This provision was inserted to enable Denmark, France or the Netherlands to alter the status of any of their territories *vis à vis* the EU without having to go through the lengthy formal Treaty amendment procedure. Referred to as the *clause passerelle*, this new provision was drafted and included at the request of these Member States to facilitate a change of status of their territories *vis à vis* the EU without the need for a formal Treaty amendment.

Curiously, the UK territories did not want to avail of this option for their territories of a status change without Treaty amendment, hence the notable exclusion of UK territories from Article 355(6). The UK was not interested in its overseas territories changing from their current OCT to Outermost Region status.

A Declaration (No. 43) in the Final Act of the Intergovernmental Conference on the Lisbon Treaty specifically provides for this change of status from OCT to Outermost Region for French Mayotte, as provided for in Article 355 TFEU.

A further Declaration (No. 60) on Article 355 TFEU, this time by the Netherlands provides that any decision initiated under Article 355 aimed at changing the status of the Netherlands Antilles and/or Aruba *vis à vis* the EU, will be taken only on the basis of a decision taken in conformity with the Charter for the Kingdom of the Netherlands. This provision is relevant specifically for the Netherlands Antilles, of which Bonaire, Saba and Sint Eustatius sought a similar

[22] Source: interview with EU Council Legal Service.

status to the Dutch municipalities. These islands will therefore become part of the EU and may fall under Outermost Region status.[23]

9.6 Conclusions

Article 299(2) is the subparagraph of Article 299 which has been most "dynamic" in that it has been amended, adapted and evolved in line with the new Member State accessions and Treaty amendments but also, more importantly, to reflect the status changes and developments with regard to the territories. In particular, the Maastricht and Amsterdam Treaties have reflected these changes. The amendments to Article 299(2) reflect the joining of new Member States and specific territories and the emergence of a new concept and group of territories—the Outermost Regions. More generally, Article 299(2) has adapted to the many socio-economic and political changes over the years out of which the concept of Outermost Regions was conceived and formulated.

However, whilst the changes and more specifically for present purposes the concerted attempt to adapt Article 299(2) to the present reality are laudable, Article 299(2) has emerged as the framework Treaty provision for the Outermost Regions only. In this way it could be argued, it has deviated from its original purpose, namely to cover all non-European overseas territories with close ties to their Member States and which have special relations with the EU. The result today is that territories not seeking to become Outermost Regions, for example, Ceuta and Melilla, are thus not covered specifically by Article 299(2) or indeed by any specific Article 299 provision.

The Lisbon Treaty does not alter the substance of Article 299(2). The specific reference to the individual territories comprising the Outermost Regions is a welcome clarification. Although the removal of the body of Article 299(2) is in line with the overall function of Article 299 as a framework provision, the creation of a new separate Article (349) to house the detailed arrangements concerning the Outermost Regions (rather than creating a new 'Part' of the Treaty as is the case for the OCTs) creates a disjointedness in the Treaty framework regarding the Outermost Regions.

Reference

Ziller J (2006) Article 299 on Extension of TEC, Hans Smit, Peter Herzog, Christian Campbell & Gudrun Zagel (eds.), Smit & Herzog on the Law of the European Union Vol. 4, Lexis-Nexis

---

[23] The other two islands of the Netherlands Antilles, Curaçao and Sint Maarten have sought the same separate status as Aruba, thus effectively falling outside the EU and remaining part of the OCT framework.

Chapter 10
Article 299(3): Overseas Countries and Territories

Abstract This chapter provides an introduction to the third paragraph of Article 299 TEC, dealing with the Overseas Countries and Territories (OCTs), just before entry into force of the corresponding Lisbon Treaty provision. The key developments since 1957 relevant to this paragraph are examined, including Member State accessions and territories, impact of and points of divergence with the EU/ACP partnership, relevant legislation and case law of the European courts, main Treaty amendments including key amendments introduced by the Lisbon Treaty. An overview of the OCT framework is also examined.

10.1 Introduction (Comparison with 1957 Version)

Article 299(3) (now Article 355(2) TFEU) has two subparagraphs compared to the original one. The first subparagraph remains essentially the same as the original except that the list of countries in Annex II (formerly Annex IV) to which Article 299(3) applies has changed as many of the original territories gained their independence and became OCTs and new territories were added with the accession of new Member States.

The second subparagraph of Article 299(3) was added upon the accession of the UK in 1972. This clarifies that the Treaty shall not apply to those UK territories not mentioned in Annex II. The subparagraph was intended to cover UK territories at the time notably Hong Kong and Rhodesia, neither of which wished to be an OCT or wished to be part of the EU like the French DOMs and thereby fall under Article 299(2).[1]

---

[1] European Commission Legal Service JUR (78) D/01681, 17 May 1978, *Territories of Member States to which the EC competition rules apply.*

F. Murray, *The European Union and Member State Territories: A New Legal Framework Under the EU Treaties*, DOI: 10.1007/978-90-6704-826-2_10,

10.2 Applicable Member States and Territories: Present Day

As mentioned above, the list of countries and territories to which Article 299(3) (Article 355(2) TFEU) and Part Four of the Treaty applies is set out in Annex II to the Treaty. Currently, only 4 EU Member States—UK, France, Netherlands and Denmark—have OCTs. The territories currently listed in Annex II are:
Danish:

- Greenland,

French:

- New Caledonia and Dependencies,
- French Polynesia,
- French Southern and Antarctic Territories,
- Wallis and Futuna Islands,
- Mayotte,
- Saint Pierre and Miquelon

Dutch:

- Aruba,
- Netherlands Antilles comprising Bonaire, Curaçao, Saba, Sint Eustatius, Sint Maarten.

British:

- Anguilla,
- Cayman Islands,
- Falkland Islands,
- South Georgia and the South Sandwich Islands,
- Montserrat,
- Pitcairn,
- Saint Helena and Dependencies,
- British Antarctic Territory,
- British Indian Ocean Territory,
- Turks and Caicos Islands,
- British Virgin Islands,
- Bermuda[2]

[2] Although formerly an OCT as listed in Annex II *infra*, TEC, Bermuda does not benefit from the EU/OCT Association.

10.3 General Characteristics of the OCTs

The following are the key features of the OCTs:

- They are not independent countries (like the ACP States). They do not have the capacity to enter into international legal relations with States or organisations. Rather, their interests are represented by their respective home countries;
- Despite lacking the capacity to enter into international relations, the OCTs are autonomous or semi-autonomous jurisdictions which are constitutionally linked to an EU Member State;
- They are not part of the Union (in contrast to the Outermost Regions, for example);
- The inhabitants of the OCTs have the nationality of the Member States to which they are related.

10.4 Overview of the OCTs

The OCTs are listed in Annex II of the Treaties. Each of the OCTs has a special link with one of the Member States of the EU but the OCTs, unlike the Outermost Regions, are not part of the EU.

The current legal framework governing the EU/OCT association is set out in Part Four of the Treaty (now Articles 198–203 TFEU, ex Article 182–188 TEC) and in a number of Council Decisions, most recently Council Decision 2001/822/EC.[3]

The basic aim of the EU/OCT association, as set out in Article 198 TFEU (ex Article 182 TEC), is "to promote the economic and social development of the countries and territories and to establish close economic relations between them and the Community as a whole".

Declaration No. 36 of the Amsterdam Treaty called on the Commission to review the EU/OCT association in the light of the inadequacy of the current legislative framework to meet the challenges of OCT development. In response to the Declaration, the Commission adopted, in November 2001, Council Decision 2001/822. Decision 2001/822, in accordance with Declaration No. 36, broadly aims to promote more effectively the economic and social development of the OCTs taking into account their specific characteristics and constraints and in the light of the changes that have occurred since the association arrangements began in 1957.

[3] Council Decision 2001/822/EC of 27 November 2001 on the association of the overseas countries and territories with the European Community, OJ L314/1 30 November 2001 and OJ L324/1 7 December 2001, as amended by Council Decision 2007/249/EC, OJ L109/33, 26.4.2007.

The OCTs are, by and large, sparsely populated. Only three of them have a population exceeding 150,000, namely, the (former) Netherlands Antilles,[4] French Polynesia and New Caledonia. Of the twelve British OCTs, five are in the Caribbean (Anguilla, the British Virgin Islands, the Cayman Islands, Montserrat and the Turks and Caicos Islands) and three are in the Atlantic (the Falkland Islands, Saint Helena and the Sandwich Islands). Bermuda is off the east coast of the United States, Pitcairn is in the Pacific Ocean and there is one British territory in the Antarctic.

Most of the French OCTs are in the Pacific Ocean (French Polynesia, New Caledonia and its dependencies, Wallis and Fortuna). The Southern and Antarctic Territories are in the Indian Ocean and the Antarctic continent. Mayotte (in the Indian Ocean) and St. Pierre and Miquelon are off the Canadian Newfoundland coast.

The two Dutch OCTs, Aruba and the Netherlands Antilles, are in the Caribbean.

Finally, the Danish OCT, Greenland stretches from the Arctic Ocean to the Labrador Sea. All of these countries and territories experience the economic disadvantages associated with their distance, low population, dependence on a few economic sectors and lack of many natural resources.

10.4.1 Constitutional Relations with Their Member State

The relationship between the OCTs and the Member States with which they have special links varies. In general, the OCTs are autonomous in legislative matters and the powers retained by the Member States tend to be in the areas of foreign affairs, defence, justice and monetary policy. That said, the powers devolved to the Governments of the OCTs vary considerably.

The OCTs are not part of the EU territory and therefore EU secondary legislation–aside from the Council Decisions adopted under Part Four of the Treaty—does not apply there. EU provisions concerning individuals (particularly as regards EU citizenship and human rights), however, do apply both to EU citizens and to those of the OCTs provided the latter have full nationality of one of the EU Member States. If OCTs fulfill this requirement, they can live, work and move freely within the Community.

The status of citizens of the OCTs *vis à vis* the relevant Member State is therefore important.

---

[4] The Netherlands Antilles was dissolved on 10 October 2010, resulting in two new constituent countries, Curaçao and Sint Maarten, with the other islands joining the Netherlands as special municipalities. This change has not however, been reflected in Annex II of the TFEU. For simplicity therefore, this book will continue to use the generic "Netherlands Antilles" to refer to the territories having that status prior to 10 October 2010.

10.4.1.1 British OCTs

The British OCTs are subject to the Crown with Queen Elizabeth II as their Head of State. The British OCTs, however, are not part of the UK and enjoy a considerable measure of autonomy. The Governors of the British OCTs, appointed by the Foreign Secretary, retain a number of powers generally in the areas of foreign affairs, defence, internal security and justice.

Until recently, most OCTs—with the exception of the citizens of the Falkland Islands-had only "British dependent territory citizenship" rather than full British citizenship. This meant that only citizens of the Falkland Islands enjoyed the same rights as UK citizens to live, work and move freely within the EU.

Since May 2002, however, following a change in UK legislation, all citizens of the British OCTs enjoy full British citizenship. They are thus entitled—like their British counterparts—to live, work and move freely with in EU.

10.4.1.2 French OCTS

As noted above,[5] the French OCTs are an integral part of the French Republic. They consist of the overseas collectivities of French Polynesia, New Caledonia and Wallis and Futuna, Mayotte, Saint Pierre et Miquelon and the French Southern and Antarctic territories. The citizens of the French OCTs have full French citizenship and are thus entitled to live, work and move freely within the EU. As the TEC provisions (apart from Articles 182–188) and secondary legislation do not apply to the OCTs, France must specifically exclude the Territorial Communities from directly applicable Community legislation.

10.4.1.3 Dutch OCTs

Relations between the Netherlands, on the one hand, and the Netherlands Antilles and Aruba, on the other, are governed by the Charter of the Kingdom of the Netherlands of 1954. Essentially, the Netherlands Antilles (as they existed prior to 10 October 2010) and Aruba each enjoy autonomy as regards internal matters. Matters of "common interest", however, are dealt with in association by the Netherlands and both the Netherlands Antilles and Aruba. Matters of "common interest" basically concern all matters falling within international law such as maintaining the country's independence, defending national territory and foreign affairs. The Dutch sovereign is Head of State of both the Kingdom of the Netherlands and of the Netherlands Antilles and Aruba where he is represented by a Governor. Citizens of the Antilles and Aruba have full Dutch nationality and

[5] See Sect. 9.4 *supra* on The DOMs, TOMs and France.

thus, like the French OCT citizens, may live, work and move freely within the Community.

The Netherlands Antilles were dissolved as a unified political entity on October 10, 2010, so that the five constituent islands will attain new constitutional statuses within the Kingdom of the Netherlands.

10.4.1.4 Greenland

Originally a Danish colony, Greenland became part of the Kingdom of Denmark in 1953. Thus, when Denmark joined the EU in 1973, Greenland, too, became part of the EU on the same footing as Denmark. In 1979, Greenland acquired the status of a separate community within the Kingdom of Denmark similar to the "home rule" status granted to the Faroe Islands in 1948.

By this Home Rule Act, nearly all responsibilities hitherto exercised by the Danish authorities were transferred to the autonomous authorities of Greenland. Greenland is broadly autonomous. Generally, local matters are handled by the Greenland authorities, for example, the organisation of local government, tax, trade regulation, fisheries, education, transport and the environment. Denmark remains responsible for defence, foreign affairs and internal security, but Greenland's involvement in these areas has gradually increased. Today, Greenland even has a relative autonomy within the Kingdom of Denmark at international level.

Citizens of Greenland have full Danish citizenship and therefore can also live, work and move freely within the Community.

10.5 Article 299(3): Developments Since 1957, Including Treaty Amendments

10.5.1 Member State Accessions and Territories

Between the signing of the Treaty in 1957 and the present day, the original list of territories (as listed in Part I above) has altered as some of the original territories gained independence and some of the new Member States brought their territories within the OCT framework. The table below ("Overseas Countries and Territories: 1957 to present day") lists all the territories that have formed part of the OCT framework since 1957 indicating those which have since gained independence, become ACPs and, in some cases, changed names. Existing OCTs are highlighted in bold. It is interesting to note the following few anomalies including, at the outset, the addition, on the occasion of the UK accession in 1972, of the second paragraph of Article 299(3) dealing with UK territories not mentioned in Annex II.

With Danish and UK accession in 1972 came a number of territories. Most of the UK's overseas territories, which had less close ties with their mother country than even the French TOMSs with France, fell naturally into the category of OCTs listed in Annex II.

At least one writer has commented that the introduction of this subparagraph on the occasion of UK accession conforms to the general spirit of Article 299 whereby other non-European territories of the Member States which are neither Outermost Regions nor OCTs listed in Annex II, do not fall within the application of Community law.[6] This was the Commission's interpretation in a response to a written question concerning the status of the French islands of Clipperton.[7]

Not all legal commentators have taken this view, however. For example, in 1979, the then Director General of the EU Council's Legal Service, Jean-Louis Dewost gave Article 299(1) a much broader interpretation, as applying to all Member States and their territories over which the exercised sovereign rights, however, limited.[8] Specifically, he noted:

> *L'article 227 par. 1 du Traite doit etre interprete selon nous en ce sens que le Traite et le droit derive, s'applique non seulement sur le territoire des Etats membres, avec ses prolongements aeriens, maritimes (mer territoriale) et de sous-sol,* mais en outre en tout lieu ou les Etats excercent, selon le droit international certains "droits souverains" meme limites. *Ceci resulte, non seulement de la lettre meme de l'article (qui se refere aux Etats et non a leurs territoires) mais egalement de la nature meme d'un Traite-cadre qui concerne potentiellement l'ensemble des activities economiques et sociales des Etats.* (Emphasis added).

10.5.1.1 Bermuda

Although one of the UK overseas territories and therefore, officially, part of the group of OCTs, Bermuda has chosen not to be subject to the Overseas Association Decision implementing Part Four of the TEC. Bermuda is however, entitled to participate in the Partnership Meetings involving British OCTs. Officially, Bermuda is an OCT because it is placed in Annex II of the TEC but does not fall under the scope of the OCT Decisions that the Council takes every 10 years, at its own request. Accordingly, the preamble to Council Decision 2001/822/EC provides: "The arrangements for association laid down in this Decision should not be applied to Bermuda in accordance with the wishes of the Government of Bermuda".[9]

10.5.1.2 Greenland

As a result of Greenland's new home rule status in 1979, the EU Council, in 1984, amended the Treaty with regard to Greenland. Thus, Greenland became an OCT

---

[6] See Megret 1987.

[7] Written Question No 1007/84 OJ C62/34, 11 March 1985 by John Ford to the Commission on the status of Clipperton Island.

[8] Dewost 1979.

[9] See also Preamble to Council Decision 2001/822/EC, *supra* footnote 3.

and Part Four of the Treaty applies to it. Unlike the other OCTs, however, Greenland is not eligible for financial and technical assistance. Instead, Greenland entered into a fisheries agreement with the EU in 1985. This agreement has been implemented by a succession of fisheries protocols concluded between the Community, on the one hand, and Denmark and Greenland, on the other.[10] These provided for compensation to Greenland for catch quotas allocated to the EU in Greenland's waters.

Another significant difference between Greenland and the other OCTs is that this financial compensation by the EU to Greenland does not come from the EDF but from the EU Budget. The compensation does not match the real value of the fishing opportunities offered to the EU (estimated to be around EUR 31.8 million in 2006) and the European Court of Auditors has noted that the financial contribution does not correspond to actual catches either. In 2006, EU aid to Greenland under the Fishing Agreement amounted therefore to around EUR 11 million.

Partly to address this imbalance and to respond also to a request for Greenland for a broader cooperation with the EU beyond fisheries, in June 2006, a Joint Declaration establishing an enlarged partnership between the EU and Greenland was signed (by Greenland, Denmark and the EU).[11] By this declaration, the parties agreed to enlarge their cooperation beyond fisheries agreements to include cooperation in sectors such as education and training, mineral resources, energy, tourism, culture, research and food safety. The partnership also aims at contributing to the sustainable development of Greenland which is particularly concerned by climate changes.

Fisheries remains a cornerstone of this arrangement, now based on a Fisheries Partnership Agreement. In June 2006, the EU and Greenland initialed a Fisheries Partnership Agreement for six years starting from 1 January 2007. The Agreement will replace the previous one which was in force since the entry into force of the Greenland Treaty in 1985.

The Joint Declaration will ensure that the funds from the EU budget allocated to Greenland remain at the same level as in previous years i.e. around EUR 42.8 million—comprising around 25 million towards cooperation in areas other than fisheries; the remaining amount to fisheries.

In July 2006, the EU Council adopted a decision, based on Article 187 TEC, approving the partnership for the period 2007–2013.[12]

---

[10] The last protocol was initialled in June 2006 and runs from January 1, 2007 to December 31, 2012.

[11] Joint Declaration by the European Community, on the one hand, and the Home Rule Government of Greenland and the Government of Denmark, on the other, on partnership between the European Community and Greenland, OJ L 208/32, 29.7.2006.

[12] Council Decision 2006/526/EC of 17 July 2006 on relations between the European Community, on the one hand, and Greenland and the Kingdom of Denmark, on the other, OJ L208/28, 29 July 2006; Commission Regulation 4391/2007/EC implementing Council Decision on relations between the European Community on the one hand, and Greenland and the Kingdom of Denmark on the other, OJ L104/20, 21 April 2007.

10.5.1.3 St Pierre et Miquelon

Originally a French Overseas Territory (TOM), St Pierre et Miquelon became a DOM in July 1976. The TEC (specifically Annex II listing the OCTs) was never amended to reflect this change. However, nine years later, in July 1985, St Pierre et Miquelon was reclassified as a territorial community[13] to comply with EU trade regulations. Later, after the constitutional reform in 2003, St. Pierre et Miquelon became a COM.[14]

10.5.1.4 Mayotte

Formerly part of the Comoros archipelago, Mayotte voted in a 1976 referendum to retain its link with France and to forgo independence. In 2001, Mayotte was granted the status of *collectivitédépartementale*—very close to the status of the *départements* of mainland France. In 2003 Mayotte became a *collectivitéd'outre mer*[15] but still retains the status of *collectivité départementale*. Mayotte has expressed a clear desire to become an EU Outermost Region and thus to become one of the French DOMs. This would entail the full applicability to Mayotte of the EU Treaties. Regarding Mayotte, Declaration No. 43 in the Final Act of the Lisbon Treaty specifically provides that the European Council will take a decision leading to the modification of the status of Mayotte with regard to the EU in order to made this territory an Outermost Region, once the French authorities have notified the Council and European Commission that the evolution currently underway in the internal status of the island so allows.

10.5.1.5 Clipperton Island and the French Scattered Islands in the Indian Ocean

On 21 February 2007, the administration of Clipperton Island was transferred from the High Commissioner of the Republic in French Polynesia (one of the OCTs) to the Minister of Overseas France thus coming under the direct authority of the French Government. Clipperton is a nine-square kilometer coral atoll in the Eastern Pacific Ocean, southwest of Mexico and west of Costa Rica. The Scattered Islands in the Indian Ocean consist of four small coral islands, an atoll, and a reef in the Indian Ocean, and since January 2005 constitute the 5th district of the French Southern and Antarctic Lands (TAAF) (currently part of the OCTs).

---

[13] *Collectivitéerritoriale.*

[14] The category of overseas collectivities (*collectivitésd'outre-mer* or *COM*), was created with the constitutional reform on 28 March 2003.

[15] The other French COMs are French Polynesia, St Pierre et Miquelon and Wallis and Futuna.

Previously the Islands fell under the administration of Réunion (one of the French Outermost Regions).

While it is not clear whether EU Treaties apply to these territories, this has few practical ramifications as they are not permanently inhabited. Since these islands are not explicitly mentioned in the list of OCTs in Annex II or in the list of Outermost Regions in the EU Treaties, it could suggest that by virtue of Article 299(1) (Article 52(1) TEU) which applies to all Member States and by implication their territories, all EU Treaties apply to them in full. However, in relation to Clipperton Island, the European Commission, in response to a written question in 1984, replied that as Clipperton is neither a European territory nor an overseas department explicitly mentioned in Article 299, it is therefore not covered by the Treaty.[16] Since Clipperton now falls under the direct authority of the French Government it could be argued that there is a stronger case today for application of the EU Treaties to this Island.

10.5.1.6 Netherlands Antilles

The Netherlands Antilles are currently in the process of constitutional reform and disbanded on 10 October 2010. The Netherlands Antilles was dissolved and replaced by the two overseas autonomous countries of Curaçao and Sint Maarten (with a status similar to Aruba) on the one hand, and the three Dutch municipalities of Bonaire, Saba and Sint Eustatius on the other hand. The latter three will have to apply most of Dutch law and could then opt to become an Outermost Region of the EU if they so wished. The former would effectively fall outside the EU and could remain part of the OCT framework. A separate Declaration by the Kingdom of the Netherlands on Article 355 TFEU (Lisbon Treaty) states that a European decision aimed at amending the status of the Netherlands Antilles and/or Aruba regarding the Union, will be submitted only on the basis of a decision taken in conformity with the Charter for the Kingdom of the Netherlands Table 10.1.

10.5.2 1958: Emergence of EU/ACP Partnership

During the five year period of validity of the OCT Implementation Agreement, the process of decolonisation began as a result of the numbers of dependent overseas countries and territories decreased (see table above). Many of these newly independent countries were concerned not to lose the benefits of their association with

[16] Supra footnote 7. Specifically, the Commission responded: "It follows from the combined provisions of Article 227(1, 2, and 3) of the Treaty establishing the European Economic Community that, as far as the French Republic is concerned, the Treaty applies to its European territory and overseas departments. As the French territory of Clipperton Island belongs to neither, it is not covered by the Treaty."

Table 10.1 Overseas Countries and Territories: 1957 to present day[17]

1957	**1958–1975**	**1972 (UK, Danish accessions)**	**1973-present**
FRENCH			
French West Africa (Senegal, French Sudan,[18] French Guinea,[19] Ivory Coast, Dahomey,[20] Mauritania, Niger and Upper Volta[21])	Gained independence in 1958. Became ACPs		
French Equatorial Africa (Middle Congo,[22] Ubangi-Shari,[23] Chad and Gabon)	Gained independence in 1960. Became ACPs		
Saint Pierre et Miquelon[24]			
The Archipelago of the Comores[25]	Gained independence in 1975. Became ACPs, except for **Mayotte,** which remained under French control and thus an OCT		Mayotte to become an Outermost Region
Madagascar and dependencies	Gained independence in 1960. Became an ACP		
The French Somali Coast[26]	Gained independence in 1967. Became an ACP		

[17] Present day OCTs outlined in bold.

[18] Now Mali.

[19] Now Guinea.

[20] Now Bénin.

[21] Now Burkina Faso.

[22] Now Republic of Congo.

[23] Now Central African Republic.

[24] St Pierre et Miquelon, originally a French TOM, became a DOM in 1976 and later, in 1985, reverted to a TOM.

[25] Now the Union of the Comoros.

[26] Now Djibouti.

Table 10.1 (continued)

1957	1958–1975	1972 (UK, Danish accessions)	1973-present
New Caledonia and dependencies			
French settlements in Oceania	Now **French Polynesia** and **Wallis and Futuna Islands**		Since February 2007, Clipperton Island, formerly under administration of French Polynesia, was transferred to the administration of the French Ministry of Overseas and thus the direct authority of the French Government
French Southern and Antarctic Territories			Since January 2005, the French Scattered Islands of the Indian Ocean, formerly under the administration of Réunion, were transferred to administration of the French Southern and Antarctic Territories.
FRENCH/ BRITISH			
Autonomous Republic of Togo	Gained independence in 1960. Became an ACP		
The trust territory of the Cameroons under French administration	Gained independence in 1961. Became an ACP		
		Anglo-French Condominium of the New Hebrides[27]	Gained independence in 1980. Became an ACP
BELGIAN			
The Belgian Congo[28] and Ruanda-Urundi[29]	Gained independence 1960–1962. Became ACPs		

[27] Now Vanuatu.

[28] Now the Republic of Congo.

[29] Now Rwanda and Burundi.

Table 10.1 (continued)

1957	1958–1975	1972 (UK, Danish accessions)	1973-present
ITALIAN			
The trust territory of Somaliland under Italian administration[30]	Gained independence in 1960. Became an ACP		
DUTCH			
Netherlands New Guinea[31]	Annexation of New Guinea to Indonesia in 1969		
Netherlands Antilles (included **Aruba**—gained a separate status in 1986)	Became an OCT in 1964		Since October 2010, Bonaire, Saba and Sint Eustatius have become Dutch Municipalities and may thus possibly become Outermost Regions. St Maarten and Curacao have assumed the status of *"Land"* like Aruba.
Surinam[32]	Became an OCT in 1962		
BRITISH			
		The Bahamas	Gained independence in 1973. Became an ACP.
		Bermuda	
		British Antarctic Territory	
		British Honduras[33]	Gained independence in 1981. Became an ACP.
		British Indian Ocean Territory	
		British Solomon Islands	Gained independence in 1978. Became an ACP
		British Virgin Islands	
		Brunei	Became fully independent in 1984. NOT an ACP

[30] Upon independence, Italian Somaliland united with British Somaliland to form the Republic of Somalia.

[31] Now part of Indonesia's provinces, Papua and West Papua.

[32] Gained independence in November 1975.

[33] Now Belize.

Table 10.1 (continued)

1957	1958–1975	1972 (UK, Danish accessions)	1973-present
		Associated States in the Caribbean: Antigua,[34] Dominica, Grenada, St Lucia, St Vincent,[35] St Kitts-Nevis-**Anguilla**[36]	Gained independence between 1974 and 1983. Became ACPs
		Cayman Islands	
		Central and Southern Line Islands[37]	
		Falkland Islands and Dependencies	
		Gilbert[38] and Ellice Islands[39]	Gained independence in 1979 and 1978 respectively. Became ACPs
		Montserrat	
		Pitcairn	
		St Helena and Dependencies	
		The Seychelles[40]	Gained independence in 1976. Became an ACP
		Turks and Caicos Islands	
DANISH			
			Greenland[41]

the Community. Therefore, the association with the now independent overseas countries and territories was continued on the basis of the Yaoundé I and II Conventions between the AAMS (Association of African and Malagasy States) and the European Community, signed in 1963 and 1969 respectively. These latter agreements constituted the first step in the creation of the EU/ACP partnership,

[34] Now Antigua and Barbuda.

[35] Now St Vincent and the Grenadines.

[36] Now Nevis and Anguilla. Currently, only Anguilla is an OCT.

[37] Now the Republic of Kiribati.

[38] Now Kiribati.

[39] Now Tuvalu.

[40] Now the Republic of Seychelles.

[41] Added to the OCT framework by Article 4 of the Treaty amending with regard to Greenland, the Treaties establishing the European Communities OJ L29 1 February 1985.

leading to the Lomé Conventions, the first concluded in 1976 with 46 ACP States and the fourth in 1990 to cover a ten-year period until 2000. In June 2000, the Cotonou Agreement was signed between the Community, its Member States and the ACP countries. The Cotonou Agreement replaced the Lomé Convention. Those countries which did not opt for independence remained part of the EU/OCT association.

10.5.3 1962 (–2001): EU/OCT Council Decisions

Following the expiry of the Implementation Agreement in 1962, the specific rules concerning the OCTs were set out in a series of Council Decisions, adopted unanimously, replaced at 5 year intervals.[42] The current implementation decision entered into force in December 2001 and, unlike its predecessors applies for 10 years until 31 December 2011,[43] for a more detailed analysis of Decision (2001/822/EC), see below, 'Current EU legal framework governing OCTs'.

10.5.4 1991: Council Decision 91/482/EEC

From the late 1980s it became clear that EU policy towards ACPs was becoming less relevant to the OCTs. For example, the OCTs differed on the whole from ACPs in their macro-economic structural adjustment, good governance and human rights. Accordingly, in 1991, the latest Council Decision 91/482/EEC[44] introduced a number of important innovations:

- Extending the duration of the Decision from 5 to 10 years
- increased financial assistance,
- the introduction of a three-way partnership between the Commission, the relevant Member State and the relevant OCT which would facilitate consultation with local communities in the OCT in question,
- greater emphasis, *inter alia*, on environmental protection, the role of women and on promoting business ventures and services,

---

[42] The first such Council Decision applicable to the OCTs was Decision 64/349/EEC of 25 February 1964, OJ 1964/1472. It was replaced by a succession of Decisions: 70/549/EEC of 25 September 1970, OJ 1970 L282/83; 76/568/EEC of 29 June 1976, OJ 1976 L176/8; 80/1186/EEC of 16 December 1980, OJ 1980 L361/1; 86/283/EEC of 30 June 1986, OJ 1986 L175/1; 91/482/EEC of 25 July 1991, OJ 1991 L263/1 as amended by Decision 97/803/EC of 24 November 1997, OJ 1997 L329/50.

[43] Council Decision 2001/822/EC of 27 November 2001 on the association of the overseas countries and territories with the European Community, *supra footnote* 3.

[44] *Supra* footnote 42.

– implementing joint regional projects for OCT and ACP States in the same geographical area and which shared similar features and were subject to similar constraints.

10.5.5 1993: Maastricht Treaty

A Declaration annexed to the Maastricht Treaty on the representation of the interests of the OCTs and (also to the Faroe Islands and the Sovereign Base Areas of the UK in Cyprus), noted that in the unusual event of divergences arising between the interests of the EU on the one hand, and those of the above-mentioned territories on the other, the EU Council of Ministers would first try to reach a solution which would be in accordance with the EU position.[45] If this were not possible, however, the Declaration went on to state that the Member State responsible for the territory in question and after giving notice to the EU Council and Commission, could act separately in the interests of the territory without this affecting the Community's interests. The Declaration also noted its application to Macao and East Timor, then Portuguese territories.[46]

10.5.6 1997: Council Decision 97/803/EC

Article 240 of Decision 91/482 provided that after 5 years the Council would adopt a Decision establishing the Community's financial assistance for the second five year period covered by Decision 91/482 and would review various aspects of the procedures governing the association. In particular, Decision 97/803 aimed to strengthen the three-way partnership by ensuring more regular consultations and by promoting local initiatives through decentralized cooperation.

10.5.7 1997: Amsterdam Treaty

The break from the traditional parallelism between the OCTs and ACPs was taken a step further by the Treaty of Amsterdam, signed in October 1997. Declaration No.36 of the Amsterdam Treaty recognized that the special arrangements for OCTs provided by the 1957 Treaty of Rome were no longer effectively meeting

---

[45] See Annex XI *infra* Declaration on the Overseas Countries and Territories, Maastricht Treaty 1992.

[46] Since Macao was returned to China in December 1999 and East Timor gained independence in May 2002, the Declaration no longer applies to these jurisdictions.

the challenges of OCT development.[47] This is because whereas formerly there were many OCTs covering vast areas of the world and with large populations, today only a few of the original OCTs remain and their total population is less than one million. Declaration No. 36 recognized that most OCTs lag far behind the EU in structural terms which is due in part to their geographical and economic disadvantages. Therefore, the Declaration called on the Council to review the association arrangements of the OCTs with four specific objectives in mind, namely:

- Promoting the economic and social development of the OCTs more effectively
- Developing economic relations between the OCTs and the EU
- Taking great account of the diversity of individual OCTs
- Improving the effectiveness of the financial instrument.

To reflect the changes in relations between the EU and the OCTs, the Amsterdam Treaty also effected a number of amendments to Part Four of the Treaty (ex Articles 131–136, which became Articles 182–188 with the Amsterdam Treaty). For example, the former Article 131 had included Member States like Belgium and Italy that no longer had overseas territories. This was therefore amended to reflect the change so that the current text only refers to the 4 Member States—Denmark, France, the Netherlands and the UK—currently having overseas territories.

10.5.8 2001: Council Decision 2001/822/EC

In November 2001, the Council adopted Council Decision 2001/822/EEC which is intended to fulfill the obligations of Declaration No. 36 and replaces Decision 91/482. Decision 2001/822/EC places greater emphasis on the EU/Member State/OCT partnership and, in particular, gives the OCTs themselves greater responsibility for programming and implementing the co-operation arrangements. For a more detailed analysis of Decisions 2001/822, see below under 'Current EU legal framework governing OCTs'.

10.5.9 2007: Lisbon Treaty Amendments to Article 299(3)

The Lisbon Treaty introduces no substantive changes to the current content of either Article 299 (3) nor to Part Four (Articles 182–188) of the TEC, which set out the legal framework of the EU/OCT association.

Significantly, however, a new paragraph is added to the current Article 299—Article 355 (6) in the Lisbon Treaty allows the European Council acting

[47] See Annex XII *infra* Declaration No. 36 on the OCTs, Amsterdam Treaty 1997.

unanimously and on the initiative of a relevant Member State, to adopt a decision amending the status, with regard to the EU, of a Danish, French or Netherlands Outermost Region or OCT.

The purpose of this provision was to take account of territories such as French Mayotte and the Netherlands Antilles and Aruba, currently OCTs, which at the time the Lisbon Treaty was agreed, were considering a possible constitutional status change *vis à vis* their Member States and the EU to become Outermost Regions and therefore part of the EU. The inclusion of Article 355(6) would permit this status change without having to formally amend the Treaty. Significantly, as none of the UK territories was interested at the time of negotiations regarding this provision in a similar status change, the UK and its OCTs chose not to be included in Article 355(6).

Regarding Mayotte, as noted above, Declaration No. 43 in the Final Act of the Lisbon Treaty specifically provides that the European Council, pursuant to Article 355(6), will take a decision leading to the modification of the status of Mayotte with regard to the EU in order to made this territory an Outermost Region within the meaning of Article 355(1) and Article 349, once the French authorities have notified the Council and European Commission that the evolution currently underway in the internal status of the island so allows.

A separate Declaration by the Kingdom of the Netherlands on Article 355 likewise states that a European decision pursuant to Article 355(6) aimed at amending the status of the Netherland Antilles and/or Aruba regarding the Union, will be submitted only on the basis of a decision taken in conformity with the Charter for the Kingdom of the Netherlands.

10.5.10 June 2008: Commission Communication

In June 2008, the European Commission tabled a Green Paper on the future relation with OCT, aimed at launching a broad debate on the EU/OCT relations.[48] The paper recognizes that for historic reasons, the current EU/OCT relationship was very much modeled on the relationship with the ACP and that such an agreement does not correspond to the specific social, economic and environmental challenges faced by OCTs today.

The Green Paper was intended to launch a broad discussion on the opportunity of replacing the current agreement with a new innovative partnership for the OCTs. Any future partnership would be tailored to their specific status, needs, challenges and potential whilst also recognising the close link, mutual interest and solidarity between the OCTs and the EU. Such partnership would fully or partly

[48] Commission Green Paper: *Future relations between the EU and the Overseas Countries and Territories*, COM (2008) 383 final, 25 June 2008; Commission staff working document accompanying the Green Paper, SEC (2008) 2067, 25 June 2008.

replace the current one when the present Overseas Association Decision expires on 31 December 2013. The Green Paper cautions, however, that the paper does not set out to create a new policy or to establish new financial instruments or detailed procedures.

The Green Paper poses questions on various aspects of the EU/OCT relationship including how to promote the sustainable development of the OCTs, how to make the partnership more active and reciprocal, in the mutual interests of both EU and OCTs, trade issues such as how to ensure greater regional economic integration of the OCTs and a review of the current EU/OCT trade arrangements.

Following the public consultation, the Commission will propose a new partnership that takes better account of the special characteristics and present economic situation in the OCTs.

10.6 EU Legal Framework and Policy Governing Relations Between the OCTs and the EU

The special arrangements for the association of the OCTs are set out in Part Four of the TEC (formerly Articles 182–188) now Articles 198–203 TFEU)[49] and in a series of Council Decisions, most recently Decision 2001/822/EC. As outlined above, the provisions of Part Four have altered little since 1957.

10.6.1 Part Four (Articles 182–188) of the TEC 2009

As noted above and in Part II of this book the special regime applying to the OCTs in Part Four of the Treaty was until the entry into force of the Lisbon Treaty set out in Articles 182 to 188 of the Treaty. The provisions of Part Four have altered little since 1957. The main changes are as follows:

Article 182 (now Article 198 TFEU): the addition of new Member States with OCTs, notably the UK and Denmark and the removal of those no longer having relevant territories, for example, Belgium and Italy.

Article 184 (now Article 200 TFEU): dealing with customs duties on imports from OCTs to Members. Whereas the original version provided for the progressive abolition of customs duties, the present version prohibits them outright. The progressive abolition in the original version was to enable the Member States to gradually adapt to the EU regime. The subject of eliminating customs duties is largely outdated as; in any event, EU customs duties are now much lower than they were.

---

[49] See Annex XIII *infra* Part Four (Articles 182–188) TEC 2009.

Article 187 (Article 203 TFEU) replaces the original Article 136. Article 136 clarified that the detailed provisions of the EU/OCT arrangement would be set out in the initial 5 year Implementing Convention and thereafter that the Council, on the basis of the experience acquired and Treaty principles, would adopt provisions for a further period. Article 187 continues the second subparagraph of Article 136 providing that the Council will adopt detailed rules and provisions governing relations between the EU and the OCTs. These rules and provisions have been set out in a series of Council Decisions, the current one being Decision 2001/822/EC.

Finally, since 1957 a new article was added to Part Four. Specifically, Article 188 (removed by the Lisbon Treaty) provided that Articles 182 to 187 (or Part Four) applied to Greenland subject to specific provisions adopted for Greenland as set out in the Protocol on Greenland annexed to the Treaty.

10.6.2 Council Decision 2001/822/EC

As already mentioned, the Treaty of Amsterdam included a Declaration on the Overseas Countries and Territories (Declaration No. 36). In the Declaration it was noted that the special arrangements for the association of the OCTs had changed little since 1957. This was despite the fact that the arrangements had originally been designed for OCTs which were more numerous, covered larger areas and larger populations than the present-day OCTs. The Declaration furthermore noted that the special arrangements conceived in 1957 were no longer appropriate since the OCTs still lagged behind in structural terms.

Specifically, the Commission, in a Communication of May 1999 identified some of the problems of the current EU/OCT association arrangements.[50] In particular, it noted the ambivalent approach of the EU towards the OCTs. On the one hand, the OCTs were given parallel treatment to the ACP countries. On the other hand, however, the OCTs were treated as part of the Community in respect of certain aspects of EU secondary legislation, for example, regarding certain trade arrangements, the right of establishment and the rights of individuals where those individuals held the nationality of a Member State. The Commission also alluded to the uncertainty of the EU role in the development of the OCTs. For example, other Member States have asked why the EU taxpayer should bear the cost of EU aid to OCTs rather than the relevant Member States. The relevant Member States, however, considered that their territories were entitled to greater attention than third countries.

The Amsterdam Treaty Declaration reaffirmed the association's basic aim, that of promoting the economic and social development of the OCTs and to establish closer economic ties between the OCTs and the EU as a whole. The Declaration

---

[50] Communication from the Commission: *The status of OCTs associated with the EC and options for "OCT* 2000", COM (1999) 163 final, 20 May 1999.

then called on the Council, on the basis of Article 136 of the Treaty (now Article 203 TFEU) to review the association arrangements in the light of the following four objectives:

- Promoting the economic and social development of the OCTs more effectively,
- developing economic relations between the OCTs and the European Union,
- taking greater account of the diversity and specific characteristics of the individual OCTs, including aspects relating to the freedom of establishment,
- ensuring that the effectiveness of the financial instrument is improved.

Following consultations with the Member States concerned and taking into account the view of the OCTs and the resolution of the European Parliament of February 11, 1999, the Council, in November 2001, adopted Decision 2001/822/EC setting out a new arrangement regarding the association of the overseas countries and territories with the EC.[51] The proposed Decision introduced a number of changes to the EU/OCT association. These included the following:

- A condensed text—42 articles instead of the 242 of the previous Council Decision (91/482/EEC),
- greater emphasis on the trilateral (EU/Member State/OCT) partnership and management by the OCTs, although the overall allocation to the OCTs under the 9th EDF (covering the period 2000–2005) did not significantly increase (from EUR 165–175 million), the Decision provided that the financial resources granted to the OCTs were to be managed more on the basis of the trilateral partnership, applying procedures based on the rules in force for the structural funds. Thus, the main responsibility for programming and implementing cooperation would be on the OCTs themselves. Until the adoption of Decision 2001/822, funds had been allocated by the EU to the three Member States concerned and the latter had redistributed those funds as they sought fit to their own OCTs. Under the new Decision, EDF funds would be distributed by the EU to each of the OCTs directly,
- the inclusion of trade in services and trade-related areas in development finance cooperation in order to help the OCTs adapt to the changing world economy,
- giving OCT citizens the opportunity to participate in all programmes normally reserved for EU citizens, specifically research, development and innovation programmes and better access to higher education in Europe,
- updating and clarifying the rules of origin. The rules regarding trade in products remain fundamentally unchanged. There was concern, however, that a rise in OCT exports made from sugar of ACP or Community origin to the EU had caused a considerable reduction in the quota for Community producers and disruption to the Community market. It was decided therefore that the origin rules would be adopted which would progressively exclude the possibility of ACP/OCT cumulation for sugar when only minimal operations are carried out.

[51] *Supra*, footnote 3.

Council Decision 2001/822/EEC sets out the details of the EC/OCT association in 64 articles and 5 annexes. The following is a summary of the key provisions:

- Articles 1–9: lay down the foundations of the EC/OCT association, covering the economic, cultural and social developments of the OCTs. Specifically, Articles 7(2) and (3) provide respectively for an EC/OCT forum for dialogue which meets annually and partnership working parties for each territory comprising, in addition to representatives of the territory, the Member State with which it is linked and the European Commission;
- Articles 10–17: concern out the substantive areas of cooperation between the Community and the OCTs, including the productive sectors, development of trade, trade in services, trade-related areas such as protection and promotion of investments, competition policy, social sectors and regional cooperation and integration;
- Articles 18–60 (Part Three): deals with the instruments of cooperation between the EU and the OCTs, including principles of the development finance cooperation, the specific regulations on the economic and trade cooperation between the Community and the OCTs—trade in goods, trade in services and the freedom of establishment, consumer health and other matters including monetary and tax and the eligibility of individuals from the OCTs to receive vocational training in the Community.

10.6.3 Application to OCTs of Other TEC Provisions

An open question up to the entry into force of the Lisbon Treaty was whether only Part Four (Articles 182–188) applied to the OCTs or whether other provisions of the Treaty also applied. The ECJ in *Kaefer & Procacci*[52] indicated that parts Five (Institutions) and Six (General and Final Provisions) applied to the OCTs, while the Court in *Eman & Sevinger*[53] clarified that Part Two (Citizenship) applied. It had been suggested by some legal commentators[54] that Part One (Principles) also applied to the OCTs. In *Antillean Rice Mills*[55] the CFI indicated that all principles of the Treaty applied to the OCTs but this application was limited to the Council Decision regulating the association. Thus, the Council Decision must apply the Community principles but the Court left open the question whether the Treaty

[52] Joined Cases C-100/89 and 101/89 *Peter Kaefer and Andréa Procacci v. French State Kaefer & Procacci, supra* footnote 23.

[53] Case C-300/04 *M.G. Eman and* O.B. *Sevinger v. College van burgemeester en wethouders van Den Haag* [2006] ECR I-8055.

[54] For example, see Ziller 2006.

[55] Joined Cases T-480/93 and T-483/93 *Antillean Rice Mills NV, Trading & Shipping Co. Ter Beek BV, European Rice Brokers AVV, Alesie Curaçao NV and Guyana Investments AVV v. Commission* [1995] ECR II-2305.

principles applied to areas not covered by the Council Decision. What is clear is that Part Three (Internal Market) did not apply.

10.6.4 Areas of EU/OCT Co-operation

The particular objectives of the EU/OCT association reflect the key objectives of the EU's development policy as set out within other development cooperation agreements, notably the Cotonou Agreement governing the EU/ACP arrangements. This cooperation focuses in particular on the following 3 objectives:

- The reduction, prevention and eradication of poverty
- sustainable development
- the gradual integration of the OCTs into the regional and global economies.

There are 6 main areas of co-operation which cover all industry sectors including transport, agriculture, environment, energy and tourism:

10.6.4.1 Economic and Trade Co-operation: Trade Arrangements

The OCTs enjoy preferential trade arrangements with the EU. Thus, although products originating in the OCTs enjoy free and unlimited access to the Community market, this arrangement is non-reciprocal. OCTs may, therefore, impose customs duties and quantitative restrictions on products originating in the EU. The only requirement under the EU/OCT association arrangement is that there is no discrimination of Community exports by the OCTs as compared with other developed countries. Likewise, OCTs may not discriminate between Member States of the EU.

According to the cumulation of origin rule, products are deemed to originate in the OCTs and therefore may benefit from preferential treatment if they originate entirely in the OCTs or are made up of products from another OCT or an ACP or EU country. In order to protect the EU market, however, Decision 2001/822 introduced specific restrictions on the application of the cumulation of origin rule in respect of certain sensitive foodstuffs, particularly rice and sugar. The Community market has been seriously disrupted by the widespread arrival of certain sensitive foodstuffs, especially rice and sugar grown by other third countries but processed and exported as originating products by OCTs, which do not grow them. Regarding sugar, therefore, the cumulation of origin rule will be removed altogether from January 2011. Concerning rice, the use of the cumulation of origin must be limited through the imposition of quotas. In general, Decision 2001/822 provides for safeguard measures which may be used if the Community or Member State markets are disrupted excessively.

The transshipment of goods system has applied to the OCTs since 1991. This provides free access to the EU for products not originating in the OCTs but which have transited through the OCTs in the unaltered state and imported into the EU. However, such products must meet certain conditions. For example, producers and importers of such products must pay customs duties to the OCTs. In addition, the transshipment procedure does not apply to agricultural products or goods resulting from the processing of agricultural products, except the import into the EU of a limited volume of fishery products from Greenland and Saint-Pierre-et-Miquelon.

10.6.4.2 Trade Development

One of the primary aims of the EU/OCT association is to integrate the OCTs in the global economy by offering support for trade development at all levels as well as integrating the OCTs into regional markets. This includes devising coherent trade strategies, strengthening trade infrastructure, for example, storage facilities and encouraging private investment.

Regarding trade in services, specifically, the EU provides assistance to support infrastructures and human resources in various sectors including transport, telecommunications, information society and tourism. The development of telecommunications and the information society in particular are viewed as necessary for the successful integration of the OCTs into the global economy.

10.6.4.3 Trade-Related Areas

The EU assists the OCTs in a number of trade-related matters, for example, in the areas of competition policy, intellectual property, information technology, consumer protection and the environment. The EU implements measures designed to enhance the capacities of the OCTs in these sectors.

10.6.4.4 Human and Social Development

Under the EU/OCT arrangement, the Community also aids human and social development, for example, education programmes to improve access to the quality of and access to education; health projects, particularly for family planning and child and maternal health; water policy and housing and integrated urban development in particular improving roads and low-income housing.

10.6.4.5 Regional Co-operation and Integration

The EU/OCT association also facilitates regional co-operation and integration both between OCTs themselves and between OCTs and third countries, including the

ACPs. Such interactivity helps promote the basic aim of the association, namely, the economic and social development of the OCTs. In particular, it accelerates economic cooperation and development and promotes the free movement of persons, goods, services and technology.

10.6.4.6 Cultural and Social Development

The association also encourages cultural and social co-operation among the citizens of the OCTs, for example, by improving their human resources and promoting cultural identities. This helps ensure the autonomous development of the OCTs.

10.6.5 Implementation of the EU/OCT Arrangements

Implementation of the EU/OCT association is based on the trilateral relationship of European Commission, relevant Member State and OCT. Two key institutions are involved in this implementation:

- The EU/OCT forum which meets annually, bringing together all 3 partners, and
- An individualized partnership for each OCT, comprising partnership working parties acting in an advisory capacity, made up of representatives of the 3 partners.

In addition, the OCTs maintain a close relationship with the ACP countries, both of which benefit from the EDF. The OCTs are kept informed of the activities of the ACP countries in the context of the Cotonou Agreement and may participate as observers in the plenary sessions of the ACP/EU Joint Parliamentary Assembly.

For each OCT a development and cooperation strategy is adopted in the form of a Single Programming Document (SPD). As the OCTs have primary responsibility for determining and implementing cooperation measures, the SPD is drafted mainly by the OCTs and is adopted jointly with the other 2 partners. All 3 partners monitor and evaluate implementation.

Finally, civil society—including non-governmental organizations, social, business and trade union organizations—also play an important part in the EU/OCT development cooperation.

10.6.6 EU Financial Assistance

The OCTs are eligible for five types of EU financial assistance:

- EU EDF grants
- Refundable aid from the Investment Facility

- European Investment Bank (EIB) loans
- Aid under the horizontal budget lines
- Aid under Community programmes.

EU EDF grants: under the 10th EDF (for the period 2007–2013), the OCTs were eligible for EDF grants totaling EUR 286 million, of which EUR 30 million was set aside for the Investment Facility. The EDF grants are managed by the European Commission, the Investment Facility by the EDF.

Horizontal budget lines: The OCTs may access EU aid provided through budget lines for sectoral development policies such as food, humanitarian aid, aid for NGOs, to raise awareness of development, for the environment, health, combating drugs etc.

Financial resources from the EU programmes: Programmes in the fields of education, training and youth, research, enterprise and the audiovisual sector are open to the OCTs.

In March 2007, the Council adopted a technical amendment to Decision 2001/822 which did two things: first, it included coverage of the EDF allocation up to 2013 (Decision 2001/822 only covered the period up to 2011). Second, whereas 2001/822 provided an exhaustive list of EU programmes to which the OCTs were eligible, the amendment opened up this applicability for OCTs to all EU programmes.[56]

10.6.7 OCT/ACP Parallelism

As noted above, the reason for the traditional parallelism in the Community relationship with the OCTs on the one hand, and the ACP countries on the other, has been their common origin. The EU/OCT association preceded the EU/ACP relationship, the details of which were set out in the Implementing Agreement annexed to the original 1957 TEC. The association was defined by Articles 131–136 TEC, which also provided for the setting up of the EDF.

As the former OCTs gained independence, most sought to continue to benefit from their relationship with the EU. As a result, the Yaoundé I and II Conventions between the AAMS (Association of African and Malagasy States) and the European Community were signed in 1963 and 1969 respectively and these constituted the first step in the EU/ACP partnership.

Thus, from 1957 to 1991, the OCT association was updated every five years in line with the Lomé Conventions.

There are, however, a number of significant differences in the EU relationship between the OCTs and the ACP countries.

---

[56] Council Decision 2007/249/EC 19 March 2007 amending Decision 2001/822/EC on the association of the overseas countries and territories with the European Community, *supra* footnote 3.

First, unlike the ACP countries, the OCTs are not independent and maintain constitutional links with Member States.

Second, unlike ACP citizens, citizens of OCTs have the nationality of the Member State to which they are related (although OCT citizens may not in all cases enjoy the benefits of full citizenship of the Member State concerned).

Third, as has been noted, Decisions 91/482, 97/803 and 2001/822 introduced a number of new initiatives which are not part of the EU/ACP relationship. Thus:

- Trade: OCT originating products, unlike their counterparts from ACP countries, enjoy totally free access to the Community,
- Transhipment: a transhipment system was introduced for OCTs (but not for ACP countries) which permits any OCT to impose EU customs duties on third country products and then treat them as products in free circulation on the Community market. Thus, the country or territory, and not the EU, receives the duty,
- Right of establishment/provision of services: OCTs were granted the right to give preference to employment of their nationals in certain sensitive areas with prior approval of the Commission and provided there is no discrimination between Member States,
- EU/Member State/OCT partnership: the final departure from the traditional OCT/ACP parallelism introduced by Decision 91/482 was the setting up of the trilateral Commission/Member State/OCT partnership in order to ensure greater participation by local authorities in OCTs,
- Finally, Decision 2001/822 provides that EDF funding should be managed on the basis of procedures similar to those used for the structural funds and with more responsibility for project management at the level of the OCTs. Until recently, the EDF had been applied to the OCTs in the same way as to the ACP countries.

The Cotonou Agreement and Decision 2001/822 for the new EU/OCT association have widened still further the differences in the EU relationship with the two groups. Thus, for example, the Cotonou Agreement has an increasingly political content compared with Decision 2001/822 on OCTs in that there is greater emphasis on human rights and good governance in that Agreement. Such provisions were not considered necessary in respect of the OCTs.

Despite the growing differences, the OCTs maintain a close relationship with the ACPs. Both groups benefit from the EDF. The OCTs are kept informed of the activities of the ACPs in the context of the Cotonou Agreement and they participate as observers in the plenary sessions of the ACP/EU Joint Parliamentary Assembly.

10.7 Conclusions

The original intention of Article 299(3) was to replace the then bilateral agreements with Member State overseas territories (mainly French) having a greater degree of autonomy than the French DOMs, with a framework that would dismantle customs duties and improve the socio-economic welfare of those territories. This framework was set out in Article 299(3) and elaborated in Part Four of the Treaty and in the original Implementing Convention.

The EU/OCT Association (as it is still known today) has evolved in the following key ways:

- More Member States and a greater variety of territories
- move from mainly developing African territories to mostly richer Caribbean jurisdictions
- replacement of original Implementing Convention with Council Decisions
- review and improvement of the Association e.g by introducing a 3 way partnership—Commission, Member State, territory in order to facilitate consultation with local OCT communities (Decision 91/482/EC) and giving OCTs more responsibility for programming and implementing funds allocated to them and giving OCT citizens the opportunity to participate in all programmes normally reserved for EU citizens
- Extension by the ECJ to the OCTs of other parts of the TEC (other than Part Four)
- finally, the Lisbon Treaty facilitates a move by the French, Dutch and Danish OCTs to move to Outermost Region status should they so wish.

The Article 299 framework governing the EU/OCT relationship has not, however, undergone any meaningful revision. The only significant change was, upon UK accession, the addition of a second subparagraph making it clear that UK territories not mentioned in what is now Annex II did not fall under the Treaty. This provision remains applicable to UK territories only and the implications of it for other territories and for the Article 299 framework generally has never been fully examined. It creates inconsistency and uncertainty as to the status of all other non-European territories not specifically mentioned in the Treaty. Neither does the latest Commission review of the EU/OCT relationship, nor the Lisbon Treaty make any attempt to review substantively Article 299(3).

References

Dewost J L (1979) L'Application Territoriale du Droit Communautaire: disparition et resurgence de la notion de frontière, Société Française pour le Droit International, Colloque de Poitiers

Megret J (1987) Le Droit de la Communauté Economique Européene, Editions de L'Université de Bruxelles, 1987, page 484

Ziller J (2006) Article 299 on Extension of TEC, Hans Smit, Peter Herzog, Christian Campbell & Gudrun Zagel (eds.), Smit & Herzog on the Law of the European Union Vol. 4, Lexis-Nexis

Chapter 11
Article 299(4): European Member State Territories for Whose External Relations a Member State is Responsible: Gibraltar

Abstract This chapter provides an introduction to the fourth paragraph of Article 299 TEC, dealing with the European territories for whose external relations a Member State is responsible, just before entry into force of the corresponding Lisbon Treaty provision. An overview of Gibraltar is provided, the only territory acknowledged to fall under this provision. The key developments since 1957 relevant to this paragraph are examined, including Member State accessions and impact of the Lisbon Treaty.

11.1 Introduction (Comparison with 1957 Provision)

As noted in Part I, the aim of Article 299(4) (now Article 355(3) TFEU) is to make the Treaty applicable to all European territories for whose foreign relations a Member State is responsible. It was also noted that in fact at the time of the Treaty's adoption in 1957, this subparagraph (ex Article 227(4)) was redundant—the dispute over the Saar land (in respect of which the corresponding provision in the ECSC Treaty had been drafted) between Germany and France having been resolved before the Treaty was signed. In fact, as will be examined below, despite the subsequent accessions of the Member States with European territories to which Article 299(4) would apply, this provision today only applies to one territory—Gibraltar—and even in this case, with qualifications.

11.2 Applicable Member State Territories: Present Day

Normally, by virtue of Article 299(4), the European territories of Member States, such as the UK Channel Islands and Isle of Man, the Danish Faroe Islands, the Finnish Alands and even Gibraltar would have automatically become part of the

F. Murray, *The European Union and Member State Territories: A New Legal Framework Under the EU Treaties*, DOI: 10.1007/978-90-6704-826-2_11,

EU without any derogations. However, since special arrangements were negotiated for these territories, currently the only European territory to which the provision applies is Gibraltar but with certain exceptions.

None of the other relevant European territories of Member States, which subsequently joined the EU after 1957, namely the UK Channel Islands and Isle of Man and Sovereign Base Areas of Cyprus and the Danish Faroe Islands wished to join the EU and therefore separate provisions were made for these (now set out in Article 355 (5) TFEU).

One could argue that the Aland Islands as a European territory for whose foreign relations a Member State is responsible, ought also to fall within Article 299(4) (Article 355(3) TFEU). Following Finnish accession in 1994, the Alands later elected to join the EU. Unlike Gibraltar, however, which is taken as falling with Article 299(4), a new subparagraph was added to Article 299(5) (now Article 355(4) TFEU) to deal with the Aland Islands.

As noted in Part I, the European micro-states San Marino, Monaco, Andorra and the Vatican are third countries, capable of entering into international agreements and therefore do not fall within this provision.

It is worth reiterating that Article 299(4) refers only to European territories for whose external relations a Member States is responsible. It does not therefore apply to non-European territories, like the UK overseas countries and territories such as Anguilla in the West Indies and the French overseas territories like French Polynesia in the Pacific Ocean. As noted above, relations between these non-European territories of the Member States and the EU are addressed in the framework of the EU/OCT.

11.3 Overview of Gibraltar

Gibraltar is one of the overseas territories of the UK but is the only one of those territories which is part of the EU. It is a Crown Colony of the UK. Gibraltar is largely self-governing with regard to internal matters. The UK, however, is responsible for the island's defence, foreign affairs and internal security.

Gibraltar is part of the EU by virtue of Article 299(4) TEC (now Article 355(3) TFEU) which provides that "The provisions of this Treaty shall apply to the European territories for whose external relations a Member State is responsible". Article 28 of the UK Act of Accession, however, provides that Gibraltar is excluded from the application of the rules on the Common Agricultural Policy (CAP) and VAT. The amendment made in Article 29 of the 1972 UK Act of Accession to incorporate the UK within the EU customs territory did not include Gibraltar. Gibraltar is therefore not part of the CCT (including the free movement of goods provisions) or the CCP.

Geography: Gibraltar is situated just south of the Iberian Peninsula facing the north coast of Africa at the entrance to the Mediterranean. It is connected to Spain by a narrow land mass. Gibraltar is approximately 4.8 kilometres long and 1.2

kilometres wide. It has a total area of 5.8 square kilometres and a population of around 30,000.

Economy: Gibraltar benefits from an extensive shipping trade, a well regulated international finance center, tourism, and has become a global leader in the virtual gaming industry. The British military presence has been sharply reduced and now contributes about 7% to the local economy. The financial sector accounts for 20% of GDP; tourism, shipping services fees, and duties on consumer goods also generate revenue.

History (including relations with Spain): Gibraltar was first settled by the Moors from North Africa in 1292. Gibraltar was fought over by the Moors and Spanish until 1462 when it became part of Spain. In 1704, during the War of Spanish Succession, Gibraltar was captured by the British and it fell under British sovereignty by virtue of Article 10 of the Treaty of Utrecht of 1713 which ended the War of Spanish Succession.

The Treaty of Utrecht clearly established British sovereignty over the area within the 1704 City Wall. It also provided that Gibraltar became part of the British Crown on condition that Spain be granted first refusal if the British Crown ever chose to relinquish its title to Gibraltar. Ownership of the land between the City wall and the present boundary fence (the southern part of the isthmus connecting Gibraltar to Spain on which Gibraltar airport is built) has been disputed between the UK and Spain. The UK has claimed title to this land on the basis of continuous possession over a long period of time on the basis that this land had been occupied by the British since 1804. Spain, however, has not accepted British title to this land and further has not accepted that the Treaty of Utrecht conveys any right to the territorial waters and airspace for Gibraltar.

The 1960s and 1970s were marked by increased tensions between the UK and Spain over Gibraltar as Spain adopted a number of restrictive measures regarding Gibraltar. Spain introduced border restrictions with Gibraltar in 1954. These were gradually intensified in 1964 following increased self-government by Gibraltarians. In 1966, the frontier gates were closed to all vehicular traffic. In 1966 and 1967, the Spanish imposed restrictions on overflying Spain in respect of flights bound for Gibraltar.

A 1967 referendum in Gibraltar made it clear that the vast majority of Gibraltarians (12,138 to 44) were in favour of British, as opposed to Spanish, rule. The referendum result led, in 1969, to the Gibraltar Government Order which resulted in a House of Assembly and a Government in Gibraltar and, in its preamble, promised that "Her Majesty's Government will never enter into arrangements under which the people of Gibraltar would pass under the sovereignty of another State against their freely and democratically expressed wishes".

In response to the Gibraltar Government Order, Spain closed completely its border with Gibraltar, including cancelling the last remaining ferry link between Gibraltar and Spain. Telephone and telegraph lines with Gibraltar were cut in October 1969.

No progress was made in relations between the UK and Spain on the Gibraltar question until the late 1970s when telephone links between Spain and Gibraltar were restored.

In April 1980, following discussions in Lisbon between the then UK Foreign Secretary, Lord Carrington, and the Spanish Foreign Minister, Mr. Oreja, a joint statement was issued in which both the UK and Spanish Governments agreed to start negotiations in order to overcome their differences on Gibraltar. The Brussels Agreement was signed by the UK and Spanish Foreign Ministers on 27 November 1984. The Agreement also provided for a process of discussions (known as "the Brussels process") on the removal of all Spanish restrictions regarding Gibraltar and on sovereignty.

In advance of Spain's entry to the EU on January 1, 1986, Spain opened its border in February 1985. Spain, however, refused to restore the sea ferry which had been removed in 1969 or to remove the air exclusion zone introduced in 1967. In 1987, the UK and Spain announced an Agreement on the joint use of Gibraltar airport (see below).

In 1985, the Spanish Foreign Minister, Mr. Moran, tabled proposals under the Brussels Process concerning the sovereignty of Gibraltar. Essentially, Spain was seeking a treaty with the UK which would "re-integrate" Gibraltar with Spain whilst preserving the Gibraltarians' way of life. The UK responded immediately that the UK would never agree to transfer the sovereignty of Gibraltar to Spain against the express wishes of the Gibraltarian people. The Spanish proposals were not formally rejected by the UK, however, until 1993.

In December 1997, Spanish Foreign Minister, Abel Matutes, tabled new sovereignty proposals which would, *inter alia*, give Gibraltar political and administrative autonomy within Spain, offer Gibraltarians Spanish citizenship (while allowing them to retain dual nationality), and provide for an indefinite transitional period of joint sovereignty. Gibraltar rejected these proposals and the UK reiterated its position that no change in the *status quo* would be made against the wishes of the Gibraltar people.

Under pressure from the EU to resolve the dispute over Gibraltar, the UK and Spain, in November 2001, began talks on sharing sovereignty over the territory. However, the Gibraltarians reject any claim and no political party or pressure group in Gibraltar supports union with Spain. In a referendum in 2002 the Gibraltarian people soundly rejected a joint sovereignty proposal. Despite this, an overwhelming majority of the population holds the view that better relations are desirable. In a mass demonstration held in March 2002, whilst condemning the idea of joint sovereignty, called for *Good, neighbourly European relations with Spain based on reasonable dialogue and mutual respect.*[1]

With the election of a moderate left-wing government in Spain (2004), Spanish officials noted that, even if Spain does not give up its claim to assume the

[1] Chief Minister's United Nations address, 5 October 2006: http://www.gibnews.net/cgi-bin/gn_view.pl/?GOGX061005_1.xml.

sovereignty of Gibraltar, no advance could be achieved without taking into account the wishes of the Gibraltarians. A new round of talks on a tri-lateral basis was proposed in October 2004 to discuss regional co-operation. In February 2005 the first talks took place at a meeting held in Malaga and subsequently in Portugal and London.

This is the first sign of formal recognition of the Gibraltar Government, and has been generally welcomed. The main issues of the talks have been a new agreement on the airport, the pensions of the Spanish workers that worked in Gibraltar during the sixties, and the removal of Spanish restrictions on telecommunications.

Those issues were successfully resolved in September 2006, with the Cordoba Agreement.[2] This package of agreements between the UK, Gibraltar and Spanish authorities agreed a number of issues. It was emphasized that the agreement had no implications on sovereignty and jurisdiction. The specific issues on which the Tripartite agreed were as follows: (a) *Pensions of former Spanish workers in Gibraltar, (b) Gibraltar airport,* specifically agreement on arrangements to facilitate the enhanced use of the Gibraltar Airport for civilian air traffic for the benefit of Gibraltar and the Campo de Gibraltar, *(c)* F*ence/Frontier:* improved access for people, vehicles and goods between Gibraltar and the surrounding area including Spain; *(d) Telecommunications*: various initiatives agreed to address the current limitation on the quantity of telephone numbers in Gibraltar accessible from and through the Spanish network, and also enable roaming agreements between networks in Spain and Gibraltar for mobile telephones, telephone calls from Spain to Gibraltar; *(e) Instituto Cervantes*: Spanish Government proposal to establish in Gibraltar an Instituto Cervantes. The Instituto Cervantes is dedicated to increasing knowledge of the Spanish language and culture; *(f) Ports*: co-operation between the port authorities of the Bay in relation to issues relating to their operations, and in continuing to explore possibilities for collaboration in fields of common interest.

11.3.1 Constitutional Relations with the United Kingdom

Following the 1967 referendum when an overwhelming majority of Gibraltarians voted to retain links with the UK, a new Gibraltar Constitution was introduced in 1969. The Constitution created in Gibraltar a separate political, administration and economic jurisdiction. The Constitution formalised the devolution to the Gibraltar Government of a wide range of "defined domestic matters". The latter include:

- municipal and public utilities (for example, markets, electricity, telephones, water supply,
- social services (including education, housing, social security and public health),

[2] Cordoba Agreement: http://www.gibnet.com/texts/trip_1.htm.

- matters which clearly affect the economy of Gibraltar (such as tourism, trade and commerce),
- public services (for example, fire-fighting and public works).

The Governor of Gibraltar, as the personal representative of Her Majesty, The Queen, has direct responsibility for all matters not specifically allocated to Gibraltar Ministers—mainly, defence, external affairs and internal security (including the Royal Gibraltar Police) and financial stability.

The Gibraltar Parliament or "House of Assembly" was established by the Gibraltar Constitution Order 1969. It consists of the Speaker and 15 elected members, the Attorney General and the Financial and Development Secretary. The life of the House of Assembly is four years, although the Governor may ask for its dissolution at any time.

Gibraltar's judicial system is based on the English system with some minor differences. The system includes a non-resident Court of Appeal which holds three sessions a year and a Supreme Court of Gibraltar.

11.4 Article 299(4): Developments Since 1957 in Relation to Article 299(4)

11.4.1 Member State Accessions

Article 299(4) remained redundant until the accession of Denmark, Ireland and the United Kingdom in 1972. Normally, by virtue of paragraph (4) (and paragraph (1)), the Treaty would have covered these Member States' European territories, namely, the Faroe Islands, the SBAs of the UK in Cyprus, the Channel Islands and the Isle of Man. For various reasons (see below under Article 299(6)), however, these territories did not wish to join the EU and specific arrangements where therefore negotiated for them and set out in a new paragraph (Article 299(6), now Article 355(5) TFEU). Only Gibraltar opted to join the EU by dint of paragraph (4).

As previously noted above in regard to Article 299(2), none of the Portuguese or Spanish territories qualified as 'European' and therefore for automatic inclusion within the Treaty. Instead, special provision was made to include these within the scope of the Treaty. In the case of the Azores and Madeira, a Joint Declaration provided for their inclusion, devoting special attention to their economic and social development and paving the way for their becoming Outermost Regions. For the Canary Islands and Ceuta and Melilla, the inclusion of these territories within the EU was ensured by Article 25 and Protocol No. 2 of the Spanish Act of Accession.

At the time of Finland's accession to the EU, the Finnish Aland Islands chose not to be part of the EU. This was reflected in the TEC, which clearly specified that the Islands were not part of the EU. Later, when the Alands decided to join the EU, a new subparagraph (now Article 355(4) TFEU) was added providing for the application of the TEC to the Islands subject to certain derogations provided for in Protocol No. 2 to the Finnish Act of Accession.

Neither the Maastricht nor Amsterdam Treaties effected any amendment to the wording or content of Article 299(4).

11.4.2 Impact of UK/Spanish Relations

One of the main reasons for Gibraltar's decision to become part of the EU when the UK joined was the view that such membership would help protect Gibraltar from pressure by Spain, which has claimed sovereignty over Gibraltar.

Gibraltar's current relationship with the EU is still dominated by the ongoing dispute between the UK and Spain concerning Gibraltar

In April 2000, the UK and Spain reached agreement on three important issues which in the past had given rise to difficulties in relations between the two States over Gibraltar. These three issues concern recognition of Gibraltar identity cards, formal police co-operation between Gibraltar and Spain and recognition of Gibraltar's competent authorities within the EU. It was made clear that agreement on these issues did not affect the issue of Gibraltar's sovereignty, nor did it diminish Gibraltar's powers of self-government. The last issue is of particular note in an EU context.

11.4.2.1 Recognition of Gibraltar Identity Cards

The Gibraltar identity card would be recognised as a valid travel document i.e. instead of a passport throughout the EU. Hitherto, only the United Kingdom and Sweden recognised the Gibraltar identity card as a valid travel document. As a condition for this recognition, it was agreed that a number of slight changes would be introduced to the Gibraltar identity card, including the inclusion of the words "United Kingdom" on the front of the card and a statement that the card is validated, for EU travel purposes, under the authority of the United Kingdom. Agreement on identity cards does not affect the continued disagreement by Spain over Gibraltar-issued passports and driving licences.

11.4.2.2 Formal Police Co-operation Between Gibraltar and Spain

Spain would formally recognise the Royal Gibraltar Police (RGP) which in turn will facilitate co-operation between the Spanish police and the RGP. Until this agreement, Spain did not recognise the RGP which meant that cross-border police co-operation arrangements between Gibraltar and Spain could not proceed under the Schengen Agreement.

11.4.2.3 Recognition of Gibraltar's Competent Authorities in the EU

Of the three agreements, this was the most far-reaching. Spain and other Member States have frequently questioned the competence of Gibraltar's competent authorities to implement EU legislation. For example, in the area of financial services, not all Member States recognised the competence of the relevant authorities in Gibraltar to issue a licence to a credit institution which in turn would allow that institution to establish a branch in any EU Member State without the need to acquire a separate banking licence in those States. Spain, in particular, argued that its claims to sovereignty over Gibraltar would be undermined if it were to recognise Gibraltar's competent authorities. This issue had led to stalemate in respect of a number of EU measures.

The UK will be able to designate Gibraltar's own authorities as the Competent Authority in Gibraltar for the purposes of EU measures. All EU Member States recognize Gibraltar's competent authorities. Acknowledging, however, that Gibraltar is not a separate Member State from the United Kingdom, it was agreed that all communications between the Gibraltar competent authorities and their counterparts in other Member States would be channeled through a special office in the United Kingdom Foreign Office known as the "post box" which would pass on the information received to the relevant competent authority either in Gibraltar or in one of the Member States. The United Kingdom post box would not re-open or have any input into these communications.

The result of this arrangement is that all Member States now, for example, recognize banking licences issued by the relevant Gibraltar competent authority. The advantage of this agreement, as far as Spain at least is concerned, is that it avoids the need for Spanish authorities to deal directly with Gibraltar.

In addition to these three agreements, the UK and Spain also cleared the way for Gibraltar to be included in all parts of the Schengen *acquis* which applies to the UK except the Schengen Information System. Hitherto, Spain had threatened to use its veto to block the UK's participation in Schengen if Gibraltar were included.

In November 2001, in response to EU pressure, the UK and Spain began talks on joint sovereignty over Gibraltar. Negotiations centred on four broad themes: respect for Gibraltar's way of life, greater co-operation, extended self-government and joint sovereignty. The agreement was due to have been finalized in July 2002 but was delayed for a number of reasons, not least of which was the situation in Iraq.

Meanwhile, in November 2002, Gibraltar pressed ahead with its own referendum on the issue of joint UK/Spanish sovereignty. A large majority of the population voted against the UK/Spanish agreement. Although both the UK and Spain publicly dismissed the referendum result (which was not legally binding), it would be difficult to ignore it since ultimately any UK/Spanish deal on sovereignty over Gibraltar would still have to be approved by the Gibraltar people.

During the course of the year 2003 arrangements were finalised for Gibraltar's first ever participation in elections to the European Parliament which would participate as part of a combined electoral region (the South West of England) with part of the United Kingdom. In 2004, for the first time, Gibraltarians took part in European Parliamentary elections.

A very major political development was the agreement in December between the governments of the UK, Spain and Gibraltar to set up a new, trilateral process of dialogue outside the Brussels Process. This followed meetings between Gibraltar's Chief Minister and the directors for Europe of both the UK and Spanish Foreign Offices.

Another important development was the start of formal constitutional negotiations with the British Government to modernise Gibraltar's constitutional relationship so that it ceases to be colonial in nature.

11.4.3 Lisbon Treaty Amendments to Article 299(4)

The corresponding provision of Article 299(4) in the Lisbon Treaty (Article 355(3)) is almost identical save for a slight word change at the beginning, namely substituting "Treaty" for "Treaties". This confirms that all three pillars apply to Gibraltar.

Otherwise, the Lisbon Treaty has made no attempt to revisit Article 299(4) or to question its usefulness or logic. There is still no mention of specific territories, notably Gibraltar, to which the provision actually applies. However, in acknowledgement of the ongoing divide between the UK and Spain concerning sovereignty over Gibraltar, the UK made a Declaration (No.55) in the Final Act of the Lisbon Treaty confirming that Gibraltar falls under Article 355(3).

To conclude, the Lisbon Treaty makes no substantive changes to Gibraltar's position *vis à vis* the EU.

11.4.4 EU Legal Framework Governing Relations Between Gibraltar and EU

Gibraltar is part of the EU by virtue of Article 355(3) TFEU which provides that "The provisions of this Treaty shall apply to the European territories for whose external relations a Member State is responsible". The specific economic and political characteristics of Gibraltar made the complete application to it of the Treaty untenable. Therefore, although Gibraltar elected to join the EU, special derogations were also made for the territory. Specifically, Article 28 of the UK Accession Act provided that Community measures relating to agricultural products listed in Annex II of the Treaty i.e. basic agricultural products, and measures relating to processed agricultural products subject to regulation because of their impact on the Community's agricultural policy, are inapplicable to Gibraltar as are measures relating to indirect taxes, unless the Council acting unanimously provides otherwise.[3]

Moreover, Annex I of the Accession Act (Part I, Customs Legislation, point 4) amended Article 1 of Regulation 1496/68 of 23 September 1968 on the customs territory of the Community, in order to exclude Gibraltar from the CCT. The amendment made in Article 29 of the 1972 UK Act of Accession to incorporate the UK within the EU customs territory did not include Gibraltar.

Gibraltar is therefore not part of the CCT (including the free movement of goods provisions) or the CCP. For the rest, the Treaties apply to Gibraltar.

11.5 Conclusions

The text of Article 299(4), taken from the ECSC Treaty, was in fact redundant when the TEC was signed in 1957, in that there were no specific Member State European territories to which it applied.

The first and in fact only territory to which Article 299(4) (Article 355(3) TFEU) has specifically applied is Gibraltar. It has been noted that, unlike other UK European territories which sought to remain outside the EU but with specific arrangements (eg the Crown Dependencies), Gibraltar chose to be part of the EU. The choice was motivated in part by Gibraltar's desire to obtain greater security from Spain's claims to sovereignty over the territory.

Article 299(4) creates a dissonance with Article 299(1) which could be argued by implication covers at the very least, in addition to Member States, their European territories.

The need for Article 299(4) was also called into question in view of the separate subparagraph—Article 299(5)—created for the Aland Islands. One would have thought that as a European territory for whose external relations a Member State—Finland—is responsible, the Aland Islands would have joined Gibraltar as one of the territories covered by Article 299(4).

Further, unlike the other Article 299 subparagraphs, which either refer specifically to the applicable territories in the text of the subparagraph or to a list in the Treaty where the relevant territories are specifically addressed, Article 299(4) did not specify to which territories it applied.

As noted, the Lisbon Treaty does not address any of these anomalies. The result is a subparagraph which was never fully considered in relation to the EU Treaty, nor reviewed or revised in the light of the many developments since 1957 and which therefore sits uneasily in the current Treaties framework for EU/Member State territories relations.

---

[3] See Annex XIV *infra*, Article 28 UK Act of Accession 1972 (Gibraltar).

Chapter 12
Art 299(5): Aland Islands

Abstract This chapter provides an introduction to the fifth paragraph of Article 299 TEC, dealing with the Finnish Aland Islands, just before entry into force of the corresponding Lisbon Treaty provision. An overview of the Aland Islands is provided.

12.1 Introduction

Article 299 (5) (now Article 355(4) TFEU), concerning the application of the Treaty to the Aland Islands was of course not a part of the 1957 Treaty as Finland was not then a Member State. Article 299(5) was one of two new subparagraphs added to the 1957 version of Article 299. Specifically, Article 299(5) provided that the Treaty shall apply to the Aland Islands in accordance with Protocol No. 2 to the Finnish Accession Act.

Article 299(5) is something of an anomaly compared with the other paragraphs of Article 299. Whereas the other paragraphs deal with the general scope (Article 299(1)) or groups of territories (Article 299(2)—the Outermost Regions, Article 299(3)—the OCTs, Article 299(4)—European territories for whose foreign relations a Member State is responsible and Article 299(6)—European territories which are not part of the EU), Article 299(5) deals with one particular European territory which, although part of the EU, has certain derogations from the Treaties. Logically, as a European territory for whose foreign relations a Member State (Finland) is responsible, one would have expected the Aland Islands, to fall within Article 299(4) (Article 355(3) TFEU), but this was not the case.

Perhaps the reason for the anomaly lies in the fact that, initially, when Finland joined the EU, the Alands decided not to join the EU. Article 28 of the Finnish Accession Act accordingly provided that the TEC would not apply to the Aland

F. Murray, *The European Union and Member State Territories: A New Legal Framework Under the EU Treaties*, DOI: 10.1007/978-90-6704-826-2_12,

Islands. This was reflected in a new subparapgraph of the TEC which added the Alands to the existing list of territories (Faroe Islands, Sovereign Base Areas of the UK in Cyprus, Channel Islands and Isle of Man) to which the TEC did not apply. That same TEC provision, (and Article 28 of the Finnish Accession Act), however, also gave the Aland Islands, the possibility of joining the EU. This could be achieved by dint of a declaration deposited by the Finnish Government when ratifying its Accession Treaty, giving notice that the TEC would apply to the Aland Islands in accordance with Protocol No. 2 of the Accession Treaty. Later, the Alands chose to join the EU and a subsequent amendment to the TEC—set out as Article 299(5)—was created to reflect this.

12.2 Background

During negotiations for Finland's accession to the EU, the Aland Islands had reservations about joining the EU. In particular, the Islands were concerned about the possible impact of EU accession on elections to its municipal and Legislative Assembly elections, on duty-free arrangements and on the Islands' special status under international law. Consequently, the Aland Islands made it clear that they would only accept EU membership in return for specific derogations. The latter would permit the Islands to maintain restrictions on participation in municipal and Legislative Assembly elections (based on regional citizenship requirements) and would allow the Islands to be exempted from Community fiscal legislation.

The reason for the latter request was to permit the continuance of duty and tax free sales on ferry traffic to and from the Alands after June 30, 1999 when all duty-free sales within the EU would be abolished. There are similar arrangements for the Canary Islands and Heligoland, Germany, partly for the same reasons. The economy of the Islands depends largely on regular transport to and from the Islands and such traffic can only be guaranteed if the duty and tax-free system continues. The Islands' economy depended to a large extent on these duty and tax-free arrangements which underpinned two of the Islands' most important industries—shipping and tourism.

Finally, the Aland Islands wanted their special status under international law (namely, the Islands' right under the Autonomy Act not to accede to international treaties concluded by Finland which impinge upon the Islands' autonomy)—including its demilitarization and neutrality—guaranteed in the Finnish Accession Treaty. This special status under international law was the basis for the requested derogations regarding restrictions on participation in municipal and Legislative Assembly elections. In the end, the derogation was not extended to Legislative Assembly elections as conditions governing elections to legislative (as opposed to municipal) elections were solely a matter for Member States.

Accordingly, the Finnish Accession Treaty provided, in Article 28, that the TEC would not apply to the Aland Islands. That same Article 28 went on to state, however, that the Finnish Government could, by dint of a declaration deposited when ratifying its Accession Treaty, give notice that the Treaty would apply to the Alands. Initially, therefore after Finnish Accession when the TEC did not formally apply to the Alands, the Islands were added, in a separate subparagraph to those other territories which had also elected not to join the EU and to which the TEC did not apply, namely, the Faroe Islands, the UK Sovereign Base Areas in Cyprus, the Channel Islands and the Isle of Man.[1] This 'provisional' arrangement for the Aland Islands was reflected in Article 227(5)(d) of the Treaty which read:

> " this Treaty shall not apply to the Aland Islands. The Government of Finland may, however, give notice, by a declaration deposited when ratifying this Treaty with the Government of the Italian Republic, that the Treaty shall apply to the Aland Islands in accordance with the provisions set out in Protocol No. 2 to the Act concerning the conditions of accession of the Republic of Austria, the Republic of Finland and the Kingdom of Sweden and the adjustments to the Treaties on which the European Union is founded."

12.3 Overview of the Aland Islands

The Aland Islands are an autonomous, Swedish-speaking archipelago which forms part of Finland. They are self-governing with respect to most matters except in certain areas, such as external affairs, which fall within the competence of Finland.

The Islands' relationship with the EU is governed by Protocol No. 2 to the Finnish Act of Accession according to which the Islands are part of the EU for all areas. Two derogations, however, were granted to the Islands, the first relating to regional citizenship of the Aland Islands, the second concerning indirect taxation.

Geography: the Aland Islands are situated in the Gulf of Bothnia in the Baltic Sea between Sweden and Finland. They consist of over 6,500 islands covering more than 300 square kilometres, of which the largest and most populated island is "Main Aland". The total population of the Islands is around 25,000, 96% of whom are Swedish speaking.

Economy: the Aland's economy is heavily dominated by shipping, trade and tourism. Shipping represents about 40% of the economy, with several international carriers owned and operated off Aland. Most companies aside from shipping are small, with fewer than ten employees. Farming and fishing are important in combination with the food industry. A few high-profile technology companies contribute to a prosperous economy.

History: the Alands formed part of the Kingdom of Sweden until 1808–1809 war when Sweden was forced to yield Finland and the Alands to Russia. The Alands then became part of the Grand Duchy of Finland. With the collapse of the Russian Empire in 1917, the Alands held discussions with a view to reuniting with

[1] At the time of Finland's accession to the EU, the relevant subparagraph was Article 227(5)—referring to those EU territories which chose not to join the EU, (following amendment by the Treaty of Amsterdam Treaty) Article 299(6).

Sweden. In that same year, however, Finland declared itself an independent republic on the basis of the same principle of national self-determination which was being invoked by the Aland Islands in support of a reunion with Sweden. Finland made it clear that it was not prepared to concede the Aland Islands to Sweden. Finland was however willing to give the Islands a certain measure of self-government.

In 1920, the Finnish Parliament passed the Autonomy Act. The Islands, however, were unwilling to accept the Act at that stage. The question of the Alands was referred to the then newly-established League of Nations in 1921 which concluded that the Islands should remain under the sovereignty of Finland but that Finland should guarantee to the Islands their Swedish language, culture and customs. It was also agreed that the Alands should remain demilitarized and should also be a neutral zone. These conclusions were supplemented by a treaty between Finland and Sweden on how these guarantees were to be implemented.

The Autonomy Act was amended in 1922 when provisions concerning voting rights, taxation and the acquisition of land were added. In that same year the first elections to the Islands' parliament (now, the *Lagting*) were held. The Autonomy Act has been substantially revised on two subsequent occasions—in 1951 and in 1993. Each reform has resulted in increased autonomy for the Islands.

12.3.1 Constitutional Relations with Finland

The Autonomy Act gives the *Lagting* wide powers to enact laws and to exercise budgetary powers regarding the Islands' internal affairs. In addition the *Lagting* appoints the Islands' Government—the *Landskapsstyrelse*. In order to safeguard the rights of Alanders within the Finnish Government, Aland has its own representative in the Finnish Parliament. The Autonomy Act provides that the *Lagting* can enact laws in most areas including the following:

- the organisation and duties of the Legislative Assembly, election of its members, of the Government of the Alands and of officials and services subordinate,
- promotion of employment,
- the police force,
- the postal service,
- education, culture, preservation of ancient monuments,
- health and medical services,
- promotion of industry,
- internal communications,
- municipal administration,
- radio and television.

In these areas, the Aland Islands function in much the same way as does an independent State with its own legislative and administrative machinery. In areas where the Autonomy Act does not give the *Lagting* authority, the Finnish Government has the power to legislate in the same way as it legislates in those areas for the rest of Finland. Those areas where the Finland is competent include:

- the administration of foreign affairs and foreign trade (including international shipping—the Islands' most important industry),
- most aspects of civil and criminal law,
- the courts of justice,
- customs and monetary matters.

The *Lagting* is made up of 30 members, elected every four years. Only those possessing regional citizenship may vote and stand for election. Finland is responsible for collecting taxes and customs duties and equivalent charges in the Aland Islands. In return, the Islands are allocated 0.45% of the Finnish budget (excluding State loans). This money is given to the *Lagting* which is free to determine how to distribute this sum. Legislation passed by the *Lagting* is forwarded to the President of Finland for his approval. The Finnish President has the power to veto such legislation but only if either the *Lagting* has exceeded its legislative competence or if the legislation in question affects the internal or external security of Finland. Finally, it is also worth noting that the official language of the Aland Islands is Swedish. Thus, official correspondence and other documentation from the Finnish authorities to the Islands must be in Swedish. As Finland in general is officially bilingual (Finnish/Swedish), this means that the Islands are the only part of Finland where there is only one official language—Swedish.

The constitutional structure of the Aland Islands is considered strong due to the fact that the Finnish Parliament cannot amend or alter the Islands' Autonomy Act without the approval of the *Lagting*. In this respect, it offers stronger protection than most other regional constitutions, including those governing the Belgian regions and German *Länder*. The Islands' autonomy, however, is generally not considered to be sufficiently flexible. Thus, unlike most regional constitutional systems in Europe which often have tailor-made fiscal initiatives for the regions in question, such special fiscal initiatives in respect of the Alands are only possibly at the municipal level.

12.4 Article 299(5): Developments Since Finnish Accession

When the Aland Islands did eventually decide to join the EU, Protocol No. 2 of the Finnish Accession Act (providing for certain derogations from the TEC in respect of the Islands), came into effect. The result was an amendment to Article 299 by the Amsterdam Treaty removing the Alands from the list of territories to which the

TEC did not apply and creating a new subparagraph—Article 299 (5)—specifying the Alands' constitutional relations with the EU.

Article 299(5), under the Lisbon Treaty became Article 355(4).[2] No substantive changes have been made to the current text. Protocol No. 2 set out in the Finnish Accession Treaty remains applicable and unchanged.[3]

12.5 EU Legal Framework Governing Relations Between the Aland Islands and the EU

Protocol No. 2 starts specifically by acknowledging the Islands' special status under international law as the basis for the derogations from the Treaty. The reference to the Islands' status under international law may indicate that the EU sought to mitigate the precedent effect of the broad derogations granted to the Islands under the Protocol.

Article 1 of Protocol No.2 permits the Islands to derogate from TEC rules in respect of:

- restrictions on the right of individuals to hold regional citizenship in the Alands and on the right to acquire and hold real property on the Islands without permission of the competent authorities of the Islands,
- restrictions on the right of establishment and the right to provide services by individuals who do not possess regional citizenship in the Aland Islands or by companies which do not have the permission of the relevant authorities of the Islands.

These restrictions must take place without discrimination.

Regional citizenship of the Aland Islands is required in order to:

- vote and stand for elections to the *Lagting*,
- own or hold real estate on the Islands,
- carry out a trade or profession without restrictions on the Islands.

These restrictions were set in place in order to protect the Islands' culture and to maintain land in the possession of Alanders. Regional citizenship is acquired by a child at birth if one of its parents possesses Aland Island citizenship. Immigrants to the Islands can apply for citizenship after five years of continuous residence on the Islands. In particular cases, the Aland Government may permit exceptions to these general rules on regional citizenship. Those living outside the Aland Islands for a period of more than five years lose their regional citizenship.

---

2 See Annex I *infra*, Lisbon Treaty provisions governing EU/Member State territories.

3 See Annex XV *infra*, Protocol No. 2 of the Finnish Act of Accession 1994 (Aland Islands).

It is clear that the first derogation only refers to the restrictions imposed by regional citizenship requirements on the right to own or hold real estate and to carry out a trade or profession on the Islands. It does not refer to the restrictions, also stemming from the regional citizenship requirement, on the right to vote and stand for elections to the *Lagting*. Nevertheless, this restriction on the right to vote and stand for elections in the Islands was incorporated in a Declaration on the Aland Islands by the then EU Member States which was included in the Finnish Act of Accession.[4] The Declaration refers to Article 19 of the Treaty (Article 22 TFEU). Article 19 permits Member States to derogate in specific cases from the general right of every EU citizen to vote and stand as a candidate in municipal elections in the Member State where he resides and of which he is not a national.

The Commission considered that the Declaration did not need to be included in Directive 96/30/EC (amending Directive 94/80/EC) laying down detailed arrangements for the exercise of the right to vote and stand as a candidate in municipal elections by citizens of the Union residing in a Member State of which they are not nationals.[5] The Commission took the view that the Aland Islands' rules on regional citizenship which granted EU citizens, including Finnish citizens without regional citizenship of the Alands, the right to vote and stand as candidates in municipal elections there after two years' residence on the Islands, were compatible with the Directive.

Article 2(a) of the Protocol No. 2 provides that the Aland Islands are exempted from EU provisions harmonising indirect taxes i.e. VAT, excise duties and other forms on indirect taxation. This derogation does not, however, extend to Community provisions relating to capital duty (as set out in Council Directive 69/335/EEC, as amended). Nor does it apply to direct taxation. In practice, this derogation permits the continuance of duty-free sales between the Islands and Finland and the Islands and Sweden even after the abolition of such sales in the EU in June 1999. (The derogation would, in practice, also benefit transport between the Islands and other Member States, for example, Germany and Denmark). The derogation also permits deviations from Community rules on VAT and excises, for example, the imposition by the Islands of tax rates lower than the minimum rates prescribed by the relevant EU legislation. The result of this derogation is that the Islands fall outside the EU fiscal area (although within the EU customs union). The Alands, however, are not permitted to act in a discriminatory manner and may not, for example, tax imported products at a higher rate than domestic products. Apart from municipal taxation—which falls within the prerogative of the Islands themselves—the taxation system of the Islands falls within the competence of Finland.

---

[4] Documents concerning the accession of the Republic of Austria, the Kingdom of Sweden, the Republic of Finland and the Kingdom of Norway to the European Union OJ C241, 29 August 1994; Protocol No.2 on the Aland Islands; Declaration No.32 on the Aland Islands.

[5] Council Directive 96/30/EC of 13 May 1996 amending Directive 94/80/EC laying down detailed arrangements for the exercise of the right to vote and to stand as a candidate in municipal elections by citizens of the Union residing in a Member State of which they are not nationals, OJ L122/14, 22 May 1996.

Article 2(b) of the Protocol contains a safeguard clause in respect of the fiscal derogation granted to the Aland Islands. It explains that this derogation is aimed at *"maintaining a viable local economy in the islands"* and should not have any adverse effects on the EU. Therefore, should the Commission take the view that the derogation is no longer justified, particularly in terms of fair competition or the Community's own resources, it shall submit appropriate proposals to the Council which shall act in accordance with relevant Treaty articles. Presumably, the latter refer to existing Treaty articles on taxation such as Article 93 (Article 113 TFEU) which concerns harmonisation of indirect taxes. To date, the Commission has not taken any action under Article 2(b).

Article 3 of Protocol No. 2 provides that Finland shall ensure that all EU nationals (both companies and individuals) are treated equally in the Aland Islands. The provision was intended mainly to prevent more favourable treatment of Finnish citizens compared to citizens of other Member States.

Since deciding to join the EU, there has been no change to the legal framework governing relations between the EU and the Aland Islands.

12.6 Conclusions

The separate Article 299 (355 TFEU) subparagraph for the Aland Islands was and remains under the Lisbon Treaty inconsistent in the EU Treaties framework. Initially, when the Aland Islands chose not to join the EU, the Islands were added to the list of those other Member State territories (later in Article 299(6)) which have elected not to join the EU. Later, when the Alands decided to join the EU, it would have seemed logical also to simply remove the Alands from the list of territories not forming part of the EU and include them under Article 299(4). Nor indeed were the Islands deemed to be part of the EU by virtue of either subparagraph (4) or subparagraph (1).

Chapter 13
Art 299(6): Faroe Islands, Sovereign Base Areas in Cyprus, Channel Islands and the Isle of Man

Abstract This chapter provides an introduction to the sixth paragraph of Article 299 TEC, dealing with those Member State European territories which have elected not to be part of the EU, just before entry into force of the corresponding Lisbon Treaty provision. An overview of each of the relevant territories is provided, namely the Danish Faroe Islands, the UK Sovereign Base Areas in Cyprus, and the UK Channel Islands and Isle of Man. The key developments since 1957 relevant to this paragraph are examined, including Member State accessions, key legislation and case law, and impact of the Lisbon Treaty.

13.1 Introduction

Like Article 299(5), Article 299(6) (now Article 355(5) TFEU) was an additional subparagraph to Article 299 which did not appear in the original 1957 Treaty. Article 299(6) deals with those Member State European territories which have chosen, for various reasons, not to be part of the EU. These territories are the Danish Faroe Islands, the Sovereign Base Areas of the United Kingdom of Great Britain and Northern Ireland in Cyprus and the UK Channel Islands and the Isle of Man. Normally, these territories would have fallen under Article 299(4) as 'European territories for whose external relations a Member State is responsible', but due to their particular political and economic concerns, these territories did not become part of the EU when their Member States (Denmark and the UK) acceded. Instead, special arrangements were negotiated for them. These territories are therefore not part of the EU. In order to accommodate these new territories, none of which chose to automatically join the EU under Article 299(4), the Danish and UK Accession Treaties added a new subparagraph—Article 299(6).

F. Murray, *The European Union and Member State Territories: A New Legal Framework Under the EU Treaties*, DOI: 10.1007/978-90-6704-826-2_13,

For each of the relevant territories, the provisions of Article 299(6) were supplemented by Protocol No. 2 on the Faroe Islands, Protocol No. 3 on the Channel Islands and the Isle of Man and a Joint Declaration on the Sovereign Base Areas of the UK in Cyprus, clarifying further the relationship of these territories with the EU. Each of these territories and their relations with the EU will now be examined in turn.

13.2 Faroe Islands

13.2.1 Introduction and Background

Article 299 (6)(a) provides that the TEC shall not apply to the Faroe Islands. At the time of Danish accession to the EU in 1972, the Faroe Islands chose not to join the EU. However, Article 25 and Protocol No. 2 of the Danish Accession Treaty left open the option for the Faroe Islands to join the EU upon submission by Denmark of a declaration to that effect by 31 December 1975. The Faroe Islands, however, decided not to join the EU and later entered into trade and fisheries agreements with the EU.

Originally, Denmark hoped that the Faroe Islands would become part of the EU subject to special arrangements for the Islands in the area of trade, fisheries, the right of establishment and State aid. Due to the Islands' dependence on the fisheries sector and the uncertainty regarding the EU's future fisheries policy, the Islands were given three years following Denmark's accession to the EU on January 1, 1973 to decide finally whether or not to join the EU. This special arrangement was acknowledged in Article 25(a) and Protocol No. 2 of the Danish Act of Accession.[1]

Article 1 provided that the existing duty-free trade arrangements between the Islands and Denmark would continue until the end of the three year period in question.

Article 2 of the Protocol provided that if the Islands were to join the EU, certain arrangements would be put into operation. These arrangements included seeking, in respect of the common organisation of the market in fishery products, "adequate solutions to the specific problems of the Faroe Islands". Article 2 permitted the Faroe Islands, under Community supervision, to retain appropriate measures with a view to ensuring supplies of milk at reasonable prices to the Faroese population.

Article 3 of the Protocol provided that if Denmark, following a resolution of the Faroese Government, decided that it would not make the declaration referred to in

---

[1] Act concerning the Conditions of Accession and the Adjustment to the Treaties, Documents concerning the Accession to the European Communities of the Kingdom of Denmark, OJ Special Edition 27 March 1972; see Annexes XVI and XVII *infra*, Article 25(a) and Protocol No. 2 Danish Act of Accession 1972 (Faroe Islands).

Article 1, the EU Council, upon request from the Danish Government, could decide arrangements or resolve the position, particularly *vis à vis* Denmark and the Faroe Islands.

Article 4 of the Protocol concerned the position of Danish nationals residing in the Faroe Islands. It stipulated that Danish nationals living in the Faroes could be regarded as EU nationals only when the Community Treaties become applicable to those islands.

As regards the fisheries issue, Denmark had sought from the EU a modification of the EU fisheries policy in respect of territories for which the fisheries industry was of vital importance. This proposal was rejected by the EU which sought instead equal and unlimited access to EU fishing waters for all Member States. Such a concept was not acceptable to the Faroe Islands and was the main reason why the Islands, in a referendum in January 1974, unanimously rejected membership of the EU. The Islands considered that the EU offer of a 10 year derogation from the principle of equal access to fishing waters agreed under the Accession Treaty in order to protect fishermen in particular areas (notably in the Faroes, Greenland, Norway and the Shetland Islands), was insufficient. The Faroe Islands were also concerned that international fishing limits of 12 nautical miles were at the time considered likely to be extended under the auspices of the UN.

Aside from specific concerns over fisheries, the Faroese innate wariness of centrally governed bodies and of external rule was an additional general factor in its refusal to become part of the EU.

13.2.2 Overview of the Faroe Islands

The Faroe Islands form part of the Kingdom of Denmark along with Greenland and, of course, Denmark. Since 1948 the Faroe Islands have enjoyed a large measure of autonomy with several matters, such as taxation and agriculture, falling solely within the Islands' jurisdiction and other matters, like education, health and social affairs, falling within the joint responsibility of both the Islands and Denmark.

The Faroe Islands have the status of a third country enjoying preferential status with the Union. By virtue of Article 299(6)(a) (Article 355(5) TFEU), the Islands are not part of the EU. The relationship between the EU and the Faroe Islands is set out in two basic agreements. The first concerns fisheries which is contained in Council Regulation 2211/80 on the conclusion of the Agreement on fisheries between the European Economic Community and the Government of Denmark and the Home Government of the Faroe Islands.[2] The second concerns trade and is set out primarily in Council Decision 97/126/EC of 6 December 1996 concerning the conclusion of an agreement between the European Community, on the one

[2] OJ L 226/11, 29 August 1980.

hand, and the Government of Denmark and the Home Government of the Faroe Islands, on the other.[3]

Geography: the Faroe Islands are situated in the North East Atlantic Ocean, 430 kilometres south-east of Iceland, 600 kilometres west of Norway and 300 kilometres north-west of Scotland. The Danish capital, Copenhagen, is around 1,300 kilometres from the Islands. The Faroe Islands comprise an area of approximately 1,400 square kilometres. There are 18 islands, 17 of which are inhabited. The largest island is Streymoy, comprising around 375 square kilometres, of which the capital is Torshavn. The total population of the Faroe Islands is approximately 45,000.

Economy: fishing remains the mainstay of the economy. However, aware that an almost total dependence on fishing means that the economy remains extremely vulnerable, the Faroese hope to broaden their economic base by building new fish-processing plants. Other than fishing, the raising of sheep is the main industry of the islands. Petroleum found close to the Faroese area gives hope for deposits in the immediate area, which may provide a basis for sustained economic prosperity. Since 2000, new information technology and business projects have been fostered in the Faroe Islands to attract new investment.

History: the original inhabitants of the Faroe Islands were Irish monks who are thought to have discovered the Islands around 800 AD. The present day Faroese descend from Norwegian settlers who replaced the Irish. The Norwegians established an assembly, the *Alting*, now known as the *Løgting*.

In 1035, the Islands passed under the Crown of Norway which included a number of islands in the North Atlantic including the Orkneys, Greenland and Iceland. Following a royal union between Norway and Denmark in 1380, the Faroe Islands became increasingly ruled by Denmark.

In 1814, following defeat in the Napoleonic wars, the Danish king ceded the Crown of Norway to the King of Sweden but retained what was left of the Norwegian islands in the North Atlantic, including the Faroes.

In 1849 Denmark became a democratic nation State and the Danish constitution was extended to the Faroe Islands. The Faroese *Løgting*, abolished by Denmark in 1816, was re-established in 1852, not, however, as a full legislative assembly, but as a mere “county council” with advisory powers.

The end of the ninetieth century saw the emergence of a Faroese nationalist movement which sought to protect the Islands' language and culture against a strong Danish influence. This movement led to the formation of two main political parties—the Home Rule Party, which called for more local powers, and the Unionist Party which favoured continued union with Denmark. Although the number of political parties has increased, the two broad political divisions remain today.

During the Second World War, the Faroe Islands were occupied by the British while Denmark was occupied by the Germans thus breaking the link between the Islands and Denmark. The *Løgting* once again assumed full legislative authority

---

[3] OJ L 53/1, 22 February1997.

and the Islands became virtually self-governing. After the war, the Islands did not want to resume their previous status with Denmark. Following a referendum for sovereignty in the Faroe Islands in 1946 (which was not accepted by Denmark), negotiations resulted in the Home Rule Act in 1948.[4] This Act defines the Faroe Islands as a "self-governing community within the Kingdom of Denmark".

13.2.3 Constitutional Relations with Denmark

The Home Rule Act is essentially a compromise which aims to satisfy both those sections of the Faroese population seeking self-government and those wishing to remain part of the Kingdom of Denmark. Thus, the administration of local matters has been transferred to the Faroese whereas matters of common interest to the Islands and Denmark are handled by the Danish Government. This compromise is reflected in the fact that the Faroe Islands have two elected members in the Danish Parliament (the *Folketing*) and that the Faroese language and the Faroese flag are recognised by the Home Rule Act. In addition, special passports issued in the Faroes indicate that the bearer is both a Danish citizen and a Faroese resident.

As regards Faroese matters, there are two types administered by the *Løgting* (which possesses the legislative power) and the *Landsstýri* (the Local Government, which possesses the executive power). First, there are matters assigned to the *Landsstýri* when the latter or the Danish Government so request. Second, there are matters which, following prior negotiations with the Danish Government, may be wholly or partly assigned to the *Landsstýri*. Examples of matters which have been assigned to the Faroe Islands include direct and indirect taxation, postal and telephone services, finance, municipal affairs, agriculture and fisheries, roads and harbours and natural resources of the sub-soil.

Examples of matters deemed to be of common interest and therefore administered by the Danish Government include foreign policy, the military, the general civil and penal codes and the judiciary. The Home Rule Act provides, however, that matters of common interest may be administered by the Faroe Islands and administered jointly by the Faroese and Danish authorities. Examples of such hybrid matters include social welfare, health and education which are administered by the Faroe Islands although legislative authority rests with the Danish Government.

Regarding foreign policy, although falling within the responsibility of the Danish Government, the Faroese authorities have the right to be consulted on external affairs which are of special concern to the Faroe Islands. Thus, the Faroese have a special adviser in the Danish Foreign Ministry and the Faroese may post attachés at Danish embassies. As a result, the Faroe Islands have not always been

---

[4] Danish Law No. 137 of 23 March 1948 (*Lov am Færøernes Hjemmesryre)*. English translation of the Home Rule Act http://www.stm.dk/Index/dokumenter.asp?o=71&n=1&d=1037&s=2&str=stor.

involved in Denmark's participation in international economic organisations. Rather, negotiations with the Islands have often been conducted at a later stage. This explains why the Islands have sometimes become members of international organisations some years after Denmark's membership of the same organisation. For example, Denmark became a member of GATT in 1950 whereas the Faroes did not become members until 1954. Likewise, whilst Denmark joined EFTA in 1959, the Faroes only joined in 1967 and withdrew from membership in 1973 after Denmark withdrew a year earlier in order to join the EU.

13.2.4 Developments Since Danish Accession

As regards trade in general, the Islands' relationship with the EU was at first a positive one. A 1974 Council Regulation upheld the duty-free regime between Denmark and the Faroe Islands. The regime extended to all goods of Faroese origin which were intended for consumption in Denmark. These goods were not, however, deemed to be in free circulation and were thus subject to EU customs rules upon re-export to another EU Member State.

In 1977, the Islands entered into a fisheries agreement with the EU which took effect from 1981 and remains in force today (see below).

In 1988, as part of its preparations for completion of the Internal Market, the European Commission questioned the validity of the 1974 trading arrangements between the Islands and the EU. In particular, the Commission challenged the legal basis for duty-free access by Faroese products into Denmark as Protocol No. 2 only permitted such access until the end of 1975. The Commission argued that the difference in customs treatment under the 1974 Regulation was incompatible with an Internal Market without trade barriers. The latter, the Commission agreed, implied the application of uniform trade and customs rules in all Member States in relation to all third countries and territories, including the Faroe Islands. The Commission, therefore, began discussions with Denmark on the establishment of a trading system for the Faroe Islands which would be compatible with the Internal Market.

In 1992, a mutual trade agreement between the EU and the Danish Government/ Faroe Islands entered into force.[5] Briefly, this agreement provided for duty-free trade between the Islands and the Community in manufactured goods, in most agricultural products and in a much broader range of Faroese fish products than previously. The agreement also set quotas and ceilings for duty-free imports of certain products, including important exports. Due to strict rules of origin, the Agreement, however, reduced the possibility for duty-free access to the

---

[5] Council Decision 91/688/EEC of 2 December 1991 concerning the conclusion of the Agreement between the European Economic Community of the one part and the Government of Denmark and the Home Government of the Faroe Islands of the other part, OJ L371/1, 31 December 1991.

Community by Faroese fish products. In addition, the rules of origin were very rigid and had the effect of reducing the scope for duty-free access by Faroese fishery products to the EU.

It was questionable whether this agreement which imposed such restrictions could qualify as a free trade agreement under WTO rules. The 1992 Agreement was subsequently replaced in 1997 by Council Decision 97/126/EC[6] which removed many of the restrictions of the 1992 Agreement. Protocol No. 1 of the 1997 Agreement (concerning tariff treatment and arrangements for fish and fishery products) was replaced in June 1999.[7]

In November 1999, a Protocol on veterinary matters to the Agreement was adopted.[8] By this Protocol, the Faroe Islands adopted the Community veterinary rules in respect of fishery products. Provisions to implement the Protocol on veterinary matters were subsequently adopted in January 2001.[9] In 2005 the Faroes joined the System of Pan-Euro-Mediterranean Cumulation.

The Lisbon Treaty has made no substantive amendments to the current legal framework governing relations between the EU and the Faroe Islands. Article 299(6)(a) has become Article 355(5)(a).

13.2.5 EU Legal Framework Governing Relations Between the Faroe Islands and the EU

Having elected not to join the EU, the Faroe Islands are now in the position of a third country. As mentioned, relations with the EU are governed by two basic agreements—one on fisheries (attached to Regulation 2211/80[10]), the other on

---

[6] Council Decision 97/126/EC of 6 December 1996 concerning the conclusion of an agreement between the European Community, on the one hand, and the Government of Denmark and the Home Government of the Faroe Islands, on the other, OJ L 53/1 22 February 1997.

[7] Decision No 1/1999 of the EC/Denmark-Faroe Islands Joint Committee of 22 June 1999 replacing Protocol No. 1 of the Agreement concerning the tariff treatment and arrangements applicable to certain fish and fishery products released for free circulation in the Community or imported into the Faroes, OJ L178/58, 14 July 1999.

[8] Council Decision of 15 November 1999 concerning the conclusion of a Protocol on veterinary matters supplementing the Agreement between the European Community, of the one part, and the Government of Denmark and the Home Government of the Faroe Islands, of the other part, OJ L305/25, 30 November 1999.

[9] Decision No. 1/2001 of the EC-Faroes Joint Committee of 31 January 2001 laying down the provisions to implement the Protocol on veterinary matters supplementing the Agreement between the European Community, of the one part, and the Government of Denmark and the Home Government of the Faroe Islands, of the other part, OJ L46/24, 16 February 2001.

[10] Council Regulation 2211/80 on the conclusion of the Agreement on fisheries between the European Economic Community and the Government of Denmark and the Home Government of the Faroe Islands, OJ L226/11, 29 August 1980.

trade (attached to Council Decision 97/126[11]). The Faroe Islands is treated as a third country with respect to each of these agreements.

13.2.5.1 The Fisheries Agreement

The Fisheries Agreement entered into force in 1980 and has remained unchanged to the present day. It broadly provides for access by the Community and the Faroe Islands to each other's coastal waters in order to fish.

The main provisions of the Agreement include:

- granting to each Party (i.e. the Faroes on the one hand and the Community on the other) jurisdiction over coastal waters extending to 200 nautical miles off their coasts,
- each Party permitting to the other access to its area of fisheries jurisdiction. Every year, each Party will determine the total allowable catch for fish stocks as well as the allotments for fishing vessels of the other Party,
- allowing each Party to impose a licence requirement on the other,
- co-operating to ensure the proper management and conservation of "the living resources of the sea".[12]

Article 12 of the Fisheries Agreement gives each Party the right to terminate the Agreement at the expiry of a given period. This provision not having been availed of so far, the original Agreement has continued unchanged.

13.2.5.2 The Trade Agreement

The current Trade Agreement between the EU and the Faroe Islands (as set out in Council Decision 97/126) entered into force on January 1, 1997. Protocol No. 1 of this Agreement (on tariff treatment and arrangements for fish and fishery products) was replaced in June 1999.[13] The Agreement covers fish and fishery products, certain agricultural products and processed agricultural products. The main provisions of the Agreement include:

- abolition of existing customs duties in imports or exports and charges having an equivalent effect in trade between the Community and the Faroe Islands and the prohibition on introducing new duties on imports or exports or charges having an equivalent effect,

---

[11] *Supra*, footnote 6.

[12] Article 6 of the Agreement.

[13] *Supra*, footnote 7.

- prohibition on introducing quantitative restrictions on imports or measures having an equivalent effect and abolition of existing quantitative restrictions on imports and charges having equivalent effect,
- exceptions permitting prohibitions/restrictions on imports, exports or goods in transit justified on the grounds, *inter alia*, of public morality, law and order or public security, protection of the life and health of humans,
- a number of protocols which, *inter alia*, set out the tariff treatment and arrangements for certain fish and fishery products and for certain products obtained by processing agricultural products, lay down special provisions applicable to imports of certain agricultural products and include provisions on mutual assistance between administrative authorities in customs matters.

13.3 Sovereign Base Areas of the UK in Cyprus

13.3.1 Introduction and Background

Article 299(6)(b) (now Article 355(5)(b)) (as amended by the Cyprus Act of Accession 2004) provided that the TEC shall not apply to the Sovereign Base Areas of the United Kingdom of Great Britain and Northern Ireland in Cyprus. Whilst, prior to Cyprus's accession to the EU, the SBAs were totally outside the scope of EU law, since Cyprus's accession in 2004, the relationship between the SBAs and the EU has been modified somewhat. Now, parts of EU law apply to the SBAs as stipulated in Protocol No. 3 to the Cyprus Accession Act, for example provisions relating to agricultural policy.

The former exclusion of the SBAs from the EU was definitive and made sense given the non-economic nature of British presence on the island. EU Member States agreed in a Declaration annexed to the UK Accession Act, to define relations between the EU and these zones in the context of any future association agreement between the Community and the Republic of Cyprus.[14] The latter took place in the context of Cyprus's accession, hence the new provisions in the Treaty.

13.3.2 Overview of the SBAs

The SBAs of Akrotiri and Dhekelia are two UK administered areas on the island of Cyprus that comprise the SBAs of the United Kingdom. The bases were retained by the UK following the transition of Cyprus's status from a colony in the British

[14] Joint Declaration on the Sovereign Base Areas of the United Kingdom of Great Britain and Northern Ireland in Cyprus, UK Accession Act, OJ Special Edition, 27 March 1972, p. 194.

Empire. The United Kingdom retained the bases because of the strategic location of Cyprus in the Mediterranean Sea.

Unlike other British overseas territories, they were not listed as Overseas Countries and Territories under the Treaty of Rome and their inhabitants (who are entitled to British Overseas Territories Citizenship) have never been entitled to British citizenship.

Prior to Cypriot accession to the EU in 2004, EU law did not apply to the SBAs (Article 299(6) (b)). This position was changed by the Cypriot accession treaty and EU law, while still not applying in principle, applies to the extent necessary to implement a Protocol attached to that treaty. In practice this Protocol applies a substantial portion of EU law to the SBAs including provisions relative to agricultural policy, customs and indirect taxation. The UK also agreed in the Protocol to keep enough control of the external (i.e. off-island and northern Cyprus) borders of the sovereign bases to ensure that the border between the sovereign bases and the Republic of Cyprus can remain fully open and will not have to be policed as an external EU border. Consequently the sovereign bases will become a *de facto* part of the Schengen Area if and when Cyprus implements it.

Geography: Cyprus is the third largest island in the Mediterranean, situated some 40 miles south of Turkey, 60 miles west of the Syrian coast and 220 miles north of Port Said in Egypt. It has a land area of 9,251 square kilometres and a total population of about 790,000.

Akrotiri and Dhekelia cover 3% of the land area of Cyprus, a total of 98 square miles (47.5 at Akrotiri and 50.5 at Dhekelia). 60% of the land is privately owned, either by British or Cypriot citizens. The other 40% is owned by the Ministry of Defence, or is classed as Crown land. In addition to Akrotiri and Dhekelia themselves, the Treaty of Establishment (see further under "History") also provides for the continued use by the British Government of certain facilities within Cyprus, known as *Retained Sites.*

Akrotiri is located in the south of the island, near the city of Limassol. Dhekelia is in the southeast, near Larnaca. Both of these areas include military bases, as well as farmland and some residential land. Akrotiri is surrounded by territory controlled by the Republic of Cyprus, but Dhekelia also borders on the UN buffer zone and the Turkish-occupied part of the island.

Around 14,000 people live in the bases. Around 7,000 native Cypriots live in the bases, who either work in the bases themselves, or on farmland within the boundaries of the bases. The British military and their families make up the rest of the population.

Economy: there are no economic statistics gathered for Akrotiri and Dhekelia. The main economic activities are the provision of services to the military, as well as limited agriculture. On 1 January 2008 Akrotiri and Dhekelia adopted the euro along with the rest of Cyprus.

History: the SBAs were created in 1960 by the Treaty of Establishment, when Cyprus, a colony within the British Empire, was granted independence. The SBAs of Akrotiri and Dhekelia, usually referred to as Western Sovereign Base Area (WSBA) and Eastern Sovereign Base Area (ESBA), are those parts of the island which have remained under British jurisdiction since the creation of an independent Republic of Cyprus in 1960. Under the 1960 Treaty of Establishment, the UK retained sovereignty over the SBAs. The United Kingdom wished to retain sovereignty over these areas, as this guaranteed the use of UK military bases in Cyprus and a garrison of the British Army. The importance of the bases to the British is based on the strategic location of Cyprus, at the eastern edge of the Mediterranean, close to the Suez Canal and the Middle East, the ability to use the RAF base as staging post for military aircraft and for general training purposes.

Following an attempted coup in 1974, the island was and remains divided with Turkey occupying the northern part of the island. Since 1974, the island has been divided by a United Nations buffer zone known as the 'Green Line'. The UK recognizes only the Government of the Republic of Cyprus, which administers the southern two-thirds of the island, but not the so-called 'Turkish Republic of Northern Cyprus' (recognised as such only by Turkey). The coup and division of the island did not affect the military bases.

13.3.3 Constitutional Relations with the United Kingdom

The SBAs are retained as military bases—not "colonial" territories. This is the basic philosophy of their administration as stated by the UK Government in 1960 in the policy declaration usually known as 'Appendix O'.[15] This stated that the policy objectives for the administration of the areas were to be:

- Effective use of the SBAs as military bases,
- Full co-operation with the Republic of Cyprus,
- Protection of the interests of those resident or working in the SBAs.

Under the Treaty of Establishment, the Bases remain Sovereign British Territory under the Crown until the Government of the United Kingdom, in view of changes in their military requirements, at any time decides to divest themselves of the sovereignty or effective control over the SBAs or any part thereof. There are no plans to withdraw from the SBAs as the military requirement still exists.

Because the SBAs are primarily required as military bases and not ordinary dependent territories, the Administration reports to the Ministry of Defence in London. It has no formal connection with the Foreign and Commonwealth Office or the British High Commission in Nicosia, although there are close informal links with both offices on policy matter.

The bases have their own legal system, distinct from the UK and Cyprus. This consists of the laws of the Colony of Cyprus as at August 1960, amended as

[15] Appendix O to the 1960 Treaty of Establishment : Declaration by Her Majesty's Government regarding the administration of the sovereign base area http://www.sba.mod.uk/web_pages/appdx-o.htm.

necessary. The laws of Akrotiri and Dhekelia are kept, as far as possible, the same as the laws of Cyprus. However, the SBA legal system and SBA law are entirely separate from those of the Republic of Cyprus and the United Kingdom. The Administration has its own court system to deal with civil and criminal matters. SBA legislation is enacted by the Administrator. Under Appendix O to the Treaty of Establishment the intention was declared on behalf of the UK Government that: "The laws applicable to the Cypriot population will be as far as possible the same as the laws of the Republic."

13.3.4 Developments Since UK Accession

13.3.4.1 2004: Accession of Cyprus to the EU

The accession of Cyprus to the EU necessitated a review of relations between the SBAs and the EU. This was because the Joint Declaration on the SBAs annexed to the UK Accession Act provided that the arrangements applicable to relations between the EU and the SBAs would be defined within the context of any agreement between the Community and the Republic of Cyprus. These special arrangements are set out in Protocol No. 3 on the SBAs and Protocol No. 10 on Cyprus of the Accession Act of Cyprus to the EU.[16] In particular, the intention was to maintain the special arrangements agreed between the UK and Cyprus under the 1960 Treaty of Establishment and to ensure that Cypriots living and working in the SBAs should have the same treatment for certain EU policies as those living and working in the Republic of Cyprus.

Protocol No. 3 amends Article 299(6)(b) (Article 355(5)(b) TFEU) to reaffirm that the TEC shall not apply to the SBAs except for the special arrangements set out in the Protocol. Briefly, Protocol No. 3 makes certain adjustments in the relationship between the SBAs and Cyprus in the light of Cyprus's accession. Thus, the Protocol provides that for certain areas—customs, indirect taxes, social security, agriculture—the SBAs will fall within the Treaties. The Protocol also deals with border control and administrative matters between the SBAs and Cyprus.

The Accession Treaty which the Republic of Cyprus signed with the EU shall not apply to the British SBAs in Cyprus, except to the extent necessary to ensure the implementation of agreed arrangements. These arrangements relate to the conditions of accession of the Republic of Cyprus and the other nine countries, who signed the Accession Treaty with the EU.

The Protocol on the SBAs in Cyprus stipulates that the arrangements provided for in this Protocol shall have the sole purpose of regulating the particular situation

---

[16] See Annexes XVIII and XIX *infra* Protocol No. 3 and Protocol No. 10 Cyprus Act of Accession 2004 (SBAs).

of the SBAs in Cyprus and shall not apply to any other territory of the Community, nor serve as a precedent, whole or in part, for any other special arrangements which either already exist or which might be set up in another European territory provided for in Article 299 of the Treaty.

According to the Protocol persons resident or employed in the territory of the SBAs, who are subject to the social security legislation of the Republic of Cyprus, shall be treated as if they were resident or employed in the territory of the Republic of Cyprus.

The Protocol notes that the Republic of Cyprus shall not be required to carry out checks on persons crossing their land and sea boundaries with the SBAs and any Community restrictions on the crossing of external borders shall not apply in relation to such persons and the United Kingdom shall exercise controls on persons crossing the external borders of the SBAs.

The European Council had repeatedly underlined its strong preference for accession by a reunited Cyprus to the EU. However, the UN plan for a comprehensive settlement of the Cyprus problem failed to gain the necessary support at the simultaneous referenda held in Cyprus on 24 April 2004. While the Turkish Cypriots approved it by a margin of 2:1, Greek Cypriots rejected it by a margin of 3:1. Thus, Cyprus acceded to the EU, as a *de facto* divided island on 1 May 2004.

In the light of Protocol No. 10 of the 2003 Accession Treaty Cyprus as a whole entered the EU, whereas the *acquis* is suspended in the northern part of the island ("areas not under effective control of the Government of the Republic of Cyprus"). This means *inter alia* that these areas are outside the customs and fiscal territory of the EU. The suspension has territorial effect, but does not concern the personal rights of Turkish Cypriots as EU citizens, as they are considered as citizens of the Member State Republic of Cyprus.

The Protocol states that in the event of a political settlement, the European Council, acting unanimously on the basis of a proposal from the Commission, shall decide on the adaptations to the terms concerning the accession of Cyprus to the European Union with regard to the Turkish Cypriot community.

It notes that nothing in the Protocol shall preclude measures with a view to promoting the economic development of the areas the Government does not exercise effective control of and that such measures shall not affect the application of the *acquis* under the conditions set out in the Accession Treaty in any other part of the Republic of Cyprus.

The Protocol underlines that the EU is ready to accommodate the terms of a settlement in line with the principles on which the EU is founded and expresses the Union's desire that the accession of Cyprus should benefit all Cypriot citizens.

The contracting parties reaffirm, in the protocol, their commitment to a comprehensive settlement of the Cyprus problem, consistent with relevant UN Security Council resolutions and their strong support for the efforts of the UN Secretary General to that end.

Thus, although the entire island of Cyprus became part of the EU on 1 May 2004, the Treaties apply only to the Greek (southern) party of the island (i.e. the Republic of Cyprus. EU legislation is suspended in the Turkish Republic of

Northern Cyprus, after a referendum on reunion failed in the south. Nationals of the Republic of Cyprus living there are nonetheless fully European citizens.

13.3.4.2 2007: Lisbon Treaty Amendments

Article 299(6)(b) became Article 355(5)(b) in the Lisbon Treaty. The Lisbon Treaty does not amend in substance this provision.

13.4 Channel Islands, Isle of Man

13.4.1 Introduction and Background

Rather than stating, as in the case of the Faroe Islands and the UK SBAs in Cyprus, that the TEC does not apply to the Channel Islands, the third subparagraph of Article 299 (6) (c) (now Article 355(5)(c)) rather cryptically provided that the Treaty shall apply to the Channel Islands and Isle of Man but only "to the extent necessary to ensure the implementation of the arrangements for those islands set out in the Treaty concerning the accession of new Member States to the European Economic Community and to the European Atomic Energy Community signed on 22 January 1972." These "arrangements" are set out in Protocol No. 3 to the UK Accession Act.[17] In a nutshell, Protocol No. 3 provides that only EU rules on customs and free movement of goods and certain aspects of the CAP are applicable to the islands. For the rest, the islands are not part of the EU.

At the time of the United Kingdom accession negotiations to the EU, Article 299 (4) (ex Article 227 (4)) of the Treaty provided: "The provisions of this Treaty shall apply to the European territories for whose external relations a Member State is responsible."

Normally, this would have meant that the Islands, as "European territories for whose external relations a Member State is responsible" would automatically have become fully part of the EU upon the United Kingdom's accession. As the Islands were not independent States they did not have the option of entering into an association agreement with the EU under Article 310 (ex Article 238) of the Treaty.

The Islands were concerned that full EU membership would have serious consequences for their economies, specifically, in respect of their then main industries, including tourism. In addition, of course, full EU membership would have considerably encroached upon the Islands' autonomy regarding internal matters.

(a) Finance: at the time of the United Kingdom accession negotiations, the Channel Islands' finance industries had not advanced to a point where EU membership would have been considered as a threat to those industries. The long term

[17] See Annex XX *infra*, Protocol No. 3 UK Act of Accession 1972 (Channel Islands and Isle of Man).

harmonisation by the EU of direct taxes at a level significantly above the Islands' 20% was a major concern to the Channel Islands. The latters' main concern regarding the application of EU direct taxation was the introduction of inheritance and gift taxes which were not imposed in the Channel Islands and which was thus a significant attraction for wealthy immigrants from the United Kingdom.

(b) Agriculture: the main concern of the Islands concerning agriculture was that if the Islands were outside the EU, they would be faced with a customs barrier to the export of agricultural produce from the Islands to the United Kingdom. The agricultural industry was concerned that it was unable to benefit from the EU's agricultural support and sought assurances from the States of Jersey and Guernsey that they would extend to the industry equivalent levels of financial support as were available to their competitors in Europe.

(c) Tourism: the introduction of VAT as a result of EU membership was considered to be a major threat to the Channel Islands' tourist industry. The Channel Islands did not apply VAT and applied considerably lower excise duties than the United Kingdom. It was feared that the introduction of VAT would markedly increase the cost of living, notably for tourist accommodation, consumer goods, tobacco, alcohol and food and would therefore be detrimental to the tourist industry of the Channel Islands. In contrast to the Channel Islands, the introduction of VAT was not perceived as a major threat to the Isle of Man. This is because the Isle of Man had opted to conform to the United Kingdom system of VAT and excise duties under a bilateral agreement. In addition, the Isle of Man was less dependent on tourism than the Channel Islands.

Finally, the Islands were able to secure a special relationship with the EU. This was achieved by abrogating from Article 299(4) TEC by providing, in a new subparagraph (Article 299(6)(c)) that the Treaty would only apply to the Dependencies in accordance with the particular arrangements negotiated for them. In essence, these arrangements provided that the Islands would become part of the CCT but would be outside the EU for all other purposes. Thus, only those Treaty provisions necessary to ensure the free movement of agricultural and manufactured goods between the Islands and EU Member States apply.

13.4.2 Overview of Channel Islands and Isle of Man

The Channel Islands and the Isle of Man ("the Islands") are dependencies of the British Crown, collectively known as the Crown Dependencies. They are neither colonies nor part of the United Kingdom. They are self-governing in all matters except international relations and defence for which the United Kingdom Government has responsibility.

The Islands' relationship with the EU is set out in Protocol No. 3 to the United Kingdom Act of Accession according to which they are part of the EU only for the purposes of customs and the free movement of goods and in relation to certain aspects of the CAP. Although their histories, their systems of Government and their links with the UK differ in varying degrees (for example the Isle of Man has opted to conform to the United Kingdom system of VAT and excise duties), nevertheless, today, there are not significant differences in the constitutional relationship between each of the Islands and the United Kingdom and less so with the EU. Therefore, for present purposes, they may be examined together.

Geography: the Channel Islands, situated within the Gulf of St. Malo, comprise the bailiwicks of Jersey and Guernsey and their islands and dependencies. The Bailiwick of Jersey consists of the island of Jersey which has an area of 72 square kilometres and a population of around 80,000 and includes also the islets of les Minquiers and les Ecréhos. The Bailiwick of Guernsey consists of three jurisdictions each with its own legislature: Guernsey, Alderney and Sark. The minor islands of Herm, Jethou and Lihou are dependencies of Guernsey and Brecqhou is a dependency of Sark. The Bailiwick covers an area of 48 square kilometres and has a population of around 60,000. The Isle of Man is situated in the Irish Sea midway between England, Scotland, Ireland and Wales. The Isle of Man has an area of 572 square kilometres and a population of around 70,000.

Economy: Jersey's economy is based on financial services, tourism, electronic commerce and agriculture. Financial services contribute approximately 60% of the Island's economy. Financial services, particularly banking, fund management and insurance, account for about 30% of total income in Guernsey. Tourism, manufacturing and horticulture, mainly tomatoes and cut flowers have been declining. For the Isle of Man, the main economy is based on financial services and tourism. Agriculture and fishing, once the mainstays of the economy, now make declining contributions to the Island's GDP. The Manx government promotes island locations for making films by contributing to the production costs.

History: the Channel Islands were subject to Norman rule in 933 and when the Duke of Normandy took the Crown of England in 1066, the Islands became subject to the King of England. When in 1204 the King of England lost mainland Normandy to the French, the Islands decided to remain loyal to the King of England. Despite repeated attacks by the French on the islands during the thirteenth and fourteenth centuries, the English claim to the islands remained. At no time, however, since the Norman conquest did the islands ever become subject to the Government of England or the United Kingdom. Thus, the islands today are associated with the United Kingdom and with the rest of the Commonwealth through the present sovereign, the Queen of England.

The Isle of Man first came under the English Crown in the fourteenth century. Formerly, it had been part of the Norwegian kingdom of the Hebrides and then came under the King of Scotland. In 1405 the Island was granted by the English Crown to Sir John Stanley and his heirs. From 1405 until 1765, the Island was ruled successively by the Stanleys, the Earls of Derby and the Dukes of Athol as Lords of Man. By Acts of Parliament passed in 1765 and 1825, the rights of the Lords of Man were revested in the Crown and the Island was for a while governed mainly from London. In 1866, an Act of Parliament was passed separating Manx revenues from those of the United Kingdom and giving the Island a certain measure of control over internal expenditure. Since then, through the adoption of a series of measures, particularly during the latter half of the twentieth century, more and more control has been transferred to the Island. Thus, today, the Isle of Man is now largely self-governing.

The precise nature of the relationship between the Islands and the United Kingdom will now be examined more closely.

13.4.3 Constitutional Relations with the United Kingdom

The Crown, through the United Kingdom Government, is ultimately responsible for the defence and international relations of the Islands and the Islands are autonomous regarding internal matters i.e. those which do not extend beyond their borders. The Crown by convention has ultimate responsibility for the "good government" of the Dependencies. By virtue of the fact that ultimate legislative authority vests in the United Kingdom Parliament, this means that in theory the United Kingdom could intervene to ensure that good governance is maintained. However, this has never happened and constitutional convention would dictate that such intervention would be limited to situations where there is a major breakdown of law and order.

Concerning international relations, in practice the Islands' consent is necessary before any international agreement entered into by the United Kingdom is extended to them. Although Her Majesty's Government is responsible for the Islands' international relations, the Islands do have limited international personality as is evident from their representation in some Commonwealth bodies and on the British Irish Council.

Regarding the enactment of legislation, although all primary insular legislation of the Islands must be submitted to the Crown (via the Department for Constitutional Affairs) for Royal Assent, secondary legislation does not need such assent. While Royal Asset could, theoretically, be withheld for primary legislation, by constitutional convention this would not happen with regard to legislation which is purely domestic. The UK has only intervened where it has judged that the relevant legislation extends to international issues.[18]

By constitutional convention, the UK Parliament does not legislate on domestic matters for the Islands without their consent. This state of affairs has been recognised by the Commission's Legal Service.[19] The Islands are not represented

---

[18] Royal Assent can only be withheld where such legislation is contrary to the United Kingdom Government. For example, in 1962, Royal Assent was withheld from the Wireless Telegraph (Isle of Man) Act. The reasons given by the United Kingdom Government for its refusal of such assent was that the legislation dealt with issues regulated by an international convention (the International Telecommunications Convention, 1959) acceded to by the United Kingdom on behalf of the Isle of Man. Therefore, the legislation exceeded the powers of the Isle of Man Government. In addition, the United Kingdom maintained that the Isle of Man legislation was contrary to the international convention.

[19] *"Le Royaume Uni a donc la capacité juridique de les liens par des traites et d'autres obligations internationals, mais il est empêchés par la Convention constitutionelle d'utiliser ce*

in the UK Parliament. The Islands' legislatures do, however, promote the adoption of legislation which is similar to UK Acts of Parliament in appropriate cases.

As regards the judiciary, the Appeal Courts of all the Islands include judges who are members of the English and Scottish Bar and final appeal from the Islands' Appeal Courts rests with the Judicial Committee of the Privy Council.

In conclusion, in practice the Islands have a large measure of freedom to manage their own domestic affairs.

13.4.4 EU Legal Framework Governing Relations Between the Channel Islands and the Isle of Man

As already mentioned, the details of the terms of the Islands' relationship with the EU are set out in Protocol No. 3 of the United Kingdom Act of Accession.

Article 1 of the Protocol provides essentially that the Islands will become part of the CCT under the same conditions as the United Kingdom. Although the articles of the Treaties which apply to the Islands are not specified in Protocol No. 3, it is generally accepted that the expression "customs matters and quantitative restrictions" referred to in Article 1.1 concerns the customs union and the prohibition of quantitative restrictions between Member States. Thus, agricultural and manufactured goods should be permitted to flow freely between the Islands and all EU Member States. All duties accruing from imports to the Islands accrue to their own budgets. Moreover, the Islands are not eligible for EU funds.

Article 1.2 concerns the application of EU agricultural rules to the Islands. Article 1.2 also provides that the Council shall determine the conditions under which EU rules on trade in agricultural products apply to the Islands. These conditions were set out subsequently in Council Regulation 706/73/EEC.[20] Article 1.1 of Regulation 706/73 provides that most of the EU rules on trade in agricultural products apply to the Islands except for the rules on refunds and on compensatory amounts granted on exports by the United Kingdom. Article 1.2 of the Regulation provides that the United Kingdom and the Islands are to be treated as one Member State in the application of the rules referred to in Article 1.1. Article 1.3 provides that refunds or compensatory amounts shall not be granted in respect of exports of (agricultural) products from the Islands where customs formalities are completed in a Member State. According to Articles 1.4 and 1.5, the Dependencies may not grant aid in excess of any refunds or compensatory amounts granted by the United Kingdom on either exports to third countries or to other Member States.

(Footnote 19 continued)
pouvoir pour des questions internes », European Commission Legal Service JUR(83)D/01290 *Etude concernant les raisons pour le statut spécial des Iles Anglo-Normandes et L'Ile de Man.*

[20] Council Regulation (EEC) No. 706/73 of 12 March 1973 concerning the Community arrangements applicable to the Channel Islands and the Isle of Man for trade in agricultural products, OJ L 68/1 15 March 1973.

Article 2 of the Regulation provides that, apart from the aids referred to in Article 1, the provisions on State aid set out in Article 88(1) (Article 108 TFEU) and the first sentence of Article 88(3) TEC shall apply to the Islands. Article 2 adds that the Council shall apply the other TEC provisions, namely, Articles 87, 88 and 89 (Articles 107-109 TFEU) on State aid to the Islands *"as this proves necessary"*.

Finally, Article 3 of Regulation 706/73 specifies the Community rules on agriculture applicable to the Islands, notably, Community legislation concerning veterinary care, animal health, plant health, marketing of seeds and seedlings, food, feeding stuffs and quality and marketing standards.

Article 2 of Protocol No. 3 provides that the free movement of persons and services will not apply to Channel Islanders or Manxmen. Nevertheless, the traditional rights of Channel Islanders and Manxmen in the United Kingdom, such as the right of employment or their right to move freely between the United Kingdom and the Islands, will be unaffected by the UK Act of Accession.

Article 3 of the Protocol simply provides that the Euratom Treaty rules, which apply to persons or undertakings as defined in Article 196 of that Treaty shall also apply to such persons or undertakings when they are established in the Islands.

Article 4 provides that the Islands are to accord all EU Member State nationals equal treatment in respect of all situations governed by EU law. This provision has been examined by the ECJ in two cases[21] (see below under 'Developments since UK Accession').

Article 5 provides for the adoption of safeguard measures by the Council where problems arise concerning the application of the arrangements set out in the Protocol. The fact that this provision provides for such measures only in relation to "arrangements defined in this Protocol" would indicate that safeguard measures could not be adopted in relation to matters falling outside the scope of the Protocol. In other words, Article 5 could not be used to extend to the Islands matters, such as EU financial services or taxation, which do not currently apply to the Islands under the Protocol.

Where safeguard measures are deemed necessary, the Commission shall submit a proposal to the Council without delay and the Council must act by a qualified majority decision within one month. Safeguard measures under Article 5 of Protocol No. 3 have been adopted by the Council on just one occasion, in relation to the Isle of Man and special import licences for sheep meat, beef and veal in Council Decision 82/530/EEC.[22] Decision 82/530 has been extended on a number of occasions, most recently by Council Decision 2006/138/EC until December 31, 2010.[23]

---

[21] Case C-355/89 *Department of Health and Social Security v. Christopher Stewart Barr and Montrose Holding Limited* [1991] ECR I-3479; Case C-171/96 *Rui Alberto Pereira Roque v. His Excellency the Lieutenant Governor of Jersey* [1998] ECR I-4607.

[22] Council Decision 82/530/EEC of 19 July 1982 authorising the United Kingdom to permit the Isle of Man authorities to apply a system of special import licences to sheepmeat and beef and veal, OJ L234/7, 9 August 1982.

[23] Council Decision 2006/138/EC of 20 February 2006 extending the period of application of Decision 82/530/EEC authorising the United Kingdom to permit the Isle of Man authorities to

Article 6, finally, defines "Channel Islander" and "Manxmen" for the purposes of Article 2 of the Protocol. The EU accepted the Islands' concern about the possible implications of EU provisions on free movement of persons and uncontrolled immigration on their limited land area. The EU then considered that, since EU nationals would not have a right of abode in the Islands, there should be some restriction on the right of abode of Island residents within the EU. The problem was that most residents in the Islands were British Nationals. Consequently, the draftsmen of Protocol No. 3 came up with a narrow definition of "Channel Islander" and "Manxmen" in order to limit the number of those who should not be permitted to have a right of abode in the EU.

Thus, a "Channel Islander" or "Manxmen" is someone who either himself or whose parent or grandparent was "born, adopted, naturalised or registered" in one of the Islands. But such a person is not regarded as a "Channel Islander" or "Manxmen" where he, a parent or grandparent was born, adopted, naturalised or registered in the United Kingdom or if he has at any time been resident in the United Kingdom for a period of five years.

13.4.5 Developments Since UK Accession

13.4.5.1 1991, 1998: Barr and Montrose and RuiRoque Judgments

Article 4 of Protocol No. 3 was the subject of scrutiny by the ECJ in two judgments in the 1990 s, *Barr and Montrose*[24] and *RuiRoque.*[25] In summary, the Court ruled that although Article 4 could not be used as the basis for extending to the Islands Community provisions such as the free movement of persons or services which do not apply to the Islands by virtue of Article 299(6) and Article 1 of Protocol No. 3, nevertheless the obligation imposed on the Islands in Article 4 to treat all Community nationals equally was not limited to those areas of Community law applying to the Islands under Article 299(6) and Protocol No. 3. Certain derogations from this general obligation were permissible, for example, in *Barr and Montrose* the fact that the general requirement of a work permit for all Community nationals did not apply to UK and Irish nationals in respect of certain types of employment did not constitute discrimination contrary to Article 4.

(Footnote 23 continued)
apply a system of special import licences to sheepmeat and beef and veal, OJ L54/32, 24 February 2006.

[24] *Supra*, footnote 21.

[25] Ibid.

13.4.5.2 2005: Jersey Produce Marketing Organisation

In *Jersey Produce Marketing Organisation,*[26] the ECJ ruled that a Jersey law regulating the terms upon which producers of Jersey potatoes could sell their produce to the UK was contrary to EU law. Specifically, the Court ruled that the fact that such a scheme was intended to apply only to purely internal affairs within the UK (with Jersey) did not prevent the scheme from infringing EU law on the free movement of goods because there was still the possibility of onward trade of the produce from the UK to other EU Member States. EU law, said the Court, sought the objective of free movement of goods within the EU as a whole, not simply in trade 'between Member States'.

13.4.5.3 2007: Lisbon Treaty Amendments

The Lisbon Treaty makes no substantive changes to the legal framework governing relations between the EU and the Channel Islands and Isle of Man. The text of Article 299(6)(a) is set out in Article 355(5)(c) of the Lisbon Treaty. As with all existing Treaty Declarations and Protocols on the Member State territories, Protocol No. 3 remains unamended.

13.5 Conclusions

In general, Article 299(6) maintained a consistency often lacking in the other Article 299 subparagraphs in that it listed those territories which are not part of the EU but which have negotiated special arrangements with the EU. It is clear also in that the specific territories are listed. Moreover, the subparagraph also distinguishes between the Faroe Islands to which EU law does not apply in its entirety, and the UK Crown Dependencies and SBAs to which, although outside the EU, parts of EU law nevertheless apply.

However, as regards the Crown Dependencies, the wording of Article 299(6) is not entirely consistent with the wording in relation to the other territories in the same paragraph which, like the Crown Dependencies, are also not part of the EU. Hence, for example, in regard to the UK SBAs in Cyprus, Article 299(6) provides that the Treaty shall not apply except to the extent necessary to ensure the implementation of the arrangements set out in the Protocol on the SBAs in the Cyprus Accession Act. In the case of the Crown Dependencies, however, Article 299(6) provides that the Treaty "shall" apply to them but only to the extent necessary to ensure the implementation of the arrangements set out for them in the UK Accession Act. The Lisbon Treaty does not resolve this anomaly.

---

[26] Case C-293/02 *Jersey Potato Marketing Organisation v States of Jersey and Another* [2005] ECR I-9543.

Part III
Assessment of Article 299 and Lisbon Treaty Amendments as a Legal Framework for EU/Territories Relations Proposed New Model EU Treaties Framework

Chapter 14
General Introduction to Part III

Abstract This chapter provides an introduction to Part III of this book, providing an overview of Parts I and II and outlining the main objectives of Part III which includes a new model EU Treaties framework for relations between the EU and Member State territories.

14.1 Overview

Part I of this book examined the origins of Article 299 as drafted and signed in 1957. Part II traced the various developments including Treaty amendments affecting Article 299. Part III has three broad aims, namely, to:

- first, summarize the main changes, both in background and content, to Article 299 since 1957;
- second, examine in the light of these changes the adequacy of Article 299 and Lisbon Treaty amendments as a legal framework for EU/Member State territories. This section will also include a comparative analysis of the changes proposed by the European Constitution and by the Lisbon Treaty to ascertain which contained the better approach to modernising Article 299 and to see what lessons, if any, can be learned from these;
- third, propose, in view of the many developments since 1957 and the present day challenges facing these territories, a new model EU Treaties framework for relations between the EU and Member State territories.

Each of these aims will be examined in turn.

F. Murray, *The European Union and Member State Territories: A New Legal Framework Under the EU Treaties*, DOI: 10.1007/978-90-6704-826-2_14,

Chapter 14
General Introduction to Part II

Chapter 15
Summary of Main Changes to Article 299 TEC Since 1957

Abstract This chapter summarises the main changes to Article 299 TEC from 1957 to the present day. This includes changes to structure and relevant Member States and territories.

15.1 Introduction

The first general and important point to note at the outset is the very different political and economic landscape today compared to that in 1957 when Article 299 was adopted. Article 299 was drafted as part of the original Treaty in the aftermath of World War II with the broad aims of helping to prevent another major war in Europe and contributing towards peace and stability in the Continent. In addition, there was the Cold War dividing East and Western Europe including two Germanys. In the post-war era, the economic climate was still recovering. This compares with today's political and economic climate with its relative prosperity and stability (the recent economic downturn notwithstanding). The end of the Cold War has brought about a reunification not only of Germany but of the whole of Europe with the East rapidly catching up economically with the West.

15.2 Structure of Article 299

As regards the provisions of Article 299, although the wording of the original four subparagraphs has altered little since 1957, the scope and relevance of each of these subparagraphs has changed and deepened over the 50 or so years since

F. Murray, *The European Union and Member State Territories: A New Legal Framework Under the EU Treaties*, DOI: 10.1007/978-90-6704-826-2_15,

signing of the Treaty. To these original four subparagraphs another two were added.

15.3 Relevant Member States and Territories

Article 299(1) refers to many more Member States (27 compared to the original 6) and, although there are not necessarily many more—or less—territories covered by Article 299 particularly since UK accession, different ‘configurations’ of territories have emerged. Several of the original territories have since gained their independence and many of the remaining and new territories have negotiated special arrangements with the EU which has resulted in more variety in the types of relationships between the EU and these territories. This variety also reflects the varied legal and constitutional relationships between the territories and their Member States.

15.4 Outermost Regions and OCTs (Article 299 (2) and (3))

Subparagraphs (2) and (3) of Article 299 were originally created to address the special position in the French Constitution of the French DOMs and Algeria on the one hand, and of the French TOMs on the other as well as the Belgian, Dutch and Italian overseas territories. Whilst the former were essentially part of metropolitan France, the latter had less close ties with the mother country and had a measure of autonomy. The application and scope of both these subparagraphs developed into two distinct groups of territories, the ‘Outermost Regions’ (which includes also the Canary Islands, Azores and Madeira), and the ‘Overseas Countries and Territories’ which, in addition to the French TOMs, also includes the UK overseas territories as well as those of the Netherlands and Denmark.

Another major change regarding the application of subparagraphs (2) and (3) is that many of the territories originally falling within their ambit, notably Algeria and many of the French and later UK territories, have since become independent countries. Out of their independence has emerged another EU association, namely the group of ACP countries, for which a particular regime under the TEC has developed.

A third significant development, introduced with UK accession, was the addition of a second paragraph to Article 299(3) clarifying that the Treaty does not apply to those UK territories not mentioned in the list of OCTs set out in Annex II to the Treaty.

Finally, in general, the EU/OCT association has also developed and deepened in scope and objective since 1957. The concept of Outermost Region has also emerged and developed.

Table 15.1 Overview of current EU/Member state territory relationship under Article 299 TEC

Territory/ Group of territories	Part of EU	Part of CCT	Special arrangements/ derogations	Primary EC law provisions (Article 299)	Key EC secondary provisions
Ceuta and Melilla	Yes	No	Derogations from CCT, CCP and CAP	Article 299(1) TEC, Article 25 and Protocol No. 2 Spanish Accession Act	
Outermost Regions	Yes	Yes	Financial assistance (EU Structural Funds); adaptation of EU policies to deal with specific constraints of these regions under POSEI	Article 299(2) TEC	
OCTs	No	No	Financial (EDF) and technical assistance under Council Decisions, except for Greenland	Article 299(3) and Part Four (Articles 182–188) TEC	Decision 2001/822/ EC
Greenland	No	No	Enlarged Partnership, Fisheries Partnership Agreement	Article 299(3) and Part Four (Articles 182–188) TEC	Joint Declaration by EC, Denmark, Greenland, 2006; Council Decision 2006/526/EC, Commission Regulation 4391/ 2007/EC
Bermuda	No	No	Though officially part of OCTs, Bermuda has opted not to be subject to the OCT Decision	Article 299(3) and Part Four (Articles 182–188) TEC	None
Gibraltar	Yes	No	Derogation from CCT, VAT, CAP and CCP	Article 299(4) TEC, Article 28 UK Accession Act	
Aland Islands	Yes	Yes	Derogations from EU direct taxation and for regional citizenship	Article 299(5) TEC, Protocol No. 2 Finnish Accession Act	
Faroe Islands	No	No	Agreements with EU on trade and fisheries	Article 299(6)(a) TEC, Protocol No. 2 Danish Accession Act	Regulation 2211/80/ EEC (fisheries) and Decision 97/ 126/EC (trade)

(continued)

Table 15.1 (continued)

Territory/Group of territories	Part of EU	Part of CCT	Special arrangements/derogations	Primary EC law provisions (Article 299)	Key EC secondary provisions
UK SBAs in Cyprus	No	Yes	Certain provisions of the TEC on CCT, indirect tax, social security and agriculture apply to the SBAs	Article 299(6)(b) TEC, Protocol No. 3 to the Cyprus Accession Act	
Channel Islands and Isle of Man	No	Yes	CCT and certain aspects of CAP apply	Article 299(6)(c) TEC, Protocol No. 3 UK Accession Act	

15.5 Territories for Whose External Relations a Member State is Responsible (Article 299(4))

As noted, Article 299(4) was in fact redundant when the Treaty was signed in 1957. The jurisdiction of the Saar region, in respect of which the equivalent provision in the ECSC Treaty had been drafted, had been resolved just prior to the signing of the TEC but subparagraph (4) was not removed. Thus, until the UK joined the EU in 1972, Article 299(4) did not apply to any specific territory. Since 1957 in fact, it has only ever directly applied to Gibraltar since other territories which would normally have fallen within the scope of the provision negotiated other arrangements with the EU.

15.6 Aland Islands and Territories not Part of the EU (Article 299(5) and (6))

The final major change to Article 299 since 1957 was the addition of two new subparagraphs, dealing with specific territories, namely subparagraph (5) dealing with the Aland Islands and (6) covering those Member State territories which are not part of the EU. Unlike the original four subparagraphs of Article 299, which deal with groups or categories of territories, whether named specifically or not, subparagraphs (5) and (6) were created to address *individual* territories.

The following chart sets out the position up to the entry into force of the Lisbon Treaty concerning relations between Member States territories and the EU under Article 299 (Table 15.1).

Chapter 16
Adequacy of Article 299 as a Legal Framework for EU/Member State Territories Relations

Abstract This chapter provides an overview of the main inadequacies and anomalies of the Article 299 TEC framework governing relations between the EU and Member State territories, as examined in greater detail in the previous chapters.

16.1 General Introduction

As noted above, the various economic, political and substantive developments concerning Member State territories since 1957 have been incorporated and absorbed in piecemeal fashion into the Treaty, including amendments to Article 299 as the legal framework governing relations between Member States territories and the EU. Each development, however, has not been accompanied by any kind of overall review of Article 299 as the framework for EU/Member State relations. The result is a framework in Article 299 that is inconsistent and replete with anomalies. These anomalies will now be discussed.

16.2 Article 299(1)

The general intention of Article 299 as drafted in 1957 was to define in the broadest terms the territorial scope of the TEC. This was reflected in Article 299(1) which defines the scope of application of the Treaty with regard to Member States which, as we have noted, includes by implication also Member State territories. Only those territories for which special provision has been made are—or should

F. Murray, *The European Union and Member State Territories: A New Legal Framework Under the EU Treaties*, DOI: 10.1007/978-90-6704-826-2_16,

be—specifically mentioned in the ensuing subparagraphs of Article 299 which were added as the 'exceptions' to Article 299(1).

In fact, when the Treaty was signed in 1957, the territories that might have fallen under Article 299(1) implicitly—namely the French territories and certain other Member State territories—were addressed in subparagraphs (2) and (3). In 1957, therefore, there do not appear to have been any other autonomous or semi-autonomous territories[1] to which the Treaty applied in its entirety in the way that it was deemed to apply to Member States as set out in Article 299 (1). At the outset therefore, exceptional arrangements were made for Member State territories.

16.2.1 Member State Accessions

It was only in 1972 when Denmark joined the EU that Greenland, then a Danish colony, also became part of the EU by virtue of Article 299(1). No specific provisions were made for Greenland in the ensuing subparagraphs of Article 299. In the Danish Accession Treaty a short Protocol (No. 4) to the Accession Act permitted Denmark to retain national provisions on obtaining a licence for certain commercial activities in Greenland and committing the EU to addressing the specific fisheries issues in Greenland.

It seems a little incongruous that Greenland, although essentially an 'overseas territory' was not from the start included either under Article 299(2) as an overseas territory like the French DOMs which had close ties to its mother country, or under Article 299(3) as an OCT. (Later, of course, when Greenland was granted "home rule" status, it did become one of the OCTs although with special conditions). Perhaps, on balance, as Protocol No. 4 did not provide for any significant derogations from the Treaty for Greenland, it made more sense at this stage for Greenland to fall under Article 299(1) than for the territory to be mentioned as one of the 'exceptions' in subsequent subparagraphs.

Also, in 1972 with UK accession, there was the issue of its many territories both in Europe and overseas. The latter, having broadly similar less close ties to their mother country as the French TOMs, became part of the OCT association, thus falling under Article 299(3). Of the UK's European territories, only Gibraltar elected to join the EU—but this was not by virtue of Article 299(1) which might have been the logical framework, but rather by Article 299(4). The remaining UK European territories, namely the Crown Dependencies and the SBAs in Cyprus which opted not to join the EU, were addressed in separate provisions.

Yet another anomaly was introduced with UK accession when a new subparagraph was added to 299(3) to ensure the exclusion of certain UK territories such as Hong Kong and Rhodesia from the application of the Treaty which might

[1] With the possible exception of French Clipperton Island and French Scattered Islands of the Indian Ocean.

otherwise have been added to the list of OCTs or assumed to be part of the EU by virtue of Article 299(1) (see further under Art 299(3) below). However, this amendment serves to reinforce the contention that territories not specifically referred to in Article 299 are therefore deemed to be part of the EU. Thus, in order to exclude any territories, specific mention had to be made of them.

With the accessions of Spain and Portugal in 1985 the Canary Islands, Ceuta and Melilla, Azores and Madeira also joined the Community. As noted in Part II above, special arrangements were negotiated for these territories as part of the accession of their Member States. In the case of the Canary Islands and Ceuta and Melilla, they were excluded from the CCT and from the application of the CCP, as set out in Article 25 and Protocol No. 2 of the Spanish Accession Act. The special position of the Azores and Madeira was recognized and set out in a Joint Declaration to the Portuguese Accession Act setting out a commitment by the EU to addressing the social and economic development of these territories.

Once again, although special provision was made for these territories in the relevant Acts of Accession, no specific reference to these special arrangements was made in Article 299. These territories were therefore assumed to be fully part of the EU under Article 299(1) like their Member States, despite the special arrangements made for them in the Acts of Accession. In the interests of consistency, as territories for which special arrangements had been agreed—as in the case of the French DOMs and TOMs—one would have expected particular reference to be made to them in the subsequent subparagraphs of Article 299, specifically under subparagraph (2) which was intended to deal with overseas territories which have closer ties with their Member States and which are formally part of the EU. Of course, this happened later when the Canary Islands, Azores and Madeira formally assumed the title of Outermost Regions but this has still left the status of Ceuta and Melilla 'ill-defined' in the context of Article 299.

There is no specific reference to Ceuta and Melilla in Article 299 or in the equivalent provision under the Lisbon Treaty, despite the derogations agreed for them. Therefore, in the absence of this special mention of these territories, it must be assumed that Ceuta and Melilla are part of the EU by virtue of Article 299(1) (Article 52(1) TEU), although as special conditions have been negotiated for them, it would have made better sense for specific reference to be made to them in a separate subparagraph for example, as overseas territories which are nevertheless part of the EU.

Finally, with Finland's accession in 1995 came the Aland Islands. Initially, due to their reservations concerning the impact of EU membership on elections to its municipal and Legislative Assembly, on duty-free arrangements and on the Islands' special status under international law, the Alands chose not to join the EU. To reflect this state of affairs, the Aland Islands was added to those other Member State territories, like the Channel Islands and Faroe Islands which were not part of the EU.

Later, when the Alands did decide to join the EU, a new subparagraph was created for them. As derogations were provided for the Islands, it is perhaps logical that they were not assumed to be part of the EU by virtue of Article 299(1) and thus not given specific mention. However, in the interests of consistency, as a European territory for whose external relations a Member State is responsible, they might have fallen more logically under subparagraph (4), like Gibraltar.

The position of Member State territories not specifically mentioned in primary EU law (including TEC and Accession Treaties) remains unclear. Two examples are French Clipperton Island and the French Scattered Islands of the Indian Ocean. Neither of these is mentioned in Article 299, neither in the Treaty generally nor in the Accession Treaties. In 1984, in response to a written question regarding the status of Clipperton Island, the Commission said that, as a non-European territory, unless mentioned as one of the Outermost Regions or OCTs, the Treaty did not apply to it.[2]

Despite this response, other commentators have taken the position that the Treaty applies to all Member State territories not specifically mentioned in Article 299.[3] This author would concur with that interpretation. Firstly, Article 299(1) was drafted as a framework applying to Member States and by implication also to their territories. The remaining subparagraphs were set out as exceptions to the general rule. The fact that the exceptions are specifically set out in the ensuing subparagraphs would lend support to the interpretation of Article 299(1) as being inclusive of all Member State territories generally.

Second, if as the European Commission suggested (in its response to the 1984 written question concerning Clipperton Island[4]) that non-EU territories not mentioned in the list of Outermost Regions or OCTs are thus excluded from the Treaty's scope, then that, by definition, could potentially exclude also Ceuta and Melilla. Whilst special provisions for the latter is made in a protocol to the Treaty, they are nevertheless, as non-EU territories, neither listed as Outermost Regions nor OCTs in Annex II of the Treaty. Thus, according to the Commission's reasoning in regard to Clipperton, Ceuta and Melilla could too in theory fall outside the scope of the Treaty. Likewise, when the Spanish and Portuguese territories of the Canary Islands, Azores and Madeira first joined the EU, no specific mention was then made for them or envisaged for them in Article 299. Yet, it is clear they were from the start part of the EU.

Third, the Commission's position with regard to Clipperton is not consistent with Article 299(3) second paragraph. This provides for the specific exclusion of UK territories not mentioned in the list of OCTs in Annex II. If it is to be assumed (according to the Commission in Clipperton) that territories not mentioned in Annex II are not part of the Treaty, then this second subparagraph was redundant since territories like UK Hong Kong and Rhodesia (at the time the provision was drafted), neither being European, nor mentioned in Article 299 or Annex II, would be assumed not to be part of the Treaty. Therefore, the addition of this subparagraph

---

[2] Written Question No 1007/84 OJ C62/34, 11 March 1985 by John Ford to the Commission on the status of Clipperton Island.

[3] For example, see Dewost 1979.

[4] *Supra* footnote 2.

upon UK accession would appear to reinforce the argument that the Treaties apply to all Member State territories unless specific provision is made to the contrary.

Fourth, the new *clause passerelle* (Article 355(6)) under the Lisbon Treaty lends further support for the argument that any exceptions to Article 299 must be specified, the implication being that if the status of a territory is not specifically mentioned in Article 299 as an exception, the territory is deemed to be covered by Article 299(1) and the Treaty applies to it.

The position of territories whose constitutional positions have altered *vis à vis* their Member State also remains uncertain in respect of their status at EU level. For example, in 2007 both French Clipperton Island and the Scattered Islands of the Indian Ocean fell under the jurisdiction of existing French OCTs, in the former case French Polynesia, in the latter the French Southern and Antarctic Lands. Previously, St Pierre et Miquelon, originally a French TOM (and an OCT) became a DOM in 1976 (thus potentially an Outermost Region), but in 2003 became once again a TOM. Other more recent examples include St Barthélemy and St Martin which in 2007 became independent of Guadeloupe (a French DOM and Outermost Region) to become French Collectivities (traditionally classified as OCTs).

The European Commission maintains the view that unless the EU Treaties have been amended to reflect such status changes to territories, their position under EU law remains unchanged. Thus, the Commission maintains, a territory, by altering its constitutional status under national law, cannot thereby alter its status under EU law.

While one can see the logic in this argument in the interests of legal certainty, practically it creates problems at EU level where the former requirement for Member State unanimity for Treaty amendment could mean that the change at national level might not be reflected in the Treaty perhaps for many years. For example, Algeria gained independence from France in 1962 but the Treaty was not amended to reflect this until the Maastricht Treaty some 20 years later. And in the case of St Pierre et Miquelon, their status change was never reflected in a Treaty amendment.

This rigidity creates confusion and inconsistency in that certain categories of territories under national law, eg the French DOMs or TOMs are accorded a different status under EU law. DOMS are traditionally classified as Outermost Regions, TOMs as OCTs. However, a French TOM which has changed its status to DOM, could potentially remain an OCT under EU law even though the other French DOMs are considered Outermost Regions, unless the Treaty is amended to reflect this. This has the added effect of blurring the traditional concept of Outermost Regions and OCTs.

The *clause passerelle* under the Lisbon Treaty offers a solution in part to this issue by permitting those French, Danish and Dutch territories which wish it, to change their status under EU law without having to go through a lengthy Treaty amendment. However, the clause only applies to status changes sought by Outermost Regions and OCTs. It would not therefore apply to a status change sought by the Danish Faroe Islands or the UK Channel Islands. And it does not apply at all to territories other than French, Danish and Dutch. Therefore it would not, for example, apply to UK territories or to the Finnish Alands or any other new territories that may emerge with further accessions. It is also worth noting here that during negotiations leading up to the Lisbon Treaty, the Spanish and Portuguese Outermost Regions (Canary Islands, Azores and Madeira) explicitly requested not to have the *clause passerelle* applied to them.

16.3 Article 299(2)

The original purpose of Article 299(2) was to address the special position of the social and economic backwardness of the French overseas territories which, despite their distance from their mother country, were an integral part of France. This subparagraph formed the basis for other Member State overseas territories which elected to join the EU and for which it was recognised that special provision should be made to address their handicaps. These territories eventually became known as the Outermost Regions. Yet, this subparagraph has also developed in a piecemeal and inconsistent fashion.

16.3.1 Member State Accessions

Thus, when in 1985 the Spanish and Portuguese territories—Canary Islands, Ceuta and Melilla, Azores and Madeira—joined the EU they were not mentioned in Article 299 at all, including subparagraph (2), even though, like the French DOMs, they were part of the EU and their Member States had already envisaged policies to address the economic and social backwardness of these regions. At the time of their accession, the EU had not developed the concept of Outermost Regions. Nevertheless, special derogations from the Treaty were negotiated for these territories at the time of their accession but not even these exceptions were specifically addressed in any other part of Article 299, which, as we have noted, was the original intention of subparagraphs (2) and subsequent subparagraphs.

Although the position of the Canary Islands, Azores and Madeira was later equated with the French DOMs as collectively 'Outermost Regions', this status (of Outermost Region) was never requested by Ceuta and Melilla which, by definition, as overseas territories which are part of the EU, one would have thought would qualify as Outermost Regions.

Finally, one might wonder whether Greenland, before it opted for home rule and non-EU status thus becoming an OCT, might more logically also have qualified to fall under Article 299(2) as an overseas territory which was part of the EU. Greenland's change of status *vis à vis* the EU came prior to the emergence of the policy on Outermost Regions but there is also the interesting question of whether it would have qualified as one of the Outermost Regions.

In summary, while the concept of Outermost Regions has been very welcome and useful for those territories which requested it, it leaves unclear the position of other territories—like Ceuta and Melilla—not mentioned in Article 299 and which nevertheless, like the Outermost Regions, are a part of the EU.

16.4 Article 299(3)

Article 299(3) was originally conceived to address the position of Member States (particularly French) overseas territories with less close ties to their mother country and which were considered to be outside the EU. Thus the EU/OCT association was formed. Many of the original OCT territories later gained independence and out of that development emerged another association, that of the EU/ACP group. Although each group of territories had a different status *vis à vis* the EU, the OCTs continued for many years to follow the ACP policy until the Amsterdam Treaty recognised the inadequacy of the legal framework for OCTs—as set out in the applicable Council Decisions—and called for a review.

This review, however, did not include an examination of Article 299(3) as an appropriate Treaty framework to take account of the differences among the territories. Nor indeed did the review consider the inconsistencies posed by, for example, Greenland, which has a different status to other OCTs, or Bermuda, which although formally an OCT has chosen not to be subject to the OCT arrangement. Territories like Bermuda which have opted not to benefit from the OCT structure could have been added to the list of other Member State territories listed in Article 299(6), like the Danish Faroe Islands and UK Crown Dependencies, which are also outside the EU. Alternately, given Bermuda's decision not to be subject to the EC/OCT association, one could have excluded Bermuda from the list of OCTs in Annex II and put Bermuda on the same footing as other UK territories at the time of accession—notably Hong Kong and Rhodesia—covered by the second paragraph of Article 299(3).

There is also the question of the second paragraph of Article 299(3) providing that the Treaty shall not apply to overseas countries and territories having special relations with the United Kingdom of Great Britain and Northern Ireland which are not included in the list in Annex II. This provision was originally conceived with former British colonies Hong Kong and to a lesser extent Rhodesia in mind. Now that these territories are no longer British territories, one questions the need for this second paragraph. In addition, the fact that this paragraph refers only to UK territories and thus has a specific application only to one Member State creates an imbalance and inconsistency by not having a general application to all Member State territories. One option would be for this subparagraph to apply to all territories. However, this would be contrary to the inclusive nature of Article 299(1) which was drafted to cover all territories unless otherwise specified in the remaining Article 299 subparagraphs. A second option would be to remove this paragraph entirely and instead to specify in Article 299(6) (Article 355(5) TFEU) any other Member State territories which are not part of the EU.

16.5 Article 299(4)

Article 299(4) was not drafted with any particular territory in mind but was simply transcribed from the ECSC equivalent provision which applied to the Saar region. As discussed above, at the time the TEC was signed the jurisdiction of the Saar region had been resolved with the result that Article 299(4) had no particular purpose. At that time, none of the founding Member States had European territories which could fall under Article 299(4).

It is worth noting that the purpose of the original ECSC provision from which Article 299(4) derived, was not to show whether or not the territory in question—namely, the Saar—was part of the EU. This was already understood. Rather, Article 79 ECSC was drafted in view of the dispute between France and Germany over the Saar land and the aim of the provision was to show that the Treaty would apply to the Saar land regardless of which Member State—Germany or France—was deemed eventually to have jurisdiction over it. In other words, if it had not been for the dispute between Member States (Germany/France) over the Saarland, Article 299(4) would almost certainly never have been drafted. Thus, all European territories would have, as at present, been deemed to be part of the EU by virtue of Article 299 TEC.

When the UK joined the EU in 1972, it had a number of European territories which should have, by virtue of Article 299(4), become part of the EU. As we have seen however, most of these territories, notably the Crown Dependencies and the SBAs in Cyprus opted to remain outside the EU with certain exceptions negotiated for them. Only Gibraltar opted to join the EU but even it was also granted a number of significant derogations.

One therefore questions the usefulness of Article 299(4). It is submitted that it would have been more logical for all European territories, not having significant derogations from the TEC, to be assumed to be part of the EU by virtue of Article 299(1). As noted previously, Article 299(1) was deliberately drafted in broad terms to implicitly cover not just all Member States but also their territories. If Greenland, as an overseas territory, could be assumed to be part of the EU by dint of Article 299(1) when Denmark joined the EU, why therefore could Member States' European territories not deemed to be part of the EU by dint of the same provision? It is superfluous to have a separate provision for Member State European territories when Article 299(1) already serves that function. In the alternative, those Member State territories with significant derogations from the TEC—like Gibraltar—could be the subject of a separate subparagraph as suggested by this thesis.

Another question to make about Article 299(4) is why the Aland Islands as a European territory did not appear to have been considered under this provision? It has been noted that initially the Alands opted to remain outside the EU and were therefore included for a time with the other European territories which also opted to remain outside the EU. Later, however, when the Alands did decide to join the EU, instead of joining Gibraltar as another European Member State territory, a new subparagraph was created for it in Article 299. Thus, in addition, to Article 299(4) another unnecessary provision exists when both of these territories could adequately and more appropriately be covered either under Article 299(1) or under an entirely new subparagraph which would apply to all Member State territories which are part of the EU.

16.6 Article 299(5)

Article 299(5) was created to address the specific position of the Aland Islands. The creation of a new subparagraph specifically to address this territory resulted in yet another anomalous provision in Article 299. The creation of a specific Article 299 subparagraph for the Aland Islands marked another change in that it was the first time that an Article 299 subparagraph had been created in reference to one specific territory which had elected to become part of the EU, as opposed to a group of territories, specified or unspecified—which was the function of the first three subparagraphs of Article 299 up to Finland's accession.

Instead of creating a new subparagraph to address the Alands, this book suggests a number of other more feasible options. One option could have been, under the Article 299 framework, to have included the Alands, like Gibraltar, under Article 299(4) as a European territory for whose external relations a Member State is responsible. There seems no obvious explanation why a separate provision was created for the Alands and not for Gibraltar. Both have significant derogations from the Treaty but for the most part the Treaty applies to them and both are part of the EU. Yet no separate provision was created for Gibraltar.

A second option, going back to the arguments set out in relation to Article 299(1), would be to argue that all European territories like the Alands and Gibraltar are assumed to be part of the EU under Article 299(1).

A third alternative (and the one proposed by this book), would be to group into a separate subparagraph the Aland Islands with those other European and non-European territories (including Gibraltar) for which significant derogations or special arrangements have been agreed.

16.7 Article 299(6)

There is a consistency in Article 299(6) that is less evident in the preceding subparagraphs. This is that Article 299(6) covers all Member States territories in Europe which are not part of the EU, namely the Faroe Islands, Crown Dependencies and SBAs in Cyprus. Despite this general consistency of Article 299(6), the wording in relation to the Faroe Islands and UK SBAs in Cyprus on the one hand, and the Crown Dependencies on the other, differs slightly. In relation to the former, Article 299(6) states that the Treaty shall *not* apply. In relation to the latter, however, Article 299(6) provides that the Treaty *shall* apply, but only to the extent necessary to ensure the implementation of the special arrangements made for them in their Accession Treaties. This difference in treatment creates confusion, giving the impression that the Treaty does apply in general to the Crown Dependencies with exceptions, when in fact the reverse is true, namely that the Treaty does *not* apply to these territories save in a limited number of specified areas.

In general, however, in the interests of creating a simpler, more logical legal framework, one question whether it might have been better to create one sub-paragraph for all Member State territories—both within and outside Europe—which are not part of the EU, for example, the OCTs. And what of those non-European territories which are formally part of the OCT arrangement but have either opted for a different relationship, like Greenland, or chosen not to be subject to the OCT Decision, like Bermuda. Should these territories not be acknowledged separately, outside of the OCT arrangement?

16.8 Conclusions

From its inception in 1957, there have been inconsistencies with the Article 299 TEC framework, notably paragraph (4) on European territories, which was redundant from the start. With new Member State accessions and the application of Article 299 to their territories, Article 299 was adapted and added to piecemeal, without any overall review of the provision as a whole. In fact, despite a number of overarching major Treaty revisions such as Maastricht and Amsterdam and latterly Lisbon, and some welcome reviews to specific groups of territories such as the Outermost Regions and OCTs, there has never been any attempt at an overall review of Article 299 itself.

This lack of review has created problems ranging from a lack of clarity as to the status of certain territories, such as Gibraltar and Ceuta and Melilla, neither of which was specifically named in Article 299, and the French island of Clipperton and French Scattered Islands of the Indian Ocean, which were not mentioned in the Treaty at all. The absence of an overall review of the Article 299 framework has further led to inconsistencies, for example, creating a new separate paragraph (Article 299(5)) for the Aland Islands despite the prior existence of another paragraph (Article 299(4)) which already covers European territories for whose external relations a Member State is responsible, which by definition could have included the Aland Islands. Finally, there is the inability of the Article 299 framework, again the product of no general review, to adequately accommodate status changes to territories at national level and/or requests for a status at EU level, as in the case for example of French Mayotte or the Netherlands Antilles.

Reference

Dewost JL (1979) L'Application Territoriale du Droit Communautaire: disparition et resurgence de la notion de frontière, Société Française pour le Droit International, Colloque de Poitiers

Chapter 17
The Lisbon Treaty and the European Constitution on Article 299: A Comparison

Abstract This chapter compares and contrasts the changes to the Article 299 TEC framework proposed by the Constitution for Europe and by the Lisbon Treaty. The objective is to see examine whether either of these Treaties improved the Article 299 TEC framework and which of the two Treaties overall made the better attempt to improve the overall Treaties framework for EU/Member State territories relations.

17.1 Introduction

It is worth recapping here on the changes introduced by the Lisbon Treaty to Article 299 to assess the adequacy of the new EU Treaties framework for Member State territories in the light of the many changes and developments outlined above since the TEC was signed in 1957. It is interesting also to contrast and compare the approach adopted by the Lisbon Treaty's predecessor—the Treaty establishing a Constitution for Europe (TCE) to see whether it promised something better.

17.2 Lisbon Treaty

The Lisbon Treaty alters how the EU works through a series of amendments to the Treaty on European Union (TEU, Maastricht) and the Treaty establishing the European Community (TEC, Rome), the latter being renamed Treaty on the Functioning of the European Union (TFEU) in the process. The two consolidated treaties form the legal basis of the EU, and together constitute most of the content of the abandoned TCE.

F. Murray, *The European Union and Member State Territories: A New Legal Framework Under the EU Treaties*, DOI: 10.1007/978-90-6704-826-2_17,

Prominent changes in the Lisbon Treaty include the replacing of the three pillar system, reduced chances of stalemate in the EU Council through more qualified majority voting, a more powerful European Parliament through extended co-decision with the EU Council, as well as new tools for greater coherence and continuity in policies, such as a long-term President of the European Council and a High Representative for Foreign Affairs.

In the Lisbon Treaty the provisions of Article 299 are split into three Articles. The main body of Article 299 (new Article 355) is retained as the legal framework for relations between the EU and Member State territories. The detailed arrangements concerning the Outermost Regions are set out in a new Article 349. A new Article 52 sets out the broad territorial scope of the Treaty. Articles 355 and 349 are set out in the TFEU which corresponds to the TEC and deals with the operational aspects of the Treaty. Article 52 is set out in the TEU setting out the broad framework principles of the Treaty.

As already noted, the Lisbon Treaty makes no substantive changes to Article 299. The principal changes are to structure, in particular:

- first, deleting Article 299(1) setting out the broad territorial scope of the Treaty to Member States and replacing it in effect with new Article 52 set out under the broad principles in the TEU
- second, removing the more detailed provisions on the Outermost Regions (set out in Article 299(2) second, third and fourth subparagraphs) into a separate new article—Article 349 TFEU
- third, inserting a new subparagraph—new Article 355(6) TFEU—permitting a status change without full Treaty amendment of the territories of Denmark, France and the Netherlands.

The various relevant provisions, including protocols and declarations, contained in the Member State Accession Treaties remain unchanged.

Although the Article 299 framework remains substantively the same under the Lisbon Treaty, the provisions concerning territorial scope of the Treaty and relations with Member State territories are set out in three Articles—Article 52, Article 349 and Article 355. Furthermore, these provisions are split up between the TEU (Article 52) and the new TFEU (Articles 349 and 355).

Overall, the proposed changes to structure do attempt to revisit the current Article 299 framework and to bring some logic into the provision, for example, by removing and putting into a separate provision the detailed provisions regarding the Outermost Regions, thus keeping Article 299 (Article 52 TEU Lisbon Treaty) as a framework measure on territorial scope that it was always intended to be. One can also see the sense in deleting Article 299(1) and replacing it with a new overarching provision—Article 52—in the TEU setting out the broad territorial scope of the Treaty to Member States.

In addition, the Lisbon Treaty addresses the issue of the application of the second and third pillars by establishing the general principle that the Treaties (i.e. encompassing all three pillars) shall apply to the Member States and, by implication, to their territories. The new provisions, incorporating the main body of Article 299 (Article 355 TFEU Lisbon Treaty), still contain the exceptions so that for example in the case of OCTs, Article 355(2) of the text refers to the "Treaty" singular, implying a narrower application of the TFEU to these territories (and therefore only the former first pillar provisions to these territories).

However, the general result of these changes, although the intentions behind them are laudable, is to create disunity and a lack of coherence in the Treaties as regards the framework for relations between the EU and Member State territories. In place of formerly one provision, Article 299 TEC, under the Lisbon Treaty there are three. In addition, by deleting 299(1) and creating a new Article 52, set out in the first part on TEU, there are now be two broad provisions (Articles 52 and 355) on territorial scope, the overarching framework referring to Member States in Article 52 and those relating to territories in Article 355. In dealing with the territorial scope of the Treaty, it would have been simpler and clearer to set this out in one provision only.

In general, the Lisbon Treaty, like all the other major Treaty revisions before it (Amsterdam, Maastricht, even the TCE) has not suggested or initiated any overall review of Article 299 *per se*. Thus, the present inconsistencies remain, including for example, the relevance of Article 299(4) (Article 355(3) TFEU) and also of the second paragraph of Article 299(3) concerning UK overseas territories and the separate provisions for the Aland Islands.

17.3 European Constitution

The TCE was an unimplemented international treaty intended to create a constitution for the EU. It was signed in 2004 by the 27 Member States but had to be ratified by all Member States in order to be brought into law. Most Member States did so, by parliamentary ratification or by referenda, but two (France and the Netherlands) rejected the Constitution in referenda. The Constitution's principal aims were to replace the overlapping set of existing treaties (Treaties of the European Union), to codify human rights throughout the EU and to streamline decision-making.

The failure of the Constitution to win popular support in France and The Netherlands caused some other countries to postpone or halt their ratification procedures, and the European Council to call a "period of reflection". Had it been ratified by all Member States, the Treaty would have come into force on 1 November 2006. In perspective, 18 Member States ratified the text (three by referendum: Spain, Luxembourg and Romania) while 7 postponed the ratification process after the 2 rejections.

Following the period of reflection, the European Council, meeting in June 2007 decided to start negotiations on a Reform Treaty, commonly referred to as the Lisbon Treaty as a replacement. While the Constitution attempted to replace all earlier EU treaties, the Lisbon Treaty amended them. Thus, whereas the TCE was

Table 17.1 Summary equivalence table Article 299 TEC: TCE, Lisbon Treaty Provisions

Numbering of the TEC community	Numbering of the TCE	N)ew numbering of the Treaty on European Union (Lisbon Treaty—TEU)
Article 299 (1)	Article IV-440(1)	Article 52 (1) and (2)
		New numbering of the Treaty on the Functioning of the European union—TFEU
Article 299 (2), second, third and fourth subparagraphs	Article III-424	Article 349
Article 299(2), first subparagraph and Articles (3)–(6)	Article IV-440 (2)–(7)	Article 355

a single piece of text, the basis of the European Union under the Treaty of Lisbon would be three treaties with equal legal value: the TEU, the TFEU and the Charter of Fundamental Rights, the latter made legally binding in Article 6 of the TEU.

Under the TCE, the main provisions of Article 299 were set out in Article IV 440. As in the case of the TEC, under the TCE, these provisions were set out in that part of the TCE—Part IV—dealing with General and Final Provisions. The following chart sets out the provisions of Article 299 under the TEC and the corresponding provisions under the TCE and the Lisbon Treaty (Tables 17.1, 17.2).

The first general point to note about Article 299 under the TCE concerns structure. In contrast to the Lisbon Treaty, which splits Article 299 into 3 provisions in two different parts of the Treaty (TEU and TFEU), the TCE took a slightly different approach. In particular, the TCE did not, as the Lisbon Treaty does, delete Article 299(1) establishing the territorial scope of the Treaty and create a new separate Article on the territorial scope as a framework provision in another part of the TCE, separate from the body of Article 299.

Like the Lisbon Treaty, however, the TCE did split Article 299 on the Outermost Regions into two parts: the first part, corresponding to the first paragraph of Article 299(2), set out in Article IV-440(2), merely provided that the Treaty should apply to the Outermost Regions named therein. The remaining paragraphs of Article 299(2), outlining the particular characteristics of the Outermost Regions, their handicaps and laying down the basis for the special relationship between the EU and the Outermost Regions were set out in another part of the TCE namely Article III-424 in Part III concerning the Policies and Functioning of the EU. However, to reflect the change in status of the French territories of Saint Barthélemy and Saint Martin since the demise of the TCE, the Lisbon Treaty (in contrast to the TCE) specifically names these territories in a revised Article 299(2).

The second point to note about the TCE is that, unlike Article 299 and the Lisbon Treaty text, the equivalent Article IV-440 is specifically entitled 'Scope'. This is an important clarification, even if an obvious one. Under the Lisbon Treaty,

Table 17.2 Full text equivalence table Article 299 TEC: TCE, Lisbon Treaty provisions

Numbering of the TEC	Numbering of the TCE	New numbering of the Treaty on European Union (Lisbon Treaty—TFEU)
Article 299	Article IV-440 Scope	Article 52 (1) and (2)
1. This Treaty shall apply to the Kingdom of Belgium, the Republic of Bulgaria, the Czech Republic, the Kingdom of Denmark, the Federal Republic of Germany, the Republic of Estonia, the Hellenic Republic, the Kingdom of Spain, the French Republic, Ireland, the Italian Republic, the Republic of Cyprus, the Republic of Latvia, the Republic of Lithuania, the Grand Duchy of Luxembourg, the Republic of Hungary, the Republic of Malta, the Kingdom of the Netherlands, the Republic of Austria, the Republic of Poland, the Portuguese Republic, Romania, the Republic of Slovenia, the Slovak Republic, the Republic of Finland, the Kingdom of Sweden and the United Kingdom of Great Britain and Northern Ireland.[1]	1. This Treaty shall apply to the Kingdom of Belgium, the Czech Republic, the Kingdom of Denmark, the Federal Republic of Germany, the Republic of Estonia, the Hellenic Republic, the Kingdom of Spain, the French Republic, Ireland, the Italian Republic, the Republic of Cyprus, the Republic of Latvia, the Republic of Lithuania, the Grand Duchy of Luxembourg, the Republic of Hungary, the Republic of Malta, the Kingdom of the Netherlands, the Republic of Austria, the Republic of Poland, the Portuguese Republic, the Republic of Slovenia, the Slovak Republic, the Republic of Finland, the Kingdom of Sweden and the United Kingdom of Great Britain and Northern Ireland.	1. The Treaties shall apply to the Kingdom of Belgium, Republic of Bulgaria, the Czech Republic, the Kingdom of Denmark, the Federal Republic of Germany, the Republic of Estonia, the Hellenic Republic, the Kingdom of Spain, the French Republic, Ireland, the Italian Republic, the Republic of Cyprus, the Republic of Latvia, the Republic of Lithuania, the Grand Duchy of Luxembourg, the Republic of Hungary, the Republic of Malta, the Kingdom of the Netherlands, the Republic of Austria, the Republic of Poland, the Portuguese Republic, Romania, the Republic of Slovenia, the Slovak Republic, the Republic of Finland, the Kingdom of Sweden and the United Kingdom of Great Britain and Northern Ireland. 2. The territorial scope of the Treaties is specified in Article 355 of the Treaty on the Functioning of the European Union.
		New numbering of the Treaty on the Functioning of the European Union—TFEU
Article 299 (2), second, third and fourth subparagraphs	Article III-424	Article 349

(continued)

[1] As amended most recently by Article 17 of the Act of Accession of Bulgaria and Romania to the EU, OJ L157/209 21 June 2005.

Table 17.2 (continued)

Numbering of the TEC	Numbering of the TCE	New numbering of the Treaty on European Union (Lisbon Treaty—TFEU)
2. However, taking account of the structural social and economic situation of the French overseas departments, the Azores, Madeira and the Canary Islands, which is compounded by their remoteness, insularity, small size, difficult topography and climate, economic dependence on a few products, the permanence and combination of which severely restrain their development, the Council, acting by a qualified majority on a proposal from the Commission and after consulting the European Parliament, shall adopt specific measures aimed, in particular, at laying down the conditions of application of the present Treaty to those regions, including common policies.	Taking account of the structural economic and social situation of Guadeloupe, French Guiana, Martinique, Réunion, the Azores, Madeira and the Canary Islands, which is compounded by their remoteness, insularity, small size, difficult topography and climate, economic dependence on a few products, the permanence and combination of which severely restrain their development, the Council, on a proposal from the Commission, shall adopt European laws, framework laws, regulations and decisions aimed, in particular, at laying down the conditions of application of the Constitution to those regions, including common policies. It shall act after consulting the European Parliament.	Taking account of the structural social and economic situation of Guadeloupe, French Guiana, Martinique, Réunion, Saint-Barthélemy, Saint-Martin, the Azores, Madeira and the Canary Islands, which is compounded by their remoteness, insularity, small size, difficult topography and climate, economic dependence on a few products, the permanence and combination of which severely restrain their development, the Council, acting by a qualified majority on a proposal from the Commission and after consulting the European Parliament, shall adopt specific measures aimed, in particular, at laying down the conditions of application of the present Treaty to those regions, including common policies. Where the specific measures in question are adopted by the Council in accordance with a special legislative procedure, it shall also act on a proposal from the Commission and after consulting the European Parliament.

(continued)

Table 17.2 (continued)

Numbering of the TEC	Numbering of the TCE	New numbering of the Treaty on European Union (Lisbon Treaty—TFEU)
The Council shall, when adopting the relevant measures referred to in the second subparagraph, take into account areas such as customs and trade policies, fiscal policy, free zones, agriculture and fisheries policies, conditions for supply of raw materials and essential consumer goods, State aids and conditions of access to Structural Funds and to horizontal Community programmes.	The acts referred to in the first paragraph concern in particular areas such as customs and trade policies, fiscal policy, free zones, agriculture and fisheries policies, conditions for supply of raw materials and essential consumer goods, State aids and conditions of access to structural funds and to horizontal Union programmes.	The measures referred to in the first paragraph concern in particular areas such as customs and trade policies, fiscal policy, free zones, agriculture and fisheries policies, conditions for supply of raw materials and essential consumer goods, State aids and conditions of access to structural funds and to horizontal Union programmes.
The Council shall adopt the measures referred to in the second subparagraph taking into account the special characteristics and constraints of the Outermost Regions without undermining the integrity and the coherence of the Community legal order, including the internal market and common policies.	The Council shall adopt the acts referred to in the first paragraph taking into account the special characteristics and constraints of the Outermost Regions without undermining the integrity and the coherence of the Union legal order, including the internal market and common policies.	The Council shall adopt the measures referred to in the first subparagraph taking into account the special characteristics and constraints of the Outermost Regions without undermining the integrity and the coherence of the Union legal order, including the internal market and common policies.
Article 299(2), first subparagraph and Articles (3)–(6)	Article IV-440 (2)–(7)	Article 355
		In addition to the provisions of Article 52 of the Treaty on European Union relating to the territorial scope of the Treaties, the following provisions shall apply:
2. The provisions of this Treaty shall apply to the French overseas departments, the Azores, Madeira and the Canary Islands.	2. This Treaty shall apply to Guadeloupe, French Guiana, Martinique, Réunion, the Azores, Madeira and the Canary Islands in accordance with Article III-424.	1. The provisions of the Treaties shall apply to Guadeloupe, French Guiana, Martinique, Réunion, Saint-Barthélemy, Saint-Martin the Azores, Madeira and the Canary Islands in accordance with Article 349.

(continued)

Table 17.2 (continued)

Numbering of the TEC	Numbering of the TCE	New numbering of the Treaty on European Union (Lisbon Treaty—TFEU)
3. The special arrangements for association set out in Part IV of this Treaty shall apply to the overseas countries and territories listed in Annex II to this Treaty	3. The special arrangements for association set out in Title IV of Part III shall apply to the overseas countries and territories listed in Annex II.	2. The special arrangements for association set out in Part IV of this Treaty shall apply to the overseas countries and territories listed in Annex II to the Treaties.
This Treaty shall not apply to those overseas countries and territories having special relations with the United Kingdom of Great Britain and Northern Ireland which are not included in the aforementioned list.	This Treaty shall not apply to overseas countries and territories having special relations with the United Kingdom of Great Britain and Northern Ireland which are not included in that list.	This Treaty shall not apply to those overseas countries and territories having special relations with the United Kingdom of Great Britain and Northern Ireland which are not included in the aforementioned list.
4. The provisions of this Treaty shall apply to the European territories for whose external relations a Member State is responsible.	4. This Treaty shall apply to the European territories for whose external relations a Member State is responsible.	3. The provisions of the Treaties shall apply to the European territories for whose external relations a Member State is responsible.
5. The provisions of this Treaty shall apply to the Åland Islands in accordance with the provisions set out in Protocol No. 2 to the Act concerning the conditions of accession of the Republic of Austria, the Republic of Finland and the Kingdom of Sweden.	5. This Treaty shall apply to the Åland Islands with the derogations which originally appeared in the Treaty referred to in Article IV-437(2)(d) and which have been incorporated in Section 5 of Title V of the Protocol on the Treaties and Acts of Accession of the Kingdom of Denmark, Ireland and the United Kingdom of Great Britain and Northern Ireland, of the Hellenic Republic, of the Kingdom of Spain and the Portuguese Republic, and of the Republic of Austria, the Republic of Finland and the Kingdom of Sweden.	4. The provisions of the Treaties shall apply to the Åland Islands in accordance with the provisions set out in Protocol No. 2 to the Act concerning the conditions of accession of the Republic of Austria, the Republic of Finland and the Republic of Finland and the Kingdom of Sweden.
6. Notwithstanding the preceding paragraphs:	6. Notwithstanding paragraphs 1 to 5:	5. Notwithstanding Article 52 of the Treaty on European Union and paragraphs 1 to 4 of this Article:

(continued)

Table 17.2 (continued)

Numbering of the TEC	Numbering of the TCE	New numbering of the Treaty on European Union (Lisbon Treaty—TFEU)
(a) this Treaty shall not apply to the Faroe Islands;	(a) this Treaty shall not apply to the Faroe Islands;	(a) the Treaties shall not apply to the Faroe Islands;
(b) this Treaty shall not apply to the United Kingdom Sovereign Base Areas of Akrotiri and Dhekelia in Cyprus except to the extent necessary to ensure the implementation of the arrangements set out in the Protocol on the Sovereign Base Areas of the United Kingdom of Great Britain and Northern Ireland in Cyprus annexed to the Act concerning the conditions of accession of the Czech Republic, the Republic of Estonia, the Republic of Cyprus, the Republic of Latvia, the Republic of Lithuania, the Republic of Hungary, the Republic of Malta, the Republic of Poland, the Republic of Slovenia and the Slovak Republic to the European Union and in accordance with the terms of that Protocol[2];	(b) this Treaty shall apply to Akrotiri and Dhekelia, the sovereign base areas of the United Kingdom of Great Britain and Northern Ireland in Cyprus, only to the extent necessary to ensure the implementation of the arrangements originally provided for in the Protocol on the Sovereign Base Areas of the United Kingdom of Great Britain and Northern Ireland in Cyprus, annexed to the Act of Accession which is an integral part of the Treaty referred to in Article IV-437(2)(e), and which have been incorporated in Title III of Part II of the Protocol on the Treaty and Act of Accession of the Czech Republic, the Republic of Estonia, the Republic of Cyprus, the Republic of Latvia, the Republic of Lithuania, the Republic of Hungary, the Republic of Malta, the Republic of Poland, the Republic of Slovenia and the Slovak Republic;	(b) the Treaties shall not apply to the United Kingdom Sovereign Base Areas of Akrotiri and Dhekelia in Cyprus except to the extent necessary to ensure the implementation of the arrangements set out in the Protocol on the Sovereign Base Areas of the United Kingdom of Great Britain and Northern Ireland in Cyprus annexed to the Act concerning the conditions of accession of the Czech Republic, the Republic of Estonia, the Republic of Cyprus, the Republic of Latvia, the Republic of Lithuania, the Republic of Hungary, the Republic of Malta, the Republic of Poland, the Republic of Slovenia and the Slovak Republic to the European Union and in accordance with the terms of that Protocol;

(continued)

[2] As amended by the Cyprus Act of Accession, OJ L236, 23 September 2003.

Table 17.2 (continued)

Numbering of the TEC	Numbering of the TCE	New numbering of the Treaty on European Union (Lisbon Treaty—TFEU)
(c) this Treaty shall apply to the Channel Islands and the Isle of Man only to the extent necessary to ensure the implementation of the arrangements for those islands set out in the Treaty concerning the accession of new Member States to the European Economic Community and to the European Atomic Energy Community signed on 22 January 1972.	(c) this Treaty shall apply to the Channel Islands and the Isle of Man only to the extent necessary to ensure the implementation of the arrangements for those islands originally set out in the Treaty referred to in Article IV-437(2)(a), and which have been incorporated in Section 3 of Title II of C 310/188 EN EU OJ 16 December 2004 the Protocol on the Treaties and Acts of Accession of the Kingdom of Denmark, Ireland and the United Kingdom of Great Britain and Northern Ireland, of the Hellenic Republic, of the Kingdom of Spain and the Portuguese Republic, and of the Republic of Austria, the Republic of Finland and the Kingdom of Sweden.	(c) the Treaties shall apply to the Channel Islands and the Isle of Man only to the extent necessary to ensure the implementation of the arrangements for those islands set out in the Treaty concerning the accession of new Member States to the European Economic Community and to the European Atomic Energy Community signed on 22 January 1972.
	7. The European Council may, on the initiative of the Member State concerned, adopt a European decision amending the status, with regard to the Union, of a Danish, French or Netherlands country or territory referred to in paragraphs 2 and 3. The European Council shall act unanimously after consulting the Commission.	6. The European Council may, on the initiative of the Member State concerned, adopt a decision amending the status, with regard to the Union, of a Danish, French or The Netherlands country or territory referred to in paragraphs 1 and 2. The European Council shall act unanimously after consulting the Commission.

neither Article 52 TEU nor Article 355 TFEU is given a specific title clarifying that they relate to the scope of the Treaty.

A third significant difference between the TCE and Lisbon Treaty is that in the case of the former, the special arrangements for the territories, currently set out in the various protocols of the Member State accession instruments, were incorporated into a single Protocol on the Treaties and Acts of Accession of the Member States. The Lisbon Treaty makes no such change and maintains the previous arrangement under the TEC. The European Constitution approach would have helped simplify and make more transparent current arrangements between the EU and various Member State territories by moving the current disparate protocols and provisions on relations with these territories, for example, those in the relevant Member State accession treaties dealing with the Aland Islands into one protocol.

Like the Lisbon Treaty, the TCE also added a new subparagraph to Article 299—the so-called "clause passerelle"—(Article IV-440(7) of the TCE) in order to facilitate a change of status for OCTs and Outermost Regions of Denmark, France and The Netherlands. Apart from slight word differences, substantively, both versions (TCE and Lisbon) are the same.

17.4 Conclusions

In conclusion, whilst neither the Lisbon Treaty nor TCE proposed any substantive revision of Article 299 and the changes proposed by both texts were largely structural, nevertheless, the following changes posed by the TCE were broadly preferable to those considered by the Lisbon Treaty:

- first, in terms of structure and transparency, the TCE kept Article 299(1) in tact within the Article 299 framework, rather than delete Article 299(1) and create a new framework provision (Article 52 TEU). This avoids the confusion created by Lisbon Treaty approach and maintains the coherency of Article 299,
- second, unlike the Lisbon Treaty, the TCE specifically entitled Article 299 as defining the 'Scope' of the Treaty, an important clarification,
- three, the TCE, by attempting to consolidate all the various protocols and declarations on territories in the accession treaties into one text, would have simplified the current structure of disparate texts, which remains unchanged under the Lisbon Treaty.

Chapter 18
Proposed New Model EU Treaties Framework for Relations Between the EU and Member State Territories and Final Observations

Abstract On the basis of the analysis undertaken and conclusions reached in the previous chapters, this chapter proposes a new model EU Treaties framework for relations between the EU and Member State territories. The new framework takes account of the many developments since 1957 when the original TEC framework was drafted, and is set in the context of the new Lisbon Treaty structure.

18.1 Introduction

In the light of the various and many anomalies outlined above, this book is proposes a new model EU Treaties framework for EU/Member State territories relations. The model seeks to be simpler, consistent and to take account of the 'new reality' today in the dynamic between the EU, relevant Member States and their territories. In so doing, the proposed new model will be formulated and discussed by reference to the Article 299 TEC structure but set in the context and using the numbering of the framework set out in the Lisbon Treaty. As outlined at the beginning of this publication, the reasons for using the Article 299 approach are primarily the relative familiarity of the provision compared to the Lisbon Treaty provisions. Secondly, like Article 299, this book proposes a single framework provision for EU/territories relations in preference to the Lisbon Treaty approach of splitting up the relevant provisions. This publication will refer to the new EU Treaties framework as model Article 355.

Nevertheless, although the model framework provision is based on the Article 299 TEC structure, in order to reflect the current post Lisbon Treaty framework, this book and the new model Article 355 will incorporate references to the current applicable (Lisbon) Treaty or Treaties as appropriate and it will be set out in the context of the Lisbon Treaty framework rather than the former TEC. It is

F. Murray, *The European Union and Member State Territories: A New Legal Framework Under the EU Treaties*, DOI: 10.1007/978-90-6704-826-2_18,

suggested that the model Article 355 would continue to be placed under the TFEU, rather than the TEU for the following reason. Although it could be argued that as a framework provision, model Article 355 should more logically be placed in the TEU, this book suggests that as the model Article 355 deals with more operational aspects and goes into detail beyond stating merely basic principles as set out in the TEU, it should be placed in the TFEU.

In summary, firstly, put simply, this book suggests that there should be only one Article (model Article 355) with 4 subparagraphs in the in the EU Treaties framework. The first 3 subparagraphs would reflect the 3 broad relationships open to Member State territories *vis à vis* the EU, namely:

i. full membership of the EU with no derogations or special conditions (model Article 355(1))
ii. membership of the EU but with specific and significant derogations (model Article 355(2))
iii. non-membership of the EU, so that in essence such territories are treated as third countries. In fact, all such territories qualifying for this category have negotiated special alternative arrangements with the EU. (model Article 355(3))

The fourth subparagraph (model Article 355(4)) would facilitate a status change for Member State territories without the necessity for a full Treaty amendment process. Unlike the new *clause passerelle* of the Lisbon Treaty, this provision would not just apply in the case of Outermost Regions and OCTs, but would apply to all territories wishing to change their status *vis à vis* the EU.

Secondly, for clarity and transparency, the model Article 355 should be clearly titled as follows: "Territorial Scope of the EU Treaties". The generic EU is used rather than the pre-Lisbon EC to reflect the model Article 355 as an 'umbrella' provision referring to all EU/Member State territories. The reference to EU also implies that, as introduced by the Lisbon Treaty, all three pillars are deemed to apply unless specifically provided to the contrary.

18.2 Model Article 355(1)

The model Article 355(1) should broadly remain as it was pre-Lisbon Treaty. However, first, as proposed by the Lisbon Treaty, the model provision would establish the general principle that the *EU Treaties*—and thus all three pillars as they existed pre-Lisbon—would apply to the Member States and their territories unless special provision is made for them in the ensuing subparagraphs of the model Article 355.

Second, the model Article 355(1) provides that the framework provision applies to *all* EU Member States thus making it clear that there are no exceptions. Unlike the present Treaty framework, the model Article 355(1) does not explicitly mention each Member State. In practical terms, the simple reference to all Member States serves both to condense the text and also to accommodate any future changes in the number and/or content of Member States to which the Treaties are applicable without the need to amend model Article 355(1). It is suggested that rather than including the full list of Member States in the body of model Article 355(1), which makes this subparagraph rather long and cumbersome, the relevant EU Member States should be listed in an Annex to the EU Treaties. This would also ensure that model Article 355(1) is short and succinct in line with the framework nature of this provision. There are currently only two annexes to the EU Treaties: Annex I dealing with the list of products to which the Common Agricultural Policy applies (internal EU policy) and Annex II listing the OCTs (external EU policy). It is suggested that the model Annex listing the EU Member States could be located as a new Annex II with the remaining Annexes numbered in sequence.

Third, in the interests of legal certainty model Article 355(1) should make some explicit reference to territories. This would serve to clarify that, unless specifically mentioned in subsequent subparagraphs, Member States *and their territories*, whether European or overseas, are assumed to be fully part of the EU in the same way and to the same extent as Member States. It would also avoid the current confusion as to the status of Member State territories such as Clipperton, not specifically referred to in the Treaties.

Relevant Member State territories covered by model Article 355(1):

Contrary to the European Commission response to the written question referred earlier:

- Clipperton Island: as an overseas possession of France now under the direct authority of the French Government, there is a strong argument for implying that the Island is covered by model Article 355(1)
- Scattered Islands of the Indian Ocean: although they fall under the administration of the senior administrator of the French Southern and Antarctic Lands which are part of the French OCTs, as the Islands are not specifically mentioned in the list of OCTs, it should be assumed unless specified otherwise that as French territories, they fall under the general application of the new model Article 355(1) and the EU Treaties.

Since October 2010 following the status change of the Netherlands Antilles, the following Dutch territories could also fall under this provision:

- Bonaire
- Saba
- Sint Eustatius

In the light of the aims of the model Article 355(1), none of the current Member State territories, with the possible of exception of the French Clipperton and Scattered Islands of the Indian Ocean, are deemed to be part of the EU solely by reference to model Article 355(1). This is because all of the current relevant territories, whether part of the EU or not, have negotiated special arrangements and/or derogations from the Treaties which therefore, according to our revised objectives of model Article 355, should be specifically referred to in the ensuing revised subparagraphs (2) or (3).

The model Article 355(1) would therefore read as follows:

Box 18.1 Model Article 355(1) TFEU

1. The Treaties shall apply to all Member States of the Union listed in model Annex II, and to their territories.

18.3 Model Article 355(2)

This book proposes, in the interests of clarity and simplicity, that model Article 355(2) addresses *all European and overseas Member territories which are part of the EU but for which special arrangements have been negotiated.*

As noted, the original version of Article 299(2) was drafted to address the position of Member State overseas territories with close and/or integral ties to their mother countries and which have chosen to be part of the EU, specifically the French DOMs and Algeria. Due to their physical and economic handicaps, it was recognised that special provision should be made for these territories and out of this recognition there later developed the concept of Outermost Regions.

The proposed model Article 355(2) should continue to address the specific position of Outermost Regions including the broad specificities of their relationship with the EU as set out in the existing Article 349 and 355(1) TFEU. However, it is proposed that the model Article 355(2) should go further in two ways. Firstly, it should address, not simply the Outermost Region territories but also, firstly, *other non-European territories* which have also chosen to be part of the EU and which have likewise negotiated special arrangements with the EU, for example, Ceuta and Melilla.

Secondly, it should also address all *European* territories which are part of the EU but for which special provision has been made under the Treaty. Thus, separate subparagraphs would address the particular arrangements negotiated for Gibraltar and the Aland Islands. This second clause would thus merge the present separate subparagraphs dealing respectively with European territories (Gibraltar) and with the Alands.

As regards the Outermost Regions specifically, it is proposed that the more detailed provisions concerning these territories should be inserted in a new Part to be added to the Treaties. As these provisions concern more the regime of the Outermost Regions rather than with policy, it is suggested that it would be more appropriate to include these detailed provisions in a new Part to be added to the EU Treaties (TFEU equivalent under the Lisbon Treaty). The proposed solution offered by the Lisbon Treaty and the TCE to move these provisions to that part of the Treaty dealing with policies and functions is misleading since the provisions address rather the special arrangements for the Outermost Regions rather than general EU policies. Moreover, by creating a new part in the Treaties for the Outermost Regions, structurally, this would create a balance with the special EU regime for the OCTs concerning which the special arrangements are set out in Part Four of the Treaty (TFEU).

Moving the body of the provisions of the Outermost Regions to a separate Part would have other advantages. Firstly, it would keep the wording of model Article 355(2) more concise and simple in line with a framework provision. This would again have the advantage of paralleling the structure in relation to the other model Article 355(2) territories where reference is made to their detailed provisions in the Treaty protocols and accession documents rather than in the body of model Article 355.

This new model Part on the Outermost Regions could be located within the TFEU for example as model Part Three A i.e. just after the current Part Three TFEU on Union Policies and Internal Actions and just before Part Four on the OCTs which in turn leads onto Part Five on External Action by the Union. Thus, its location would reflect its position as part of the EU but with a specific status like the special status of the OCTs, which are nevertheless outside the EU. The numbering of the new model Part on the Outermost Regions would follow from the Lisbon Treaty approach. Thus the three new paragraphs of the model Part Three A would normally be numbered Article 198. However, for simplicity and to avoid confusion with the present Lisbon Treaty numbering, this book has numbered the relevant model Part Three A as Article 197A.

It is suggested that the specific Outermost Region territories should not be listed either in the model Article 355(2) or in the new model Part Three A setting out the more detailed arrangements of the Outermost Regions regime. Rather, this book proposes that the territories and their relevant Member States should be listed in a new model Annex to the Treaties. This new Annex could be located after the model Annex II listing the EU Member States and thus numbered model Annex III.

Under the new model framework, there would thus be 4 Annexes to the Treaties instead of the current two, as follows:

- Annex I: list (of products) referred to in Article 38 of the TFEU
- Annex II: list of current EU Member States (see above point 17.2)
- Annex III: list of Outermost Regions
- Annex IV: list of OCTs

This arrangement would have several advantages over the present one: in particular, it would parallel the present structure for the OCTs, which as another special group of territories should, in the interests of consistency, be formatted in the same way. Thus, each special group—Outermost Regions and OCTs—would have a short general framework provision (model Article 355(2) and (3)) which makes no specific reference to the individual territories concerned. The relevant territories and, for transparency, their Member States, would be listed in separate Annexes to the Treaties. Finally, the special arrangements for each group would be set out in two Parts of the Treaty TFEU.

Finally, as proposed by the Lisbon Treaty, the model Article 355(2) would clarify that it is the EU Treaties which shall as a rule apply to these territories.

The relevant Member State territories are:

- Outermost Regions (Guadeloupe, French Guiana, Martinique, Réunion, Saint-Barthélemy and Saint-Martin, also possibly in time Bonaire, Saba and Sint Eustatius)
- Ceuta and Melilla
- Gibraltar
- Aland Islands

The model Article 355(2) would therefore read as follows:

The model Part Three A on the Outermost Regions would read as follows:

Box 18.2: Model Article 355(2) TFEU

2. The provisions of the Treaties shall apply to the following Member State territories:
(a) the Outermost Regions listed in model Annex III to the Treaties, in accordance with the model Part Three A concerning the Outermost Regions
(b) Ceuta and Melilla in accordance with Article 25 and Protocol No. 2, as amended, to the Act concerning the conditions of accession of the Kingdom of Spain and the Portuguese Republic
(c) Gibraltar in accordance with Article 28 to the Act concerning the conditions of accession of the Kingdom of Denmark, Ireland and the United Kingdom of Great Britain and Northern Ireland
(d) Aland Islands in accordance with Protocol No. 2 to the Act concerning the conditions of accession of the Republic of Austria, the Republic of Finland and the Kingdom of Sweden.

The model Annex III on the Outermost Regions would read as follows:

18.4 Model Article 355(3)

As a logical and consistent corollary to model Article 355(2) dealing with Member States territories (non-European as well as European) which are part of the EU but with special arrangements, it is submitted that the model Article 355(3) address the position of *Member State territories which are not part of the EU but which likewise may have also negotiated special arrangements.*

Box 18.3: Model Part Three A on the Outermost Regions

Model Part Three A on the Outermost Regions

Article 197A

Taking into account the special status of the Outermost Regions under EU law, the EU Treaties shall apply to the Outermost Regions listed in model Annex III with the following special arrangements:

1. Taking account of the structural social and economic situation of the Outermost Regions, which is compounded by their remoteness, insularity, small size difficult topography and climate, economic dependence on a few products, the permanence and combination of which severely restrain their development, the Council, acting by a qualified majority on a proposal from the Commission and after consulting the European Parliament, shall adopt specific measures aimed, in particular, at laying down the conditions of application of the present Treaty to those regions, including common policies. Where the specific measures in question are adopted by the Council in accordance with a special legislative procedure, it shall also act on a proposal from the Commission and after consulting the European Parliament.
2. The measures referred to in the first paragraph concern in particular areas such as customs and trade policies, fiscal policy, free zones, agriculture and fisheries policies, conditions for supply of raw materials and essential consumer goods, State aids and conditions of access to structural funds and to horizontal Union programmes.
3. The Council shall adopt the measures referred to in the first subparagraph taking into account the special characteristics and constraints of the Outermost Regions without undermining the integrity and the coherence of the Union legal order, including the internal market and common policies.

As with model subparagraph (2), model subparagraph (3) starts by stating the general principle concerned, namely the non-application to specific Member States territories of the Treaties, with the qualifications of the specific EU/territory relationship outlined. Thus, where possible, again in the interests of greater clarity, reference to the specific protocols or provisions of the Treaties addressing the position of individual territories are included in the text.

As regards the OCTs specifically, in parallel with the model Part on the Outermost Regions, it is proposed, in the interests of clarity and consistency, that the detailed arrangements for the OCTs currently set out in Part Four of the TFEU, be retained. The wording of Part Four is updated and amended to reflect reference to the EU Treaties. The reference to Greenland in the final paragraph of Part Four

Box 18.4: Model Annex III Outermost Regions

Model Annex III

OUTERMOST REGIONS

to which the provisions of model Part Three A of the Treaty on the Functioning of the European Union apply

French territories:

- French overseas departments
  - Guadeloupe
  - French Guiana
  - Martinique
  - Reunion
  - Saint-Barthélemy
  - Saint-Martin

Portuguese territories:

- Azores
- Madeira

Spanish territories:

- Canary Islands

TFEU (i.e Article 188 TEC removed by the Lisbon Treaty) is not included in the interests of consistency and simplification as Greenland's position is addressed separately in the model Article 355(3) framework. Likewise, a general reference is made to Member States rather than only to those specific Member States having OCTs. Elsewhere the non-substantive changes to wording proposed by the Lisbon Treaty are included. The Netherland Antilles are maintained in the list of Dutch OCTs as their status under EU law is still to be determined and, at the time of writing, it is still unclear whether the constituent Dutch territories will remain OCTs or whether some of them (notably Bonaire, Saba and Sint Eustatius) will become Outermost Regions.

Second, greater consistency of wording is sought where similarities exist. Thus, for example, reference is made to the specific protocols in respect of the UK SBAs in Cyprus and the Channel Islands and Isle of Man. This would correct the current inconsistency in the Lisbon Treaty framework, which refers (in Article 355(4)) to the specific Protocol No. 2 in the case of the Aland Islands but makes no such specific reference in Article 355 (5) (b) and (c) to the relevant Protocols by number in the case of the SBAs and the Channel Islands.

In both these cases and in relation to the Aland Islands, reference in the model Article 355 is made to the specific Member State accession treaties. The Lisbon Treaty text is inconsistent in this regard where, for example, Article 355(4) on the Aland Islands refers to the accession treaties of Austria, Finland and Sweden, whereas in relation to the UK Channel Islands and Isle of Man, Article 355(5)(c) refers not to the corresponding accession treaties of Denmark, Ireland and the UK, but to the "Treaty concerning the accession of new Member States to the European Community and to the European Atomic Energy Community". Also, in the case of the SBAs, the wording in the new model framework is changed to reflect the same wording used in relation to the Channel Islands and Isle of Man in order to clarify that the Treaty does not apply to either.

Third, in relation to the OCTs, Greenland is mentioned separately as, although an OCT, a different arrangement is in place for it compared to the other OCTs. Bermuda, on the other hand, although nominally an OCT, has chosen not to have the Association applied to it. Therefore, in practice it is not an OCT, whatever its constitutional status with the UK. Thus, it is proposed that Bermuda be listed separately from the OCTs simply as a territory to which the Treaties do not apply.

Fourth, the second subparagraph of Article 299(3) TEC (Article 355(2) TFEU) in relation to the UK territories specifically would be excluded as superfluous.

Finally, the present Annex II list of territories would, for transparency and in parallel with the model Annex III for the Outermost Regions, also refer to the relevant Member States and be renumbered as Annex IV.

Therefore, for the purposes of the model Article 355(3), the relevant territories are:

- the OCTs
- Greenland
- Faroe Islands
- the UK SBAs in Cyprus of Akrotiri and Dhekelia
- Channel Islands and Isle of Man
- Bermuda

The model Article 355(3) would therefore read as follows:

Part Four of the TFEU in relation to the OCTs would read as follows:

The model Annex IV on the OCTs would read as follows:

18.5 Model Article 355(4)

Both the TCE and the Lisbon Treaty proposed the addition of a new subparagraph in Article 355 (6) TFEU which would permit a status change for Danish, Dutch and French Outermost Regions or OCTs. Although welcome (for reasons already

Box 18.5: Model Article 355(3) TFEU

3. The provisions of the Treaties shall not apply to the following Member State territories:

(a) The Overseas Countries and Territories listed in model Annex IV to the Treaties. However, the special arrangements for association set out in Part Four of this Treaty on the Functioning of the European Union shall apply to the overseas countries and territories with the following exception:

- Greenland save to the extent necessary to ensure the implementation of the special arrangements with the Union set out in the Joint Declaration of 2006 on a partnership with the Union and the Fisheries Partnership Agreement of 2006

(b) Faroe Islands

(c) Akrotiri and Dhekelia, the Sovereign Base Areas of the United Kingdom of Great Britain and Northern Ireland in Cyprus, save to the extent necessary to ensure the implementation of the arrangements set out in Protocols No. 3 and No. 10 to the Act concerning the conditions of accession of the Czech Republic, the Republic of Estonia, the Republic of Cyprus, the Republic of Latvia, the Republic of Lithuania, the Republic of Hungary, the Republic of Malta, the Republic of Poland, the Republic of Slovenia and the Slovak Republic

(d) the Channel Islands and the Isle of Man save to the extent necessary to ensure the implementation of the arrangements for those islands set out in Protocol No. 3 to the Act concerning the accession of the Kingdom of Denmark, Ireland and the United Kingdom of Great Britain and Northern Ireland

(e) Bermuda

Box 18.6: Model Part Four TFEU OCTs

Part Four on the Association of the Overseas Countries and Territories

Article 198

The Member States agree to associate with the EU the non-European countries and territories which have special relations with Member States. These countries and territories (hereinafter called the 'countries and territories') are listed in Annex II. Treaties.

The purpose of association shall be to promote the economic and social development of the countries and territories and to establish close economic relations between them and the EU as a whole.

In accordance with the principles set out in the preamble to the EU Treaties, the association shall serve primarily to further the interests and prosperity of the inhabitants of these countries and territories in order to lead them to the economic, social and cultural development to which they aspire.

Article 199

The Association shall have the following objectives.

1. Member States shall apply to their trade with the countries and territories the same treatment as they accord each other pursuant to the Treaties.
2. Each country or territory shall apply to its trade with Member States and with the other countries and territories the same treatment as that which it applies to the European State with which has special relations.
3. The Member States shall contribute to the investments required for the progressive development of these countries and territories.
4. For investments financed by the EU, participation in tenders and supplies shall be open on equal terms to all natural and legal persons who are nationals of a Member State or of one of the countries and territories.
5. In relations between Member States and the countries and territories the right of establishment of nationals and companies or firms shall be regulated in accordance with the provisions and procedures laid down in the Chapter relating to the right of establishment and on a non-discriminatory basis, subject to any special provisions laid down pursuant to Article 203.

Article 200

1. Customs duties on imports into the Member States of goods originating in the countries and territories shall be prohibited in conformity with the prohibition of customs duties between Member States in accordance with the provisions of the Treaties.
2. Customs duties on imports into each country or territory from Member States or from the other countries or territories shall be prohibited in accordance with the provisions of Article 30.
3. The countries and territories may, however, levy customs duties which meet the needs of their development and industrialisation or produce revenue for their budgets.

   The duties referred to in the preceding subparagraph may not exceed the level of those imposed on imports of products from the Member State with which each country or territory has special relations.

4. Paragraph 2 shall not apply to countries and territories which, by reason of the particular international obligations by which they are bound, already apply a non-discriminatory customs tariff.
5. The introduction of or any change in customs duties imposed on goods imported into the countries and territories shall not, either in law or in fact, give rise to any direct or indirect discrimination between imports from the various Member States.

Article 201

If the level of the duties applicable to goods from a third country on entry into a country or territory is liable, when the provisions of Article 3(1) have been applied, to cause deflections of trade to the detriment of any Member State, the latter may request the Commission to propose to the other Member States the measures needed to remedy the situation.

Article 202

Subject to the provisions relating to public health, public security or public policy, freedom of movement within Member States for workers from the countries and territories, and within the countries and territories for workers from Member States, shall be regulated by acts adopted in accordance with Article 203.

Article 203

The Council, acting unanimously on a proposal from the Commission, shall, on the basis of the experience acquired under the association of the countries and territories with the Union and of the principles set out in the Treaties, lay down provisions as regards the detailed rules and the procedure for the association of the countries and territories with the Union. Where the provisions in question are adopted by the Council in accordance with a special legislative procedure, it shall act unanimously on a proposal from the Commission and after consulting the European Parliament.

stated), this clause as worded in the TCE/Lisbon Treaty, has two significant flaws which create further inconsistency and disjointedness in the overall framework for EU/Member State territories relationship. First, the new subparagraph applies only to Outermost Regions and OCTs and thus not to other territories which fall into neither of these categories. Second, it applies only to the territories of those Member States specifically mentioned i.e Danish, Dutch and French and thus not to the UK and potentially other Member State territories.

It is suggested, therefore, in the interests of consistency and legal certainty, that a general *passerelle* clause covering all Member State territories would be more balanced and more consistent. This general clause would permit any Member State

Box 18.7: Model Annex IV OCTs

Model Annex IV

OVERSEAS COUNTRIES AND TERRITORIES
to which the provisions of Part Four of the Treaty on the Functioning of the European Union apply

Danish territories:

- Greenland

French territories:

- New Caledonia and Dependencies
- French Polynesia
- French Southern and Antarctic Territories
- Wallis and Futuna Islands
- Mayotte
- Saint Pierre and Miquelon

Dutch territories:

- Aruba
- Netherlands Antilles:
  - Bonaire
  - Curaçao
  - Saba
  - Sint Eustatius
  - Sint Maarten

UK territories:

- Anguilla
- Cayman Islands
- Falkland Islands
- South Georgia and the South Sandwich Islands
- Montserrat
- Pitcairn
- Saint Helena and Dependencies
- British Antarctic Territory
- British Indian Ocean Territory
- Turks and Caicos Islands
- British Virgin Islands

territory to change its status whether from Outermost Region to OCT and *vice verse* but also to accommodate other categories of status, without the need for a Treaty amendment.

Another important issue could be addressed by permitting a general *clause passerelle*, namely how to address and reflect in new model Article 355 changes in the constitutional status of territories *vis à vis* their Member State including the addition or removal of existing or new territories. For example, as already noted, St Pierre et Miquelon changed status from TOM to DOM and back to TOM. This status change was never reflected in an amendment to the TEC, notably by removal of St Pierre et Miquelon from the list of OCTs in Annex II. And although one could argue that the practical effects of the status change were negligible at EU level (since the concept of Outermost Region was not yet then conceived and developed), nevertheless the status change did create some confusion at the time as regards St Pierre's status at EU level.[1] Similarly, Aruba changed its status in 1986 within the Kingdom of The Netherlands when it was granted the status of *Land*, separate from the other islands of the Antilles. Algeria's independence from France was not reflected in the Treaty until the Maastricht Treaty. The Treaty was not initially amended to reflect this. The recent change of status of the French territories of Saint Barthélemy and Saint Martin to TOMs under French law—even though they are technically Outermost Regions under the EU framework—could create similar confusion unless clarified by corresponding amendments to the Treaty to reflect these changes.

It has been noted that the *clause passerelle* proposed under the Lisbon Treaty was drafted to accommodate the anticipated status changes of Mayotte and the Netherlands Antilles specifically. Whilst the clause would be a welcome amendment to help address the confusion caused by status changes of Outermost Regions and OCTs, it should not be limited to these categories of territories. In the interests of consistency and a harmonious application of the Treaties to Member State territories, therefore, an alternative *clause passerelle* is proposed.

Finally, the *clause passerelle* proposed by the Lisbon Treaty provided that the power to adopt a decision amending the status of a Member State territory rested with the European Council i.e heads of State and Government meeting four times per year. This book suggests that, as any such decision would be part of the

---

[1] For example, see Commission Regulation (EEC) No 73/87 of 12 January 1987 amending the list of ACP countries in Regulation (EEC) No 486/85 on the arrangements applicable to agricultural products and certain goods resulting from the processing of agricultural products originating in the African, Caribbean and Pacific States or in the overseas countries and territories (OCT), OJ L11/23, 13 January 1987, where the purpose of the amendment to Regulation 486/85 is to add St Pierre et Miquelon to its Annex to reflect the fact that St Pierre is included in the list of OCTs annexed to Annex I of Council Decision No 86/283/EEC of 30 June 1986, relating to the association of the OCTs with the EC. Previously, due to confusion over the status of St Pierre, that territory had not been included with other OCTs in the Annex to Regulation 486/85.

legislative rather than the political process, that power should more properly rest with the EU Council of Ministers rather than the European Council. As the decision relates to Member State sovereignty, rather than to ordinary policy-making legislation, the co-decision procedure would not be appropriate. Nevertheless, to avoid a situation where other Member States (including those currently with no territories) could block a decision under this provision, it is proposed that any decision under this provision could be adopted on the basis of a qualified majority vote, rather than by unanimity. Moreover, as the matter does not fall within the co-decision procedure and therefore the European Parliament would not have co-legislative powers with the Council, nevertheless, in line with the greater powers accorded to the European Parliament under the EU decision-making process, it is proposed that the European Parliament—as well as the European Commission—should be consulted on any such decision to amend the status of Member State territories as set out in the Treaties.

The model Article 355(4) would provide:

Box 18.8: Model Article 355(4) TFEU

4. The Council may, on the initiative of the Member State concerned, adopt a decision amending the status, with regard to the Union, of any Member State territory. The Council shall act by qualified majority after consulting the Commission and the European Parliament.

Accordingly, for the purposes of comparison and cross-reference, the following table sets out the TEC, Lisbon Treaty and proposed new model Article 355 provisions:

Box 18.9: Full text equivalence table Article 299 TEC, Lisbon Treaty, Model Article 355 TFEU

Pre Lisbon Treaty numbering of Article 299 TEC	**Lisbon Treaty numbering of corresponding provisions**	*Territorial Scope of the EU Treaties* **Model numbering of Article 355 TFEU** **Territorial Scope of the Treaties**
Article 299 **TEC**	Article 52 **TEU**	Article 355 **TFEU**
1. This Treaty shall apply to the Kingdom of Belgium, the Republic of Bulgaria, the Czech Republic, the Kingdom of Denmark, the Federal Republic of Germany, the Republic of Estonia, the Hellenic Republic, the Kingdom of Spain, the French Republic, Ireland, the Italian Republic, the Republic of Cyprus, the Republic of Latvia, the Republic of Lithuania, the Grand Duchy of Luxembourg, the Republic of Hungary, the Republic of Malta, the Kingdom of the Netherlands, the Republic of Austria, the Republic of Poland, the Portuguese Republic, Romania, the Republic of Slovenia, the Slovak Republic, the Republic of Finland, the Kingdom of Sweden and the United Kingdom of Great Britain and Northern Ireland.	1. The Treaties shall apply to the Kingdom of Belgium, the Republic of Bulgaria, the Czech Republic, the Kingdom of Denmark, the Federal Republic of Germany, the Republic of Estonia, the Hellenic Republic, the Kingdom of Spain, the French Republic, Ireland, the Italian Republic, the Republic of Cyprus, the Republic of Latvia, the Republic of Lithuania, the Grand Duchy of Luxembourg, the Republic of Hungary, the Republic of Malta, the Kingdom of the Netherlands, the Republic of Austria, the Republic of Poland, the Portuguese Republic, Romania, the Republic of Slovenia, the Slovak Republic, the Republic of Finland, the Kingdom of Sweden and the United Kingdom of Great Britain and Northern Ireland 2. The territorial scope of the Treaties is specified in Article 355 of the Treaty on the Functioning of the European Union.	1. The Treaties shall apply to all Member States of the Union listed in model Annex II to the Treaties, and to their territories
	Article 349 **TFEU**	
2. The provisions of this Treaty shall apply to the French overseas departments, the Azores, Madeira and the Canary Islands. However, taking account of the structural social and economic	Taking account of the structural social and economic	2. The provisions of the Treaties shall apply to the following Member State territories: (a) the Outermost Regions, listed in model Annex III to the Treaties in accordance with

(continued)

Pre Lisbon Treaty numbering of Article 299 TEC	Lisbon Treaty numbering of corresponding provisions	*Territorial Scope of the EU Treaties* **Model numbering of Article 355 TFEU Territorial Scope of the Treaties**
situation of the French overseas departments, the Azores, Madeira and the Canary Islands, which is compounded by their remoteness, insularity, small size, difficult topography and climate, economic dependence on a few products, the permanence and combination of which severely restrain their development, the Council, acting by a qualified majority on a proposal from the Commission and after consulting the European Parliament, shall adopt specific measures aimed, in particular, at laying down the conditions of application of the present Treaty to those regions, including common policies.	situation of Guadeloupe, French Guiana, Martinique, Réunion, Saint-Barthélemy, Saint-Martin, the Azores, Madeira and the Canary Islands, which is compounded by their remoteness, insularity, small size, difficult topography and climate, economic dependence on a few products, the permanence and combination of which severely restrain their development, the Council, acting by a qualified majority on a proposal from the Commission and after consulting the European Parliament, shall adopt specific measures aimed, in particular, at laying down the conditions of application of the present Treaty to those regions, including common policies. Where the specific measures in question are adopted by the Council in accordance with a special legislative procedure, it shall also act on a proposal from the Commission and after consulting the European Parliament.	model Part Three A concerning the Outermost Regions (b) Ceuta and Melilla in accordance with Article 25 and Protocol No. 2 as amended, to the Act concerning the conditions of accession of the Kingdom of Spain and the Portuguese Republic (c) Gibraltar in accordance with Article 28 to the Act concerning the conditions of accession of the Kingdom of Denmark, Ireland and the United Kingdom of Great Britain and Northern Ireland (d) Aland Islands in accordance with Protocol No. 2 to the Act concerning the conditions of accession of the Republic of Austria, the Republic of Finland and the Kingdom of Sweden.
The Council shall, when adopting the relevant measures referred to in the second subparagraph, take into account areas such as customs and trade policies, fiscal policy, free zones, agriculture and fisheries policies, conditions for supply of raw materials and essential consumer goods, State aids and conditions of access to Structural Funds and to	The measures referred to in the first paragraph concern in particular areas such as customs and trade policies, fiscal policy, free zones, agriculture and fisheries policies, conditions for supply of raw materials and essential consumer goods, State aids and conditions of access to structural funds and to horizontal Union programmes	

(continued)

Pre Lisbon Treaty numbering of Article 299 TEC	**Lisbon Treaty numbering of corresponding provisions**	***Territorial Scope of the EU Treaties*** **Model numbering of Article 355 TFEU Territorial Scope of the Treaties**
horizontal Community programmes.		
The Council shall adopt the measures referred to in the second subparagraph taking into account the special characteristics and constraints of the Outermost Regions without undermining the integrity and the coherence of the Community legal order, including the internal market and common policies.	The Council shall adopt the measures referred to in the first subparagraph taking into account the special characteristics and constraints of the Outermost Regions without undermining the integrity and the coherence of the Union legal order, including the internal market and common policies.	
	Article 355 **TFEU**	
	In addition to the provisions of Article 52 of the Treaty on European Union relating to the territorial scope of the Treaties, the following provisions shall apply: 1. The provisions of the Treaties shall apply to Guadeloupe, French Guiana, Martinique, Réunion, Saint-Barthélemy, Saint-Martin the Azores, Madeira and the Canary Islands in accordance with Article 349.	
3. The special arrangements for association set out in Part Four of this Treaty shall apply to the overseas countries and territories listed in Annex II to this Treaty. This Treaty shall not apply to those overseas countries and territories having special relations with the United Kingdom of Great Britain and Northern Ireland which are not included in the aforementioned list.	2. The special arrangements for association set out in Part Four of this Treaty shall apply to the overseas countries and territories listed in Annex II to the Treaties. This Treaty shall not apply to those overseas countries and territories having special relations with the United Kingdom of Great Britain and Northern Ireland which are not included in the aforementioned list.	3. The provisions of the Treaties shall not apply to the following Member State territories: (a) the Overseas Countries and Territories listed in model Annex IV to the Treaties. However, the special arrangements for association set out in Part Four of the Treaty on the Functioning of the European Union shall apply to the overseas countries and territories, with the following exception:
4. The provisions of this Treaty shall apply to the European	3. The provisions of the Treaties shall apply to the	- Greenland, save to the extent

(continued)

Pre Lisbon Treaty numbering of Article 299 TEC	**Lisbon Treaty numbering of corresponding provisions**	*Territorial Scope of the EU Treaties* **Model numbering of Article 355 TFEU Territorial Scope of the Treaties**
territories for whose external relations a Member State is responsible.	European territories for whose external relations a Member State is responsible.	necessary to ensure the implementation of the special arrangements with the Union set out in the Joint Declaration of 2006 on a partnership with the Union and the Fisheries Partnership Agreement of 2006
5. The provisions of this Treaty shall apply to the Åland Islands in accordance with the provisions set out in Protocol No 2 to the Act concerning the conditions of accession of the Republic of Austria, the Republic of Finland and the Kingdom of Sweden.	4. The provisions of the Treaties shall apply to the Åland Islands in accordance with the provisions set out in Protocol No. 2 to the Act concerning the conditions of accession of the Republic of Austria, the Republic of Finland and the Kingdom of Sweden.	(b) Faroe Islands (c) Akrotiri and Dhekelia, the Sovereign Base Areas of the United Kingdom of Great Britain and Northern Ireland in Cyprus, save to the extent necessary to ensure the arrangements set out in Protocols No. 3 and No. 10 to the Act concerning the conditions of accession of the Czech Republic, the Republic of Estonia, the Republic of Cyprus, the Republic of Latvia, the Republic of Lithuania, the Republic of Hungary, the Republic of Malta, the Republic of Poland, the Republic of Slovenia and the Slovak Republic
6. Notwithstanding the preceding paragraphs: (a) this Treaty shall not apply to the Faroe Islands; (b) this Treaty shall not apply to the United Kingdom Sovereign Base Areas of Akrotiri and Dhekelia in Cyprus except to the extent necessary to ensure the implementation of the arrangements set out in the Protocol on the Sovereign Base Areas of the United Kingdom of Great Britain and Northern Ireland in Cyprus annexed to the Act concerning the conditions of accession of the Czech Republic, the Republic of Estonia, the Republic of Cyprus, the Republic of Latvia, the Republic of Lithuania, the Republic of Hungary, the Republic of Malta, the Republic of Poland, the Republic of Slovenia and the Slovak Republic to the European Union and in	5. Notwithstanding Article 52 of the Treaty on European Union and paragraphs 1–4 of this Article: (a) the Treaties shall not apply to the Faroe Islands; (b) the Treaties shall not apply to the United Kingdom Sovereign Base Areas of Akrotiri and Dhekelia in Cyprus except to the extent necessary to ensure the implementation of the arrangements set out in the Protocol on the Sovereign Base Areas of the United Kingdom of Great Britain and Northern Ireland in Cyprus annexed to the Act concerning the conditions of accession of the Czech Republic, the Republic of Estonia, the Republic of Cyprus, the Republic of Latvia, the Republic of Lithuania, the Republic of Hungary, the Republic of Malta, the Republic of Poland, the Republic of Slovenia and the	(d) the Channel Islands and the Isle of Man save to the extent necessary to ensure the implementation of the arrangements for those islands set out in Protocol No. 3 to the Act concerning the accession of the Kingdom of Denmark, Ireland and the United Kingdom of Great Britain and Northern Ireland (e) Bermuda

(continued)

Pre Lisbon Treaty numbering of Article 299 TEC	**Lisbon Treaty numbering of corresponding provisions**	***Territorial Scope of the EU Treaties*** **Model numbering of Article 355 TFEU Territorial Scope of the Treaties**
accordance with the terms of that Protocol[2]; (c) this Treaty shall apply to the Channel Islands and the Isle of Man only to the extent necessary to ensure the implementation of the arrangements for those islands set out in the Treaty concerning the accession of new Member States to the European Economic Community and to the European Atomic Energy Community signed on 22 January 1972.	Slovak Republic to the European Union and in accordance with the terms of that Protocol; (c) the Treaties shall apply to the Channel Islands and the Isle of Man only to the extent necessary to ensure the implementation of the arrangements for those islands set out in the Treaty concerning the accession of new Member States to the European Economic Community and to the European Atomic Energy Community signed on 22 January 1972	
	6. The European Council may, on the initiative of the Member State concerned, adopt a decision amending the status, with regard to the Union, of a Danish, French or Netherlands country or territory referred to in paragraphs 1 and 2. The European Council shall act unanimously after consulting the Commission.	4. The Council may, on the initiative of the Member State concerned, adopt a decision amending the status, with regard to the Union, of any Member State territory. The Council shall act by qualified majority after consulting the Commission and the Parliament

18.6 Final Observations

This book has attempted to trace the origins and development of Article 299 TEC from its inception in 1957 to the present day. This has included an analysis of the intentions behind the original drafters of the Article. It has reviewed the developments, including Member State accessions and major Treaty revisions that have impacted Article 299.

[2] As amended by the Cyprus Act of Accession, OJ L236, 23 September 2003.

The overall objective in this review has been to examine and assess the adequacy of the present EU Treaties framework for relations between the EU and Member State territories. As the focus of this publication has been therefore primarily on the EU treaties framework, it has not examined in any detail specific policy areas. Nevertheless, it is worth noting here that all of these territories have negotiated derogations and special arrangements in regard to policy areas such as taxation, customs and agriculture. For example, Ceuta and Melilla obtained derogations from the CCT, CCP and CAP, Gibraltar also for VAT and the Aland Islands for direct taxation. Such special provisions have usually been agreed in order to protect the small fragile economies of these territories and to ensure their ongoing competitiveness within the EU and/or globally.

For the purposes of this analysis, the book has been structured into three parts. Part I reviewed the origins and content of Article 299 as drafted and set out in the 1957 TEC. Part II looked at the major political and legal developments since 1957 including those introduced by the Lisbon Treaty to the present, assessing their impact on the Article 299 framework. Part III, using the information from the previous two parts, proposed a new model Article 355 TFEU that attempts to create a modern and dynamic legal framework that both reflects the present relations with Member States and their territories, but also more easily accommodates any future changes in this structure and relationship.

For each of the three parts of this book, key conclusions can be drawn:

Part I: Original Version of Article 299 TEC, 1957

It is clear that from its inception in 1957 Article 299 TEC (ex Article 227 TEC) was drafted with little thought to structure or indeed to future amendment. Whilst it is probable that Article 299(1) was intended to set a general principle of application of the Treaty to all Member States and their territories, the exceptions set out in the ensuing subparagraphs (2) and (3) were addressed to and created for specific categories of territories rather than to general categories of territories or situations that could more easily adapt to future change. And subparagraph (4) had no clear specific application.

Thus, from the start, Article 299 was ill thought out and poorly structured and ill-suited to the many and disparate future developments relating to it.

Part II: Article 299 TEC and Developments Since 1957

Part Two reviewed Article 299 TEC (and equivalent provisions under the Lisbon Treaty) and the key developments relevant to Article 299—including political and social changes, Member State accessions, European Court judgments, major

Treaty amendments including those of the Lisbon Treaty. Some of these developments resulted in amendments to Article 299 itself but not all.

In particular, two key points were noted: first, in general, amendments to Article 299 have been piecemeal and have not usually taken account of how such amendments fit with the overall structure of Article 299. Second, most of the major Treaty amendments, with the possible exception of the Amsterdam Treaty amendments in relation to Article 299(2) on the Outermost Regions, have not taken advantage of the opportunity to in addition conduct an overall review of Article 299 as a legal framework for relations between the EU and Member State territories.

Part III: Proposed New Model Article 355 TFEU

Based on the research and analysis undertaken in Parts I and II, this book formulates a new alternative Article 355 set within the new Lisbon Treaty TFEU. This model Article 355 attempts to achieve the following:

- a *modern* framework for relations between the EU and Member State territories that reflects all the developments that have taken place since 1957 including new Member States and territories
- a *dynamic* framework particularly through the model subparagraph (4) which more easily accommodates future changes and developments including new and departing territories
- a *simplified* provision with just four subparagraphs each with a clear objective including one relating to those territories which are part of the EU and one concerning those which are not but which have negotiated special arrangements with the EU
- a *transparent* framework in that the territories that are covered by Article 355 are either clearly stated in that provision or are easy to identify. Transparent also in showing clearly to which territories the Treaties apply and to which they do not
- a more *balanced* structure in that each of the four subparagraphs states a general principle and the detailed provisions if any are set out in other parts, protocols and annexes appended to the Treaties
- a more *concise* framework with just 4 subparagraphs (as opposed to the current 6) and close to half the number of words (441 words compared to 794 under the present Lisbon Treaty equivalent provisions), setting out general principles rather than detailed provisions.

Annexes

F. Murray, *The European Union and Member State Territories: A New Legal Framework Under the EU Treaties*, DOI: 10.1007/978-90-6704-826-2,

Annex I

Lisbon Treaty Provisions Governing EU/Member State Territories

Article 52 (1) and (2) Treaty on the European Union

1. *The Treaties shall apply to the Kingdom of Belgium, Republic of Bulgaria, the Czech Republic, the Kingdom of Denmark, the Federal Republic of Germany, the Republic of Estonia, the Hellenic Republic, the Kingdom of Spain, the French Republic, Ireland, the Italian Republic, the Republic of Cyprus, the Republic of Latvia, the Republic of Lithuania, the Grand Duchy of Luxembourg, the Republic of Hungary, the Republic of Malta, the Kingdom of the Netherlands, the Republic of Austria, the Republic of Poland, the Portuguese Republic, Romania, the Republic of Slovenia, the Slovak Republic, the Republic of Finland, the Kingdom of Sweden and the United Kingdom of Great Britain and Northern Ireland.*
2. *The territorial scope of the Treaties is specified in Article 355 of the Treaty on the Functioning of the European Union.*

Article 349 Treaty on the Functioning of the European Union (TFEU)

Taking account of the structural social and economic situation of Guadeloupe, French Guiana, Martinique, Réunion, Saint-Barthélemy, Saint-Martin,the Azores, Madeira and the Canary Islands, which is compounded by their remoteness, insularity, small size, difficult topography and climate, economic dependence on a few products, the permanence and combination of which severely restrain their development, the Council, acting by a qualified majority on a proposal from the Commission and after consulting the European Parliament, shall adopt specific measures aimed, in particular, at laying down the conditions of application of the present Treaty to those regions, including common policies. Where the specific measures in

F. Murray, *The European Union and Member State Territories: A New Legal Framework Under the EU Treaties*, DOI: 10.1007/978-90-6704-826-2,

question are adopted by the Council in accordance with a special legislative procedure, it shall also act on a proposal from the Commission and after consulting the European Parliament.
The measures referred to in the first paragraph concern in particular areas such ascustoms and trade policies, fiscal policy, free zones, agriculture and fisheries policies, conditions for supply of raw materials and essential consumer goods, State aids and conditions of access to structural funds and to horizontal Union programmes.
The Council shall adopt the measures referred to in the firstsubparagraph taking into account the special characteristics and constraints of the Outermost Regions without undermining the integrity and the coherence of the Unionlegal order, including the internal market and common policies.

Article 355 TFEU

In addition to the provisions of Article 52 of the Treaty on European Union relating to the territorial scope of the Treaties, the following provisions shall apply:

1. *The provisions of the Treaties shall apply to Guadeloupe, French Guiana, Martinique, Réunion, Saint-Barthélemy, Saint-Martin the Azores, Madeira and the Canary Islands in accordance with Article 349.*
2. *The special arrangements for association set out in part four of this Treaty shall apply to the overseas countries and territories listed in Annex II to the Treaties.*

This Treaty shall not apply to those overseas countries and territories having special relations with the United Kingdom of Great Britain and Northern Ireland which are not included in the aforementioned list.

3. *The provisions of the Treaties shall apply to the European territories for whose external relations a Member State is responsible.*
4. *The provisions of the Treatiesshall apply to the Åland Islands in accordance with the provisions set out in Protocol No. 2 to the Act concerning the conditions of accession of the Republic of Austria, the Republic of Finland and the Kingdom of Sweden.*
5. *Notwithstanding Article 52 of the Treaty on European Union and paragraphs 1 to 4 of this Article:*
   (a) *the Treaties shall not apply to the Faroe Islands;*
   (b) *the Treaties shall not apply to the sovereign base areas of the United Kingdom of Great Britain and Northern Ireland in Cyprus;*

(c) the Treaties shall apply to the Channel Islands and the Isle of Man only to the extent necessary to ensure the implementation of the arrangements for those islands set out in the Treaty concerning the accession of new Member States to the European Economic Community and to the European Atomic Energy Community signed on 22 January 1972.

6. *The European Council may, on the initiative of the Member State concerned, adopt a decision amending the status, with regard to the Union, of a Danish, French or Netherlands country or territory referred to in paragraphs 1 and 2. The European Council shall act unanimously after consulting the Commission.*

Annex II

Article 227 TEC 1957

1957 TEC—Article 227 (original version)
(Part Six: General and Final Provisions)

Article 227:

1. *This Treaty shall apply to the Kingdom of Belgium, the Federal Republic of Germany, the French Republic, the Italian Republic, the Grand Duchy of Luxembourg and the Kingdom of the Netherlands.*
2. *With regard to Algeria and the French overseas departments, the general and particular provisions of this Treaty relating to:*

   - the free movement of goods;
   - agriculture, save for Article 40(4);
   - the liberalisation of services;,
   - the rules of competition :
   - the protective measures provided for in Articles 108, 109 and 226;
   - the institutions,
   Shall apply as soon as this Treaty enters into force.

The conditions under which the other provisions of this Treaty are to apply shall be determined, within two years of the entry into force of this Treaty, by decisions of the Council, acting unanimously on a proposal from the Commission.

The institutions of the Community will, within the framework of the procedures provided for in this Treaty, in particular Article 226, take care that the economic and social development of these areas is made possible.

3. *The special arrangements for association set out in Part Four of this Treaty shall apply to the overseas countries and territories listed in Annex IV to this Treaty.*
4. *The provisions of this Treaty shall apply to the European territories for whose external relations a Member State is responsible.*

F. Murray, *The European Union and Member State Territories: A New Legal Framework Under the EU Treaties*, DOI: 10.1007/978-90-6704-826-2,

Annex III

Article 226 TEC 1957

Article 226 TEC

1. *If during the transitional period, difficulties arise which are serious and liable to persist in any sector of the economy or which could bring about serious deterioration in the economic situation of a given area, a Member State may apply for authorisation to take protective measures in order to rectify the situation and adjust the sector concerned to the economy of the common market.*
2. *On application by the State concerned, the Commission shall, by emergency procedure, determine without delay the protective measures which it considers necessary, specifying the circumstances and the manner in which they are to be put into effect.*
3. *The measures authorised under paragraph 2 may involve derogations from the rules of this Treaty, to such an extent and for such periods as are strictly necessary in order to attain the objectives referred to in paragraph 1. Priority shall be given to such measures as will least disturb the functioning of the common market.*

F. Murray, *The European Union and Member State Territories: A New Legal Framework Under the EU Treaties*, DOI: 10.1007/978-90-6704-826-2,

Annex IV

Part Four (Articles 131–136) TEC 1957

Part Four (Articles 131—136)

Article 131
The Member States agree to associate with the Community the non-European countries and territories which have special relations with Belgium, France, Italy and the Netherlands. These countries and territories (hereinafter called the 'countries and territories') are listed in Annex IV to this Treaty.
The purpose of association shall be to promote the economic and social development of the countries and territories and to establish close economic relations between them and the Community as a whole.
In accordance with the principles set out in the preamble to this Treaty, association shall serve primarily to further the interests and prosperity of the inhabitants of these countries and territories in order to lead them to the economic, social and cultural development to which they aspire.

Article 132
The Association shall have the following objectives:

1. *Member States shall apply to their trade with the countries and territories the same treatment as they accord each other pursuant to this Treaty.*
2. *Each country or territory shall apply to its trade with Member States and with the other countries and territories the same treatment*
3. *The Member States shall contribute to the investments required for the progressive development of these countries and territories*
4. *For investments financed by the Community, participation in tenders and supplies shall be open on equal terms to all natural and legal persons who are nationals of a Member State or of one of the countries and territories.*

F. Murray, *The European Union and Member State Territories: A New Legal Framework Under the EU Treaties*, DOI: 10.1007/978-90-6704-826-2,

5. *In relations between Member States and the countries and territories the right of establishment of nationals and companies or firms shall be regulated in accordance with the provisions and procedures laid down in the Chapter relating to the right of establishment and on a non-discriminatory basis, subject to any special provisions laid down pursuant Article 136.*

Article 133

1. *Customs duties on imports into the Member States of goods originating in the countries and territories shall be completely abolished in conformity with the progressive abolition of customs duties between Member States in accordance with the provisions of this Treaty.*
2. *Customs duties on imports into each country or territory from Member States or from the other countries or territories shall be progressively abolished in accordance with the provisions of Articles 12, 13, 14, 15 and 17.*
3. *The countries and territories may, however, levy customs duties which meet the needs of their development and industrialisation or produce revenue for their budgets.*
   The duties referred to in the preceding subparagraph shall nevertheless be progressively reduced to the level of those imposed on imports of products from the Member State with which each country or territory has special relations. The percentages and the timetable of the reductions provided for under this Treaty shall apply to the difference between the duty imposed on a product coming from the Member States which has special relations with the country or territory concerned and the duty imposed on the same product coming from within the Community on entry into the importing country or territory.
4. *Paragraph 2 shall not apply to countries and territories which, by reason of the particular international obligations by which they are bound, already apply a non-discriminatory customs tariff when this Treaty enters into force.*
5. *The introduction of or any change in customs duties imposed on goods imported into the countries and territories shall not, either in law or in fact, give rise to any direct or indirect discrimination between imports from the various Member States.*

Article 134
If the level of the duties applicable to goods from a third country on entry into a country or territory is liable, when the provisions of Article 133(1) have been applied, to cause deflections of trade to the detriment of any Member State, the latter may request the Commission to propose to the other Member States the measures needed to remedy the situation.

Article 135
Subject to the provisions relating to public health, public security or public policy, freedom of movement within Member States for workers from the countries and territories, and within the countries and territories for workers from Member States, shall be governed by agreements to be concluded subsequently with the unanimous approval of Member States.

Article 136
For an initial period of five years after entry into force of this Treaty, the details of and procedure for the association of the countries and territories with the Community shall be determined by an Implementing Convention annexed to this Treaty.

Before the Convention referred to in the preceding paragraph expires, the Council shall, acting unanimously, lay down provisions for a further period, on the basis of the experience acquired and of the principles set out in this Treaty.

Annex V

Implementing Convention on the Association of Overseas Countries and Territories of the Community 1957

Article 1
The Member States shall, under the conditions laid down below, participate in measures which will promote the social and economic development of the countries and territories listed in Annex IV to this Treaty, by supplementing the efforts made by the authorities responsible for those countries and territories.
For this purpose, a Development Fund for the Overseas Countries and Territories is hereby established, into which the Member States shall, over a period of five years, pay the annual contributions set out in Annex A to this Convention.
The Fund shall be administered by the Commission.

Article 2
The authorities responsible for the countries and territories shall, in agreement with the local authorities or with the representatives of the peoples of the countries and territories concerned, submit to the Commission the social or economic projects for which financing by the Community is requested.

Article 3
The Commission shall draw up annually general programmes for allocation to the different classes of project of the funds made available in accordance with Annex B to this Convention.
The general programmes shall contain projects for financing:

(*a*) *certain social institutions, in particular hospitals, teaching or technical research establishments and institutions for vocational guidance and advancement among the peoples concerned;*

F. Murray, *The European Union and Member State Territories: A New Legal Framework Under the EU Treaties*, DOI: 10.1007/978-90-6704-826-2,

(b) economic investments which are in the public interest and are directly connected with the implementation of a programme containing specific productive development projects.

Article 4
At the beginning of each financial year the Council shall, acting by a qualified majority after consulting the Commission, determine what funds will be devoted to financing:

(a) the social institutions referred to in Article 3(a);
(b) the economic investments in the public sector referred to in Article 3(b).

The decision of the Council shall aim at a rational geographical distribution of the funds made available.
Article 5

1. *The Commission shall determine how the funds made available under Article 4(a) shall be allocated according to the various requests received for the financing of social institutions.*
2. *The Commission shall draw up proposals for financing the economic investment projects which it is considering under Article 4(b).*

It shall submit these proposals to the Council.
If, within one month, no Member State requests that the Council examine the proposals, they shall be deemed to be approved.
If the Council examines the proposals, it shall act by a qualified majority within two months.

3. *Any funds not allocated during any one year shall be carried forward to the following years.*
4. *The funds allocated shall be made available to the authorities responsible for carrying out the work concerned. The Commission shall ensure that such funds are used for the purposes which have been decided upon, and are expended to the best economic advantage.*

Article 6
Within six months of the entry into force of this Treaty, the Council shall, acting by a qualified majority on a proposal from the Commission, lay down rules for the collection and transfer of financial contributions, for budgeting and for the administration of the resources of the Development Fund.

Article 7
The qualified majority referred to in Article 4, 5 and 6 shall be 67 votes. Member States shall have the following votes:
Belgium.................... 11 votes
Germany...................33 votes
France ....33 votes

Italy.........................11 votes
Luxembourg...............1 vote
Netherlands...............11votes

Article 8
The right of establishment shall, in each country or territory, be progressively extended to nationals, companies or firms of Member States other than the State which has special relations with the country or territory concerned. During the first year in which this Convention is applied, the manner in which this is to be effected shall be so determined by the Council, acting by a qualified majority on a proposal from the Commission, as to ensure the progressive abolition during the transitional period of any discrimination.

Article 9
The customs treatment to be applied to trade between member States and the countries and territories shall be that provided for in Articles 133 and 134 of this Treaty.

Article 10
For the duration of this Convention, Member States shall apply to their trade with the countries and territories those provisions of the Chapter of this Treaty relating to the elimination of quantitative restrictions between the Member States which they apply to trade with one another during the same period.

Article 11

1. *In each country or territory where import quotas exist, one year after this Convention enters into force, the quotas open to States other than the State with which such country or territory has special relations shall be converted into global quotas open without discrimination to the other Member States. As from the same date, these quotas shall be increased annually in accordance with Article 32 and Article 33(1), (2), (4), (5), (6) and (7) of this Treaty.*
2. *Where, in the case of a product which has not been liberalized the global quota does not amount to 7% of total imports into a country or territory, a quota equal to 7% of such imports shall be introduced not later than one year after the entry into force of this Convention, and shall be increased annually in accordance with paragraph.*
3. *Where, in the case of certain products, no quota has been opened for imports into a country or territory, the Commission shall, by means of a decision, determine the manner in which the quotas to be offered to other Member States shall be opened and increased.*

Article 12
Where import quotas established by Member States cover both imports from a State having special relations with a country or territory and imports from the

country or territory concerned, the share of imports from the countries and territories shall be the subject of a global quota based on import statistics. Any such quota shall be established during the first year in which this Convention is in force and shall be increased as provided for in Article 10.

Article 13
The provisions of Article 10 shall not preclude prohibitions or restrictions on imports, exports or goods in transit justified on grounds of public morality; public policy or public security; the protection of health and life of humans, animals or plants; the protection of national treasures possessing artistic, historic or archaeological value; or the protection of industrial and commercial property. Such prohibitions or restrictions shall not, however, constitute a means of arbitrary discrimination or a disguised restriction on trade.

Article 14
After the date of expiry of this Convention and until provisions covering association for a further period have been adopted, quotas for imports into the countries and territories on the one hand, and into the Member States on the other, of products originating in the countries and territories shall remain at the level set for the fifth year. The arrangements in respect of the right of establishment in force at the end of the fifth year shall also be maintained.

Article 15

1. *Tariff quotas for imports from third countries of raw coffee into Italy and the Benelux countries, and of bananas into the Federal Republic of Germany, shall be introduced in accordance with the Protocols annexed to this Convention.*
2. *If this Convention expires before the conclusion of a new agreement, the Member States shall, pending such new agreement, enjoy tariff quotas for bananas, cocoa beans and raw coffee at the rates of duty applying at the beginning of the second stage; such quotas shall be equal to the volume of imports from third countries in the course of the latest year for which statistics are available.*

Such quotas shall, where appropriate, be increased in proportion to the increase in consumption within the importing countries.

3. *Member States enjoying tariff quotas at the rates of duty applied within this Treaty enters into force under the Protocols relating to imports of raw coffee and bananas from third countries may require that, instead of the treatment provided for in paragraph 2, the tariff quotas for these products be maintained at the level reached at the date of expiry of this Convention.*

Such quotas shall, where appropriate, be increased as provided in paragraph 2.

4. The Commission shall, at the request of the States concerned, determine the size of the tariff quotas referred to in the preceding paragraphs.

Article 16

The provisions contained in Article 1—8 of this Convention shall apply to Algeria and the French overseas departments.

Article 17

Without prejudice to cases in which the provisions of Articles 14 and 15 apply, this Convention is concluded for a period of five years.

Annex A referred to in Article 1 of this Convention

Percentages	*1st year*	*2nd year*	*3rd year*	*4th year*	*5th year*	*Total*
	10%	*12.5%*	*16.5%*	*22.5%*	*38.5%*	*100%*
Countries	*MILLIONS*	*OF*	*EPU*	*UNITS*	*OF*	*ACCOUNT*
Belgium	7	8.75	11.55	15.75	26.95	70
Germany	20	25	33	45	77	200
France	20	25	33	45	77	200
Italy	4	5	6.60	9	15.40	40
Luxembourg	0.125	0.15625	0.20625	0.28125	0.48125	1.25
Netherlands	7	8.75	11.55	15.75	26.95	*70*

Annex B referred to in Article 3 of this Convention

Percentages	*1st year*	*2nd year*	*3rd year*	*4th year*	*5th year*	*Total*
	10%	*12.5%*	*16.5%*	*22.5%*	*38.5%*	*100%*
OCTs of	*MILLIONS*	*OF*	*EPU*	*UNITS*	*OF*	*ACCOUNT*
Belgium	3	3.75	4.95	6.75	11.55	30
France	51.125	63.906	84.356	15.031	196.832	511.25
Italy	0.5	0.625	0.825	1.125	1.925	5
Netherlands	3.5	4.375	5.775	7.875	13.475	35

Annex VI

Article 299 TEC 2009

Article 299

1. *This Treaty shall apply to the Kingdom of Belgium, the Republic of Bulgaria, the Czech Republic, the Kingdom of Denmark, the Federal Republic of Germany, the Republic of Estonia, the Hellenic Republic, the Kingdom of Spain, the French Republic, Ireland, the Italian Republic, the Republic of Cyprus, the Republic of Latvia, the Republic of Lithuania, the Grand Duchy of Luxembourg, the Republic of Hungary, the Republic of Malta, the Kingdom of the Netherlands, the Republic of Austria, the Republic of Poland, the Portuguese Republic, Romania, the Republic of Slovenia, the Slovak Republic, the Republic of Finland, the Kingdom of Sweden and the United Kingdom of Great Britain and Northern Ireland.*[1]
2. *The provisions of this Treaty shall apply to the French overseas departments, the Azores, Madeira and the Canary Islands.*

However, taking account of the structural social and economic situation of the French overseas departments, the Azores, Madeira and the Canary Islands, which is compounded by their remoteness, insularity, small size, difficult topography and climate, economic dependence on a few products, the permanence and combination of which severely restrain their development, the Council, acting by a qualified majority on a proposal from the Commission and after consulting the European Parliament, shall adopt specific measures aimed, in particular, at laying down the conditions of application of the present Treaty to those regions, including common policies.

[1] As amended most recently by Article 17 of the Act of Accession of Bulgaria and Romania to the EU, OJ L157/209 21 June 2005.

F. Murray, *The European Union and Member State Territories: A New Legal Framework Under the EU Treaties*, DOI: 10.1007/978-90-6704-826-2,

The Council shall, when adopting the relevant measures referred to in the second subparagraph, take into account areas such as customs and trade policies, fiscal policy, free zones, agriculture and fisheries policies, conditions for supply of raw materials and essential consumer goods, State aids and conditions of access to Structural Funds and to horizontal Community programmes.
The Council shall adopt the measures referred to in the second subparagraph taking into account the special characteristics and constraints of the Outermost Regions without undermining the integrity and the coherence of the Community legal order, including the internal market and common policies.

3. *The special arrangements for association set out in Part Four of this Treaty shall apply to the overseas countries and territories listed in Annex II to this Treaty.*

This Treaty shall not apply to those overseas countries and territories having special relations with the United Kingdom of Great Britain and Northern Ireland which are not included in the aforementioned list.

4. *The provisions of this Treaty shall apply to the European territories for whose external relations a Member State is responsible.*
5. *The provisions of this Treaty shall apply to the Åland Islands in accordance with the provisions set out in Protocol No. 2 to the Act concerning the conditions of accession of the Republic of Austria, the Republic of Finland and the Kingdom of Sweden.*
6. *Notwithstanding the preceding paragraphs:*

   (a) This Treaty shall not apply to the Faroe Islands;
   (b) This Treaty shall not apply to the United Kingdom Sovereign Base Areas of Akrotiri and Dhekelia in Cyprus except to the extent necessary to ensure the implementation of the arrangements set out in the Protocol on the Sovereign Base Areas of the United Kingdom of Great Britain and Northern Ireland in Cyprus annexed to the Act concerning the conditions of accession of the Czech Republic, the Republic of Estonia, the Republic of Cyprus, the Republic of Latvia, the Republic of Lithuania, the Republic of Hungary, the Republic of Malta, the Republic of Poland, the Republic of Slovenia and the Slovak Republic to the European Union and in accordance with the terms of that Protocol[2]*;*
   (c) This Treaty shall apply to the Channel Islands and the Isle of Man only to the extent necessary to ensure the implementation of the arrangements for those islands set out in the Treaty concerning the accession of new Member States to the European Economic Community and to the European Atomic Energy Community signed on 22 January 1972.

---

[2] As amended by the Cyprus Act of Accession, OJ L236, 23 September 2003.

Annex VII

Article 25 Spanish Act of Accession 1985 (Ceuta and Melilla)

Article 25, Spanish Act of Accession

1. *The Treaties and the acts of the institutions of the European Communities shall apply to the Canary Islands and to Ceuta and to Melilla, subject to the derogations referred to in paragraphs 2 and 3 and to the other provisions of this Act.*
2. *The conditions under which the provisions of the EEC and ECSC Treaties concerning the free movement of goods and the acts of the institutions of the Community concerning customs legislation and commercial policy, shall apply to the Canary Islands Ceuta and to Melilla are set out in Protocol 2.*
3. *Without prejudice to the specific provisions of Article 155, the acts of the institutions of the European Communities concerning the common agricultural policy and the common fisheries policy shall not apply to the Canary Islands and Ceuta or Melilla.*

The Council acting by a qualified majority on a proposal from the Commission shall determine the provisions of a socio-structural nature, which, in the sphere of agriculture, shall apply to the Canary Islands, whilst ensuring that these provisions are compatible with the general objectives of the common agricultural policy.

4. *At the request of the Kingdom of Spain, the Council, acting unanimously on a proposal from the Commission and after consulting the Assembly, may:*

   - *decide to include the Canary Islands and Ceuta and Melilla in the customs territory of the Community;*

F. Murray, *The European Union and Member State Territories: A New Legal Framework Under the EU Treaties*, DOI: 10.1007/978-90-6704-826-2,

- *define the appropriate measures aimed at extending to the Canary Islands and to Ceuta and Melilla the provisions of Community law in force.*

On a proposal from the Commission acting on its own initiative or at the request of a Member State, the Council acting unanimously and after consulting the Assembly, may decide to make such adjustments applicable to the Canary Islands and Ceuta and to Melilla as may prove necessary.

Annex VIII

Protocol No. 2 Spanish Act of Accession 1985 (Ceuta and Melilla)

Protocol No. 2
concerning the Canary Islands and Ceuta and Melilla

Article 1

1. *Products originating in the Canary Islands or in Ceuta and Melilla and products coming from third countries imported into the Canary Islands or into Ceuta and Melilla under the arrangements which are applicable there to them shall not be deemed, when released for free circulation in the customs territory of the Community, to be goods fulfilling the conditions of Articles 9 and 10 of the ETEC, nor goods in free circulation under the ECSC Treaty.*
2. *The customs territory of the Community shall not include the Canary Islands and Ceuta and Melilla.*
3. *Except where otherwise provided for in this Protocol, the acts of the institutions of the Community regarding customs legislation for foreign trade shall apply under the same conditions to trade between the customs territory of the Community, on the one hand, and the Canary Islands and Ceuta and Melilla, on the other.*
4. *Except where otherwise provided for in this Protocol, the acts of the institutions of the Community regarding the common commercial policy, be they autonomous or enacted by agreement, directly linked to the import or export of goods, shall not be applicable to the Canary Islands or to Ceuta and Melilla.*
5. *Except where otherwise provided for in the Act of Accession, including this Protocol, the Community shall apply in its trade with the Canary Islands and with Ceuta and Melilla, for products falling within Annex II to the ETEC, the general arrangements which it applies in its foreign trade.*

F. Murray, *The European Union and Member State Territories: A New Legal Framework Under the EU Treaties*, DOI: 10.1007/978-90-6704-826-2,

Article 2

1. *Subject to Articles 3 and 4 of this Protocol, products originating in the Canary Islands and in Ceuta and Melilla, shall, when released for free circulation in the customs territory of the Community, qualify for exemption from customs duties under the conditions defined in paragraphs 2 and 3.*
2. *In that part of Spain which is included in the customs territory of the Community, the exemption from customs duties referred to in paragraph 1 shall be granted as from 1 January 1986. With regard to the remainder of the customs territory of the Community, customs duties on the import of products originating in the Canary Islands or in Ceuta and Melilla shall be abolished in accordance with the same timetable and under the same conditions as those provided for in Articles 30, 31 and 32 of the Act of Accession.*
3. *By way of derogation from paragraphs 1 and 2, manufactured tobacco falling within heading No 24.02 of the Common Customs Tariff which is processed in the Canary Islands shall qualify, in the customs territory of the Community, for exemption from customs duties within the limit of tariff quotas. These quotas shall be opened and allocated by the Council, acting by a qualified majority on a proposal from the Commission, taking as the reference base the average of the three best of the last five years for which statistics are available. The Council shall act in good time so as to provide for the opening and allocation of these quotas on 1 January 1986.*

In order to avoid a situation whereby this arrangement results in economic difficulties in one or more Member States because of the reconsignment of manufactured tobacco imported into another Member State, the Commission shall adopt, after consulting the Member States, all methods of administrative co-operation which prove necessary.

Article 3

1. *Fishery products falling within heading Nos 03.01, 03.02, 03.03, 16.04, 16.05 and subheadings 05.15 A and 23.01 B of the Common Customs Tariff and originating in the Canary Islands or Ceuta and Melilla, shall, within the limit of tariff quotas calculated by product and on the average quantities actually disposed of during 1982, 1983 and 1984, benefit from the arrangements hereinafter defined, intended respectively for that part of Spain which is included in the customs territory of the Community, on one hand, and for the Community as at present constituted, on the other :*

   - *Where the said products are imported into that part of Spain which is included in the customs territory of the Community, they shall qualify for exemption from customs duties. They may not be deemed to be in free circulation in that part of Spain within the meaning of Article 10 of the ETEC when they are reconsigned to another Member State.*

- *Where the said products are released for free circulation in the remainder of the customs territory of the Community, they shall qualify for the progressive reduction of customs duties according to the same timeable and under the same conditions as those provided for in Article 173 of the Act of Accession, provided that the reference prices are complied with.*

2. *As from 1 January 1993 for the fishery products referred to in paragraph 1, and from 1 January 1996 for the sardine preparations and preserved sardines falling within subheading 16.04 D of the Common Customs Tariff, the products concerned shall qualify for exemption from customs duties in the whole of the customs territory of the Community up to the limit of the tariff quotas calculated by product and on the average quantities actually disposed of during 1982, 1983 and 1984 in that part of Spain which is included in the customs territory of the Community or exported to the Community as at present constituted. The release for free circulation for products imported into the customs territory of the Community, under these tariff quotas, shall be subject to compliance with the rules laid down by the common organization of markets and in particular with respect to reference prices.*
3. *The Council, acting by qualified majority on a proposal from the Commission, shall each year adopt provisions opening and allocating tariff quotas in accordance with the detailed rules laid down in paragraphs 1 and 2. For 1986 the Council shall act in good time so as to provide for the opening and allocation of the quotas by 1 January 1986.*

Article 4

1. *The agricultural products appearing in Annex A, originating in the Canary Islands, shall, when they are released for free circulation in the customs territory of the Community, qualify under the conditions laid down in this Article, for exemption from customs duties within the limit of tariff quotas calculated on the average quantities actually disposed of during 1982, 1983 and 1984 respectively, intended for that part of Spain which is included in the customs territory of the Community, on the one hand, and for the Community as at present constituted on the other:*

   (a) until 31 December 1995, for those of the products referred to above falling within Regulation (EEC) No 1035/72 and until 31 December 1992 for the other products referred to, the products in question shall qualify:

- *in that part of Spain which is included in the customs territory of the Community, for an exemption from customs duties, without application, where this arises, of the system of reference prices,*

- in the remainder of the customs territory of the Community, for the same conditions as those adopted for the same products coming from that part of Spain which is included in the customs territory of the Community, as long as the system of reference prices is complied with, where they are applicable;

(b) as from 1 January 1996 for those of the products referred to above falling within Regulation (EEC) No 1035/72 and from 1 January 1993 for the other products referred to, the products in question shall qualify for exemption from customs duties in the whole of the customs territory of the Community as long as the system of reference prices is complied with, where they are applicable.

The Council, acting by a qualified majority on a proposal from the Commission, shall adopt in good time measures so as to provide for the opening and allocation of those quotas by 1 January 1986.

2. *(a) By way of derogation from paragraph 1, when bananas falling within subheading 08.01 B of the Common Customs Tariff, originating in the Canary Islands, are released for free circulation in that part of Spain which is included in the customs territory of the Community, they shall qualify for exemption from customs duties. Bananas imported under the abovementioned arrangements may not be deemed to be in free circulation in the said part of Spain within the meaning of Article 10 of the ETEC when they are reconsigned to another Member State.*

   (b) Until 31 December 1995, the Kingdom of Spain may maintain, for the bananas referred to in (a) which are imported from the other Member States, the quantitative restrictions and measures having equivalent effect which it applied on the import of these products under the previous national arrangements. Notwithstanding Article 76 (2) of the Act of Accession and until the setting up of a common organization of the market for that product, the Kingdom of Spain may retain, to the extent that is strictly necessary to ensure the maintenance of the national organization, quantitative restrictions on imports of bananas referred to in (a) imported from third countries.

Article 5

1. *Where application of the arrangement referred to in Article 2 (2) could lead to a substantial increase in the import of certain products originating in the Canary Islands or in Ceuta and Melilla such as might prejudice Community producers, the Council, acting by qualified majority on a proposal from the Commission, may subject the access of these products to the customs territory of the Community to special conditions.*
2. *Where, because the Common Commercial Policy and the Common Customs Tariff are not applied to the import of raw materials or*

intermediate products into the Canary Islands or Ceuta and Melilla, imports of a product originating in the Canary Islands or in Ceuta or Melilla cause, or may cause, serious injury to a producer activity exercised in one or more Member States, the Commission, at the request of a Member State or on its own initiative, may take the appropriate measures.

Article 6

1. *On import into the Canary Islands or into Ceuta and Melilla, products originating in the customs territory of the Community shall qualify for exemption from the customs duties and charges having equivalent effect under the conditions defined in paragraphs 2 and 3.*
2. *The customs duties existing in the Canary Islands and in Ceuta and Melilla and the charge known as the " arbitrio insular—tarifa generall" existing in the Canary Islands shall be abolished progressively, with regard to products originating in the customs territory of the Community, according to the same timeable and under the same conditions as those provided for in Articles 30, 31 and 32 of the Act of Accession.*
3. *The so-called " arbitrio insular—tarifa especial" of the Canary Islands shall be abolished with regard to products originating in the customs territory of the Community on 1 March 1986. However, the said charge may be maintained, on the import of the products listed in Annex B, at a rate corresponding to 90% of the rate indicated opposite each of the products on the said list and on condition that this reduced rate is applied on a uniform basis to all imports of the products concerned originating in the whole of the customs territory of the Community. The said charge will be abolished by 1 January 1993 at the latest unless the Council, acting by qualified majority on a proposal from the Commission, decides that it should be prolonged on the basis of the trend in the economic situation in the Canary Islands for each of the products concerned.*

The said charge may at no time be higher than the level of the Spanish customs tariff as modified with a view to the progressive introduction of the Common Customs Tariff.

Article 7

The customs duties and charges having an effect equivalent to such duties and the trade arrangements applied, on the import to the Canary Islands and to Ceuta and Melilla, of goods coming from a third country may not be less favourable than those applicable by the Community in accordance with its international commitments or its preferential arrangements with regard to such third country, providing that the same third country grants, to imports from the Canary Islands and from Ceuta and Melilla, the same treatment as that which it grants to the Community. However, the arrangements applied to imports into the Canary Islands and into Ceuta and Melilla with regard to goods coming from such third country may not be more favourable than those applied with regard to the imports of products originating in the customs territory of the Community.

Article 8

The arrangements applicable to trade in goods between the Canary Islands, on the one hand, and Ceuta and Melilla, on the other, shall be at least as favourable as those applicable pursuant to Article 6.

Article 9

1. *The Council, acting by a qualified majority on a proposal from the Commission, shall, before 1 March 1986, adopt the rules for the application of this Protocol and in particular the rules of origin applicable to trade, as referred to in Articles 2, 3, 4, 6 and 8, including the provisions concerning the identification of originating products and the control of origin.*

The rules will include, in particular, provisions on marking and/or labelling of products, on the conditions of registration of vessels, on the application of the rule on mixed origin for fishery products, and also provisions enabling the origin of products to be determined.

2. *The following shall remain applicable until 28 February 1986:*

- *the rules of origin provided for by the 1970 Agreement between the European Economic Community and Spain, to trade between the customs territory of the Community as at present constituted, on the one hand, and the Canary Islands and Ceuta and Melilla, on the other,*
- *the rules of origin provided for by the national provisions in force as at 31 December 1985, to trade between that part of Spain included in the customs territory of the Community, on the one hand, and the Canary Islands and Ceuta and Melilla, on the other.*

Annex IX

Joint Declaration on the Azores and Madeira, Portuguese Act of Accession 1985

Joint Declaration on the Azores and Madeira
Article 299(2) TEC

The High Contracting Parties recall that the fundamental objectives of the European Economic Community comprise the constant improvement of living and working conditions of the peoples of the Member States and the harmonious development of their economies by reducing the variation between the different regions.

They note the fact that the Government of the Portuguese Republic and the autonomous regions of the Azores and Madeira are pursuing an economic and social development policy the object of which is to overcome the handicaps of these regions, which arise from their geographical situation, far away from the mainland of Europe, their physical geographical features, the serious deficiency of infrastructures and their economic backwardness.

They recognize that it is in their common interest that the final objectives set by this policy be attained and recall that specific provisions concerning the autonomous regions have been adopted in the instruments of accession.

The High Contracting Parties agree to recommend to this end that the Community institutions devote special attention to the realization of the above objectives.[3]

---

[3] Joint Declaration concerning the economic and social development of the autonomous regions of the Azores and Madeira, Act of Access of Portugal to the EC, OJ L 302, 15 November 1985.

F. Murray, *The European Union and Member State Territories: A New Legal Framework Under the EU Treaties*, DOI: 10.1007/978-90-6704-826-2,

Annex X

Declaration on the Outermost Regions, Maastricht Treaty 1992

Declaration on the Outermost Regions, Maastricht Treaty

The Conference acknowledges that the Outermost Regions of the Community (the French overseas departments, Azores and Madeira and Canary Islands) suffer from major structural backwardness compounded by several phenomena (remoteness, island status, small size, difficult topography and climate, economic dependence on a few products), the permanence and combination of which severely restrain their economic and social development.

It considers that, while the provisions of the Treaty establishing the European Community and secondary legislation apply automatically to the Outermost Regions, it is nonetheless possible to adopt specific measures to assist them inasmuch and as long as there is an objective need to take such measures with a view to the economic and social development of those regions. Such measures should have as their aim both the completion of the internal market and a recognition of the regional reality to enable the Outermost Regions to achieve the average economic and social level of the Community.

F. Murray, *The European Union and Member State Territories: A New Legal Framework Under the EU Treaties*, DOI: 10.1007/978-90-6704-826-2,

Annex XI

Declaration on the Overseas Countries and Territories, Maastricht Treaty 1992

Declaration on OCTs—Maastricht Treaty

The Conference, noting that in exceptional circumstances divergences may arise between the interests of the Union and those of the overseas countries and territories referred to in Article 227(3) and (5)(a) and (b), agrees that the Council will seek to reach a solution which accords with the position of the Union. However, in the event that this proves impossible, the Conference agrees that the Member State concerned may act separately in the interests of the said overseas countries and territories, without this affecting the Community's interests. The Member State concerned will give notice to the Council and the Commission where such a divergence of interests is likely to occur and, when separate action proves unavoidable, make it clear that it is acting in the interests of an overseas territory mentioned above.
This declaration also applies to Macao and East Timor.

F. Murray, *The European Union and Member State Territories: A New Legal Framework Under the EU Treaties*, DOI: 10.1007/978-90-6704-826-2,

Annex XII

Declaration No. 36 on the Overseas Countries and Territories, Amsterdam Treaty 1997

Declaration No. 36, Amsterdam Treaty

The Conference recognises that the special arrangements for the association of the overseas countries and territories (OCTs) under Part Four of the Treaty establishing the European Community were designed for countries and territories that were numerous, covered vast areas and had large populations. The arrangements have changed little since 1957.

The Conference notes that there are today only 20 OCTs and that they are extremely scattered island territories with a total population of approximately 900 000. Moreover, most OCTs lag far behind in structural terms, a fact linked to their particularly severe geographical and economic handicaps. In these circumstances, the special arrangements for association as they were conceived in 1957 can no longer deal effectively with the challenges of OCT development.

The Conference solemnly restates that the purpose of association is to promote the economic and social development of the countries and territories and to establish close economic relations between them and the Community as a whole.

The Conference invites the Council, acting in accordance with the provisions of Article 136 of the Treaty establishing the European Community, to review the association arrangements by February 2000, with the fourfold objective of:

- *promoting the economic and social development of the OCTs more effectively;*
- *developing economic relations between the OCTs and the European Union;*
- *taking greater account of the diversity and specific characteristics of the individual OCTs, including aspects relating to freedom of establishment;*
- *ensuring that the effectiveness of the financial instrument is improved.*

F. Murray, *The European Union and Member State Territories: A New Legal Framework Under the EU Treaties*, DOI: 10.1007/978-90-6704-826-2,

Annex XIII

Part Four (Articles 182–188) TEC 2009

Part Four of the TEC (Articles 182-188)

Article 182
The Member States agree to associate with the Community the non-European countries and territories which have special relations with Denmark, France, the Netherlands and the United Kingdom. These countries and territories (hereinafter called the 'countries and territories') are listed in Annex II to this Treaty.
The purpose of association shall be to promote the economic and social development of the countries and territories and to establish close economic relations between them and the Community as a whole.
In accordance with the principles set out in the preamble to this Treaty, the association shall serve primarily to further the interests and prosperity of the inhabitants of these countries and territories in order to lead them to the economic, social and cultural development to which they aspire.

Article 183
Association shall have the following objectives.

1. *Member States shall apply to their trade with the countries and territories the same treatment as they accord each other pursuant to this Treaty.*
2. *Each country or territory shall apply to its trade with Member States and with the other countries and territories the same treatment as that which it applies to the European State with which is has special relations.*
3. *The Member States shall contribute to the investments required for the progressive development of these countries and territories.*

F. Murray, *The European Union and Member State Territories: A New Legal Framework Under the EU Treaties*, DOI: 10.1007/978-90-6704-826-2,

4. *For investments financed by the Community, participation in tenders and supplies shall be open on equal terms to all natural and legal persons who are nationals of a Member State or of one of the countries and territories.*
5. *In relations between Member States and the countries and territories the right of establishment of nationals and companies or firms shall be regulated in accordance with the provisions and procedures laid down in the Chapter relating to the right of establishment and on a non-discriminatory basis, subject to any special provisions laid down pursuant to Article 187.*

Article 184

1. *Customs duties on imports into the Member States of goods originating in the countries and territories shall be prohibited in conformity with the prohibition of customs duties between Member States in accordance with the provisions of this Treaty.*
2. *Customs duties on imports into each country or territory from Member States or from the other countries or territories shall be prohibited in accordance with the provisions of Article 25.*
3. *The countries and territories may, however, levy customs duties which meet the needs of their development and industrialisation or produce revenue for their budgets.*
   The duties referred to in the preceding subparagraph may not exceed the level of those imposed on imports of products from the Member State with which each country or territory has special relations.
4. *Paragraph 2 shall not apply to countries and territories which, by reason of the particular international obligations by which they are bound, already apply a non-discriminatory customs tariff.*
5. *The introduction of or any change in customs duties imposed on goods imported into the countries and territories shall not, either in law or in fact, give rise to any direct or indirect discrimination between imports from the various Member States.*

Article 185
If the level of the duties applicable to goods from a third country on entry into a country or territory is liable, when the provisions of Article 184(1) have been applied, to cause deflections of trade to the detriment of any Member State, the latter may request the Commission to propose to the other Member States the measures needed to remedy the situation.

Article 186
Subject to the provisions relating to public health, public security or public policy, freedom of movement within Member States for workers from the countries and territories, and within the countries and territories for workers

from Member States, shall be governed by agreements to be concluded subsequently with the unanimous approval of Member States.

Article 187

The Council, acting unanimously, shall, on the basis of the experience acquired under the association of the countries and territories with the Community and of the principles set out in this Treaty, lay down provisions as regards the detailed rules and the procedure for the association of the countries and territories with the Community.

Article 188

The provisions of Articles 182–187 shall apply to Greenland, subject to the specific provisions for Greenland set out in the Protocol on special arrangements for Greenland, annexed to this Treaty.

Annex XIV

Article 28 UK Act of Accession 1972 (Gibraltar)

Article 28 UK Act of Accession to EU

Acts of the institutions of the Community relating to the products in Annex II to the ETEC and the products subject, on importation into the Community, to specific rules as a result of the implementation of the common agricultural policy, as well as the acts on the harmonization of legislation of Member States concerning turnover taxes, shall not apply to Gibraltar unless the Council, acting unanimously on a proposal from the Commission, provides otherwise.

F. Murray, *The European Union and Member State Territories: A New Legal Framework Under the EU Treaties*, DOI: 10.1007/978-90-6704-826-2,

Annex XV

Protocol No. 2 Finnish Act of Accession 1994 (Aland Islands)

Protocol No. 2 on the Aland Islands

Taking into account the special status that the Åland islands enjoy under international law, the Treaties on which the European Union is founded shall apply to the Åland islands with the following derogations:

Article 1
The provision of the TEC shall not preclude the application of the existing provisions in force on 1 January 1994 on the Åland islands on:

- *restrictions, on a non-discriminatory basis, on the rights of natural persons who do not enjoy hembygdsrätt/kotiseutuoikeus (regional citizenship) in Åland, and for legal persons, to acquire and hold real property on the Åland islands without permission by the competent authorities of the Åland islands;*
- *restrictions, on a non-discriminatory basis, on the right of establishment and the right to provide services by natural persons who do not enjoy hembygdsrätt/kotiseutuoikeus (regional citizenship) in Åland, or by legal persons without permission by the competent authorities of the Åland islands.*

Article 2

a) The territory of the Åland islands being considered as a third territory, as defined in Article 3(1) third indent of Council Directive 77/388/EEC as amended, and as a national territory falling outside the field of application of the excise harmonization directives as defined in Article 2 of Council directive 92/12/EEC shall be excluded from the territorial application of the EC provisions in the fields of harmonization of the laws of the Member States on turnover taxes and on excise duties and other forms of indirect

F. Murray, *The European Union and Member State Territories: A New Legal Framework Under the EU Treaties*, DOI: 10.1007/978-90-6704-826-2,

taxation. This exemption shall not have any effect on the Community's own resources. This paragraph shall not apply to the provisions of Council Directive 69/335/EEC, as amended, relating to capital duty.

b) This derogation is aimed at maintaining a viable local economy in the islands and shall not have any negative effects on the interests of the Union nor on its common policies. If the Commission considers that the provisions in paragraph (a) are no longer justified, particularly in terms of fair competition or own resources, it shall submit appropriate proposals to the Council, which shall act in accordance with the pertinent articles of the TEC.

Article 3

The Republic of Finland shall ensure that the same treatment applies to all natural and legal persons of the member States in the Åland islands.

Annex XVI

Article 25(a) Danish Act of Accession 1972 (Faroe Islands)

Article 25(a)

This Treaty shall not apply to the Faroe Islands. The Government of the Kingdom of Denmark may, however, give notice, by a declaration deposited by 31 December 1975 at the latest with the Government of the French Republic, which shall transmit a certified copy thereof to each of the Governments of the other Member States, that this Treaty shall apply to those Islands. In that event, this Treaty shall apply to those Islands from the first day of the second month following the deposit of the declaration.

F. Murray, *The European Union and Member State Territories: A New Legal Framework Under the EU Treaties*, DOI: 10.1007/978-90-6704-826-2,

Annex XVII

Protocol No. 2 Danish Act of Accession 1972 (Faroe Islands)

Protocol No. 2 Danish Act of Accession 1972

Article 1
So long as the Danish Government has not made declarations referred to in Articles 25, 26 and 27 of the Act of Accession and until 31 December 1975 at the latest, no alteration shall be required in the customs treatment applicable at the time of accession to imports of products originating in and coming from the Faroe Islands into other regions of Denmark.
Products imported from the Faroe Islands into other regions of Denmark under the above-mentioned arrangement shall not be considered as being in free circulation in that State, within the meaning of Article 10 of the ETEC, when they are re-exported to another Member State.

Article 2
If the Danish Government makes the declarations referred to in Article 1, the provisions of the Act of Accession shall apply to the Faroe Islands, taking into account the following provisions:
- *imports into the Faroe Islands shall be subject to the customs duties which would have been applicable if the Treaty and Decision concerning the Accession had been applied from 1 January 1973;*
- *the institutions of the Community shall seek, within the framework of the common organization of the market in fishery products, adequate solutions to the specific problems of the Faroe Islands;*
- *the authorities of the Faroe Islands may, under Community supervision, retain appropriate measures with a view to ensuring supplies of milk at reasonable prices to the Faroese population.*

F. Murray, *The European Union and Member State Territories: A New Legal Framework Under the EU Treaties*, DOI: 10.1007/978-90-6704-826-2,

Article 3
If, during the period referred to in Article 1, the Danish Government, following a resolution of the local Faroese Government, informs the Council that it cannot make the declarations referred to in Article 1, the Council shall, at the request of the Danish Government, examine the situation thus created. The Council shall, on a proposal from the Commission, decide the arrangements to be made for solving the problems which could arise out of this situation for the Community and especially for Denmark and the Faroe Islands.

Article 4
Danish nationals resident in the Faroe Islands shall be considered to be nationals of a Member State within the meaning of the originally Treaties only from the date on which those original Treaties become applicable to those Islands.

Article 5
The declaration referred to in Article 1 must be made simultaneously and can only give rise to a simultaneous application of the original Treaties to the Faroe Islands.

Annex XVIII

Protocol No. 3 Cyprus Act of Accession 2004 (UK Sovereign Base Areas)

Protocol No. 3

on the Sovereign Base Areas of the United Kingdom of Great Britain and Northern Ireland in Cyprus

THE HIGH CONTRACTING PARTIES,
RECALLING that the Joint Declaration on the Sovereign Base Areas of the United Kingdom of Great Britain and Northern Ireland in Cyprus annexed to the Final Act of the Treaty concerning the Accession of the United Kingdom to the European Communities provided that the arrangements applicable to relations between the European Economic Community and the Sovereign Base Areas will be defined within the context of any agreement between the Community and the Republic of Cyprus,
TAKING ACCOUNT of the provisions concerning the Sovereign Base Areas set out in the Treaty concerning the Establishment of the Republic of Cyprus (hereafter referred to as the 'Treaty of Establishment') and the associated Exchanges of Notes dated 16 August 1960,
NOTING the Exchange of Notes between the Government of the United Kingdom and the Government of the Republic of Cyprus concerning the administration of the Sovereign Base Areas, dated 16 August 1960, and the attached Declaration by the United Kingdom Government that one of the main objects to be achieved is the protection of the interests of those resident or working in the Sovereign Base Areas, and considering in this context that the said persons should have, to the extent possible, the same treatment as those resident or working in the Republic of Cyprus,

F. Murray, *The European Union and Member State Territories: A New Legal Framework Under the EU Treaties*, DOI: 10.1007/978-90-6704-826-2,

NOTING FURTHER the provisions of the Treaty of Establishment regarding customs arrangements between the Sovereign Base Areas and the Republic of Cyprus and in particular those of Annex F to the said Treaty,

NOTING ALSO the commitment of the United Kingdom not to create customs posts or other frontier barriers between the Sovereign Base Areas and the Republic of Cyprus and the arrangements made pursuant to the Treaty of Establishment whereby the authorities of the Republic of Cyprus administer a wide range of public services in the Sovereign Base Areas, including in the fields of agriculture, customs and taxation,

CONFIRMING that the accession of the Republic of Cyprus to the European Union should not affect the rights and obligations of the parties to the Treaty of Establishment,

RECOGNISING therefore the need to apply certain provisions of the Treaty establishing the European Community and related EC law to the Sovereign Base Areas and to make special arrangements regarding the implementation of these provisions in the Sovereign Base Areas,

HAVE AGREED UPON THE FOLLOWING PROVISIONS:

Article 1

Article 299(6)(b) of the Treaty establishing the European Community shall be replaced by the following:

(b) This Treaty shall not apply to the United Kingdom Sovereign Base Areas of Akrotiri and Dhekelia in Cyprus except to the extent necessary to ensure the implementation of the arrangements set out in the Protocol on the Sovereign Base Areas of the United Kingdom of Great Britain and Northern Ireland in Cyprus annexed to the Act concerning the conditions of accession of the Czech Republic, the Republic of Estonia, the Republic of Cyprus, the Republic of Latvia, the Republic of Lithuania, the Republic of Hungary, the Republic of Malta, the Republic of Poland, the Republic of Slovenia and the Slovak Republic to the European Union and in accordance with the terms of that Protocol.'

Article 2

1. *The Sovereign Base Areas shall be included within the customs territory of the Community and, for this purpose, the customs and common commercial policy acts listed in Part One of the Annex to this Protocol shall apply to the Sovereign Base Areas with the amendments set out in the Annex.*
2. *The acts on turnover taxes, excise duties and other forms of indirect taxation listed in Part Two of the Annex to this Protocol shall apply to the Sovereign Base Areas with the amendments set out in the Annex as well as the relevant provisions applying to Cyprus as set out in the Act concerning the conditions of accession of the Czech Republic, the*

Republic of Estonia, the Republic of Cyprus, the Republic of Latvia, the Republic of Lithuania, the Republic of Hungary, the Republic of Malta, the Republic of Poland, the Republic of Slovenia and the Slovak Republic to the European Union.

3. *The acts listed in Part Three of the Annex to this Protocol shall be amended as set out in the Annex to enable the United Kingdom to maintain the reliefs and exemptions from duties and taxes on supplies to its forces and associated personnel which are granted by the Treaty of Establishment.*

Article 3

The following Treaty and related provisions shall apply to the Sovereign Base Areas:

(a) Title II of Part Three of the TEC, on agriculture, and provisions adopted on that basis;
(b) *Measures adopted under Article 152(4)(b) of the TEC*

Article 4

Persons resident or employed in the territory of the Sovereign Base Areas who, under arrangements made pursuant to the Treaty of Establishment and the associated Exchange of Notes dated 16 August 1960, are subject to the social security legislation of the Republic of Cyprus shall be treated for the purposes of Council Regulation (EEC) No 1408/71 of 14 June 1971 on the application of social security schemes to employed persons, to self-employed persons and to members of their families moving within the Community(11) as if they were resident or employed in the territory of the Republic of Cyprus.

Article 5

1. *The Republic of Cyprus shall not be required to carry out checks on persons crossing their land and sea boundaries with the Sovereign Base Areas and any Community restrictions on the crossing of external borders shall not apply in relation to such persons.*
2. *The United Kingdom shall exercise controls on persons crossing the external borders of the Sovereign Base Areas in accordance with the undertakings set out in Part Four of the Annex to this Protocol.*

Article 6

The Council, acting unanimously on a proposal from the Commission, may, in order to ensure effective implementation of the objectives of this Protocol, amend Articles 2 to 5 above, including the Annex, or apply other provisions of the TEC and related Community legislation to the Sovereign Base Areas on such terms and subject to such conditions as it may specify. The Commission shall consult the United Kingdom and the Republic of Cyprus before bringing forward a proposal.

Article 7

1. *Subject to paragraph 2, the United Kingdom shall be responsible for the implementation of this Protocol in the Sovereign Base Areas. In particular:*

(a) *the United Kingdom shall be responsible for the application of the Community measures specified in this Protocol in the fields of customs, indirect taxation and the common commercial policy in relation to goods entering or leaving the island of Cyprus through a port or airport within the Sovereign Base Areas;*
(b) *customs controls on goods imported into or exported from the island of Cyprus by the forces of the United Kingdom through a port or airport in the Republic of Cyprus may be carried out within the Sovereign Base Areas;*
(c) *the United Kingdom shall be responsible for issuing any licences, authorisations or certificates which may be required under any applicable Community measure in respect of goods imported into or exported from the island of Cyprus by the forces of the United Kingdom.*

2. *The Republic of Cyprus shall be responsible for the administration and payment of any Community funds to which persons in the Sovereign Base Areas may be entitled pursuant to the application of the common agricultural policy in the Sovereign Base Areas under Article 3 of this Protocol and the Republic of Cyprus shall be accountable to the Commission for such expenditure.*
3. *Without prejudice to paragraphs 1 and 2, the United Kingdom may delegate to the competent authorities of the Republic of Cyprus, in accordance with arrangements made pursuant to the Treaty of Establishment, the performance of any functions imposed on a Member State by or under any provision referred to in Articles 2–5 above.*
4. *The United Kingdom and the Republic of Cyprus shall cooperate to ensure the effective implementation of this Protocol in the Sovereign Base Areas and, where appropriate, shall conclude further arrangements concerning the delegation of the implementation of any of the provisions referred to in Articles 2–5 above. A copy of any such arrangements shall be submitted to the Commission.*

Article 8

The arrangements provided for in this Protocol shall have the sole purpose of regulating the particular situation of the Sovereign Base Areas of the United

Kingdom in Cyprus and shall not apply to any other territory of the Community, nor serve as a precedent, in whole or in part, for any other special arrangements which either already exist or which might be set up in another European territory provided for in Article 299 of the Treaty.

Article 9

The Commission shall report to the European Parliament and the Council every five years on the implementation of the provisions of this Protocol.

Annex XIX

Protocol No. 10 Cyprus Act of Accession 2004 (UK Sovereign Base Areas)

Protocol No. 10 on Cyprus

THE HIGH CONTRACTING PARTIES,
REAFFIRMING their commitment to a comprehensive settlement of the Cyprus problem, consistent with relevant United Nations Security Council Resolutions, and their strong support for the efforts of the United Nations Secretary General to that end,
CONSIDERING that such a comprehensive settlement to the Cyprus problem has not yet been reached,
CONSIDERING that it is, therefore, necessary to provide for the suspension of the application of the acquis in those areas of the Republic of Cyprus in which the Government of the Republic of Cyprus does not exercise effective control,
CONSIDERING that, in the event of a solution to the Cyprus problem this suspension shall be lifted,
CONSIDERING that the European Union is ready to accommodate the terms of such a settlement in line with the principles on which the EU is founded,
CONSIDERING that it is necessary to provide for the terms under which the relevant provisions of EU law will apply to the line between the abovementioned areas and both those areas in which the Government of the Republic of Cyprus exercises effective control and the Eastern Sovereign Base Area of the United Kingdom of Great Britain and Northern Ireland,
DESIRING that the accession of Cyprus to the European Union shall benefit all Cypriot citizens and promote civil peace and reconciliation,
CONSIDERING, therefore, that nothing in this Protocol shall preclude measures with this end in view,

F. Murray, *The European Union and Member State Territories: A New Legal Framework Under the EU Treaties*, DOI: 10.1007/978-90-6704-826-2,

CONSIDERING that such measures shall not affect the application of the acquis under the conditions set out in the Accession Treaty in any other part of the Republic of Cyprus,
HAVE AGREED UPON THE FOLLOWING PROVISIONS:
Article 1

1. *The application of the acquis shall be suspended in those areas of the Republic of Cyprus in which the Government of the Republic of Cyprus does not exercise effective control.*
2. *The Council, acting unanimously on the basis of a proposal from the Commission, shall decide on the withdrawal of the suspension referred to in paragraph 1.*

Article 2

1. *The Council, acting unanimously on the basis of a proposal from the Commission, shall define the terms under which the provisions of EU law shall apply to the line between those areas referred to in Article 1 and the areas in which the Government of the Republic of Cyprus exercises effective control.*
2. *The boundary between the Eastern Sovereign Base Area and those areas referred to in Article 1 shall be treated as part of the external borders of the Sovereign Base Areas for the purpose of Part IV of the Annex to the Protocol on the Sovereign Base Areas of the United Kingdom of Great Britain and Northern Ireland in Cyprus for the duration of the suspension of the application of the acquis according to Article 1.*

Article 3

1. *Nothing in this Protocol shall preclude measures with a view to promoting the economic development of the areas referred to in Article 1.*
2. *Such measures shall not affect the application of the acquis under the conditions set out in the Accession Treaty in any other part of the Republic of Cyprus.*

Article 4

In the event of a settlement, the Council, acting unanimously on the basis of a proposal from the Commission, shall decide on the adaptations to the terms concerning the accession of Cyprus to the European Union with regard to the Turkish
Cypriot Community.

Annex XX

Protocol No. 3 UK Act of Accession 1972 (Channel Islands and Isle of Man)

Protocol No. 3
On the Channel Islands and the Isle of Man

Article 1

1. *The Community rules on customs matters and quantitative restrictions, in particular those of the Act of Accession, shall apply to the Channel Islands and the Isle of Man under the same conditions as they apply to the United Kingdom. In particular customs duties and charges having equivalent effect between those territories and the Community as originally constituted and between those territories and the new Member States shall be progressively reduced in accordance with the timetable laid down in Articles 32 and 36 of the Act of Accession. The Common Customs Tariff and the ECSC unified tariff shall be progressively applied in accordance with the timetable laid down in Articles 39 and 59 of the Act of Accession, and account being taken of Articles 109, 110 and 119 of that Act.*
2. *In respect of agricultural products and products processed therefrom which are the subject of a special trade regime, the levies and other import measures laid down in Community rules and applicable by the United Kingdom shall be applied to third countries.*

Such provisions of Community rules, in particular those of the Act of Accession, as are necessary to allow free movement and observance of normal conditions of competition in trade in these products shall also be applicable.
The Council, acting by a qualified majority on a proposal from the Commission, shall determine the conditions under which the provisions referred to in the preceding subparagraphs shall be applicable to these territories.

F. Murray, *The European Union and Member State Territories: A New Legal Framework Under the EU Treaties*, DOI: 10.1007/978-90-6704-826-2,

Article 2
The rights enjoyed by Channel Islanders or Manxmen in the United Kingdom shall not be affected by the Act of Accession. However, such persons shall not benefit from Community provisions relating to the free movement of persons and services.

Article 3
The provisions of the Euratom Treaty applicable to persons or undertakings within the meaning of Article 196 of that Treaty shall apply to those persons or undertakings when they are established in the aforementioned territories.

Article 4
The authorities of these territories shall apply the same treatment to all natural and legal persons of the Community.

Article 5
If, during the application of the arrangements defined in this Protocol, difficulties appear on either side in relations between the Community and these territories, the Commission shall without delay propose to the Council such safeguard measures as it believes necessary, specifying their terms and conditions of application.
The Council shall act by a qualified majority within one month.

Article 6
In this Protocol, Channel Islanders or Manxmen shall mean any citizen of the United Kingdom and Colonies who holds that citizenship by virtue of the fact that he, a parent or grandparent was born, adopted, naturalised or registered in the island in question; but such a person shall not for this purpose be regarded as a Channel Islander or Manxman if he, a parent or a grandparent was born, adopted,
naturalised or registered in the United Kingdom. Nor shall he be so regarded if he has at any time been ordinarily resident in the United Kingdom for five years.
The administrative arrangements necessary to identify these persons will be notified to the Commission.

Source Materials

Selected Bibliography

- BRINKHORST L.J. *Special Relationships and the European Communities: Netherlands Antilles and Surinam*, British Institute of Studies in International and Comparative Law, No.6, 1972
- DEWOST J.L. *L'Application Territoriale du Droit Communautaire: disparition et resurgence de la notion de frontière,* Société Française pour le Droit International, Colloque de Poitiers, 17-19 May 1979
- CHALMERS D., DAVIES G., and MONTI G. *European Union Law*, 2nd Ed. Cambridge University Press, 2010
- CRAIG P. and De BURCA, G. *EU Law : Text Cases and Materials*, 4th Ed., Oxford University Press, 2008
- GROUX J. *Territorialité et droit communautaire*, RTD eur. 1987
- *HILLEBRINK, S. The right to Self-Determination and Post-Colonial Governance, The Asser Press, The Hague, 2008*
- KARAGIANNIS S. *A propos du règlement des conflits d'intérêts entre les territoires dépendants d'Etats members et les Communautés européennes* 75 Revue du Droit Internationale et de Droit Comparé at 340 (1998)
- KOCHENOV D. *Substantive and Procedural issues in the application of European law in the overseas possessions of European Union Member States*, 17 Michigan State Journal of International Law 2, 2008–2009, pp 195–288
- MEGRET J. *Le Droit de la Communauté Economique Européene,* Editions de L'Université de Bruxelles, 1987
- MURRAY F. *EU and Member State Territories: The Special Relationship under Community Law,* Sweet & Maxwell, June 2004
- MURRAY F. *Micro-states (Andorra, Monaco, San Marino and the Vatican City), The European Union and its Neighbours,* Editors Steven Blockmans and Adam Lazowski, TMC Asser Press, 2006

F. Murray, *The European Union and Member State Territories: A New Legal Framework Under the EU Treaties*, DOI: 10.1007/978-90-6704-826-2,

- OLIVIER Case Law Note 39 *Common Market Law Review (2002) 337* (Joined Cases T-332/00 and T-350/00, *Rica Foods (Free Zone) NV and Free Trade Foods NV v. Commission,* [2002] ECR II4755)
- PLENDER R. *The Rights of European Citizens in Jersey*, The Jersey Law Review, October 1998
- RIGAUX A. *Territoire communautaire : Rép. Communautaire,* Dalloz 1995
- STEINER J. and WOOD L. *EU Law*, 10th Ed. Oxford University Press, 2006
- VAN RIJN A.B. *Dimensions under International Law linked to the Dissolution of the Netherlands Antilles,* Netherlands Yearbook of International Law, Vol 40 2009, 75–109 Cambridge University Press
- WEATHERILL S. and BEAUMONT P. *EU Law: the essential guide to the legal workings of the European Union*, 3rd Ed. EU Law Penguin Books, 1999
- ZILLER J. *TEC, Article 299 on Extension of TEC*, Hans Smit, Peter Herzog, Christian Campbell & Gudrun Zagel (eds.), Smit & Herzog on the Law of the European Union Vol. 4, Lexis-Nexis, 2006
- ZILLER J. *Champ d'application du droit communautaire et de l'union—Application territoriale,* Paris, Lexis-Nexis, Juris-Classeur Europe Traité, 2006, fasc 470, 31
- ZILLER J. *The European Union and the Territorial Scope of the European Territories*, 38 Vict. U. Wellington L. Rev 51 (2007)
- ZIMMERMAN *Vorbemerkungen, Articles 182 bis 188* in H. Von der Groeben and J. Schwarze (eds), Kommentar zum Vertrag über die Europäische Union und zur Gründung der Europäische Gemeinschaft (2004)

Table of Treaties

- Exchange of Letters between the Government of the Federal Republic of Germany and the Government of the French Republic concerning the Saar, Treaty establishing the European Coal and Steel Community (ECSC), 1951
- Traité sur la Sarre du 29 octobre 1956; Gesetz uber die Eingliederung des Saarlandes vom 23 Juni 1956
- The Treaty establishing the European Economic Community (EEC), signed in Rome on 25 March 1957, and entered into force on 1 January 1958 (Treaty of Rome)
- Protocol relative to the application of the ETEC to the non-European parties of the Kingdom of the Netherlands (Netherlands Antilles and Surinam), 1957
- French Constitution, Title XII on territorial units, Article 73 on the French overseas departments and regions, 4 October 1958
- Rijkswet, Staatsbland 1962, NO. 285 Netherlands ratification of TEC on behalf of Surinam
- Convention amending the ETEC with a view to making applicable to the Netherlands Antilles the special regime of association defined in Part IV of the

ETEC, concluded at Brussels, 13 November 1962 (entered into force 1 October 1964) Trb. 1963, no.11; JO No. 2414/64, 1 October 1964
- Act concerning the Conditions of Accession and the Adjustment to the Treaties, Documents concerning the Accession to the European Communities of the Kingdom of Denmark, OJ Special Edition 27 March 1972
- Joint Declaration on the Sovereign Base Areas of the United Kingdom of Great Britain and Northern Ireland in Cyprus, UK Accession Act, OJ Special Edition, 27 March 1972, p. 194
- Treaty amending with regard to Greenland, the Treaties establishing the European Communities OJ L29 1 February 1985
- Joint Declaration concerning the economic and social development of the autonomous regions of the Azores and Madeira, Act of Accession of Portugal to the EC, OJ L 302, 15 November 1985
- Treaty on European Union (Maastricht Treaty) OJ C 191, 29 July 1992 (entered into force November 1993)
- Declaration on the Outermost regions of the Community, Maastricht Treaty, OJ C191, 29 July 1992
- Declaration 25 on the representation of the interests of the overseas countries and territories referred to in Article 227(3) and (5)(a) and (b) of the Treaty establishing the European Community appended to the Final Act of the Maastricht Treaty, 7 February 1992, OJ C191/103, 29 July 1992
- Documents concerning the accession of the Republic of Austria, the Kingdom of Sweden, the Republic of Finland and the Kingdom of Norway to the European Union OJ C241, 29 August 1994; Protocol No. 2 on the Aland Islands; Declaration No.32 on the Aland Islands
- Statute of the Autonomy of the Canary Islands, Basic Law 10/1982, 10 August 1982, amended by Basic law 4/1996,10 December 1996
- Amsterdam Treaty OJ C340, 10 November 1997. Treaty entered into force 1 May 1999
- Documents concerning the accession of the Czech Republic, the Republic of Estonia, the Republic of Cyprus, the Republic of Latvia, the Republic of Lithuania, the Republic of Hungary, the Republic of Malta, the Republic of Poland, the Republic of Slovenia and the Slovak Republic to the European Union, OJL236, 23 September 2003
- Act of Accession of Bulgaria and Romania to the EU, OJ L157/209, 21 June 2005
- Joint Declaration by the European Community, on the one hand, and the Home Rule Government of Greenland and the Government of Denmark, on the other, on partnership between the European Community and Greenland, OJ L 208/32, 29 July 2006
- Treaty of Lisbon amending the Treaty on European Union and the Treaty establishing the European Community, OJ C306 17 December 2007

Table of Legislation

- Danish Faroe Islands, Home Rule Act, Danish Law No. 137 of 23 March 1948 (*Lov am Færøernes Hjemmesryre)*
- Charter of the Kingdom of the Netherlands, 1954 *(Statuut voor het koninkrijk der Nederlanden)*
- Appendix O to the 1960 Treaty of Establishment : Declaration by Her Majesty's Government regarding the administration of the UK Sovereign Base Areas in Cyprus
- Council Decision 64/349/EEC of 25 February 1964, OJ 1964/1472
- Council Decision 70/549/EEC of 25 September 1970, OJ L282/83
- Council Regulation (EEC) No. 706/73 of 12 March 1973 concerning the Community arrangements applicable to the Channel Islands and the Isle of Man for trade in agricultural products, OJ L 68/1 15 March 1973
- Council Decision 76/568/EEC of 29 June 1976, OJ L176/8
- Council Regulation 2211/80 on the conclusion of the Agreement on fisheries between the European Economic Community and the Government of Denmark and the Home Government of the Faroe Islands, OJ L226/11, 29 August 1980
- Council Decision 80/1186/EEC of 16 December 1980 on the association of the overseas countries and territories with the European Economic Community, OJ 1980 L361/1
- Council Decision 82/530/EEC of 19 July 1982 authorising the United Kingdom to permit the Isle of Man authorities to apply a system of special import licences to sheepmeat and beef and veal, OJ L234/7, 9 August 1982
- Council Decision 86/283/EEC of 30 June 1986 on the association of the overseas countries and territories with the European Economic Community, OJ 1986 L175/1
- Statute of Autonomy of the Canary Islands, Basic Law 10/1982 of 10 August 1982, amended by Basic Law 4/1996 of 10 December 1996
- Council Regulation 2151/1984 of 27 July 1984 on the customs territory of the Community, OL L197/1
- Council Decision 86/283/EEC of 30 June 1986, OJ L175/1, 1986
- Council Decision 89/687/EEC of 22 December 1989 establishing a programme of options specific to the remote and insular nature of the French overseas departments (POSEIDOM), OJ L399/39, 30 December 1989
- Commission Regulation (EEC) No 73/87 of 12 January 1987 amending the list of ACP countries in Regulation (EEC) No 486/85 on the arrangements applicable to agricultural products and certain goods resulting from the processing of agricultural products originating in the African, Caribbean and Pacific States or in the overseas countries and territories (OCT), OJL11/23, 13 January 1987
- Council Decision 91/314/EEC of 26 June 1991 setting up a programme of options specific to the remote and insular nature of the Canary Islands (POSEICAN), OJ L171/5, 29 June 1991

- Council Decision 91/315/EEC of 26 June 1991 setting up a programme of options specific to the remote and insular nature of Madeira and the Azores (POSEIMA), OJL 171/10, 29 June 1991
- Council Decision 91/482/EEC of 25 July 1991, OJ L263/1 1991 as amended by Decision 97/803/EC of 24 November 1997, OJ L329/50 1997
- Council Regulation 1911/91 of 26 June 1991 on the application of the provisions of Community law to the Canary Islands, OJL 171/1, 29 June 1991
- Council Regulation 3763/91, OJ L 356, 24 December 1991, in respect of the French DOMs (*Départements d'Outre Mer*) and Council Regulations (EEC) Nos 1600/92 and 1601/92 OJ L173 27 June 1992, concerning Madeira, the Azores and the Canary Islands
- Council Decision 91/688/EEC of 2 December 1991 concerning the conclusion of the Agreement between the European Economic Community of the one part and the Government of Denmark and the Home Government of the Faroe Islands of the other part, OJ L371/1, 31 December 1991
- Council Regulation (EEC) No 2408/92 of 23 July 1992 on access for Community air carriers to intra-Community air routes, OJ L 240, 28 August 1992
- Council Regulation 2913/92 of 12 October 1992 (as amended) establishing the Community Customs Code, OL L302/1, 19 October 199
- Council Directive 96/30/EC of 13 May 1996 amending Directive 94/80/EC laying down detailed arrangements for the exercise of the right to vote and to stand as a candidate in municipal elections by citizens of the Union residing in a Member State of which they are not nationals, OJ L122/14, 22 May 1996
- Decision 1254/96/EC of the European Parliament and of the Council of 5 June 1996 laying down a series of guidelines for trans-European energy networks, OJ L 161/147 29 June 1996
- Council Decision 97/126/EC of 6 December 1996 concerning the conclusion of an agreement between the European Community, on the one hand, and the Government of Denmark and the Home Government of the Faroe Islands, on the other, OJ L 53/1 22 February 1997
- Council Decision 1999/95/EC of 31 December 1998 concerning the monetary arrangements in the French territorial communities of St Pierre et Miquelon and Mayotte, OJ L30/29 4 February 1999
- Decision No. 1/1999 of the EC/Denmark-Faroe Islands Joint Committee of 22 June 1999 replacing Protocol No. 1 of the Agreement concerning the tariff treatment and arrangements applicable to certain fish and fishery products released for free circulation in the Community or imported into the Faroes, OJ L178/58, 14 July 1999
- Council Decision of 15 November 1999 concerning the conclusion of a Protocol on veterinary matters supplementing the Agreement between the European Community, of the one part, and the Government of Denmark and the Home Government of the Faroe Islands, of the other part, OJ L305/25 30 November 1999

- Community Guidelines for state aid in the agriculture sector OJ C 28/2 1 February 2000
- Commission Guidelines on national regional aid, OJ C258/5 9 September 2000
- Decision No. 1/2001 of the EC-Faroes Joint Committee of 31 January 2001 laying down the provisions to implement the Protocol on veterinary matters supplementing the Agreement between the European Community, of the one part, and the Government of Denmark and the Home Government of the Faroe Islands, of the other part, OJ L46/24 16 February 2001
- Guidelines for the examination of state aid to fisheries and acquaculture, OJ C 19/7 20 January 2001
- Council Decision 2001/822/EC of 27 November 2001 on the association of the overseas countries and territories with the European Community, OJ L314/1 30 November 2001 and OJ L324/1, 7 December 2001
- Council Decision 2002/166/EC of 18 February 2002 authorising France to extend the application of a reduced rate of excise duty on "traditional" rum produced in its overseas departments, OJ L 55/33 26 February 2002
- Council Decision 2002/167/EC of 18 February 2002 authorising Portugal to apply a reduced rate of excise duty in the autonomous region of Madeira on locally produced and consumed rum and liquers and in the autonomous region of the Azores on locally produced and consumed liquers and eaux-de-vie, OJ L 55/36 26 February 2002
- Council Decision 2002/546/EC of 20 June 2002 on the AIEM tax applicable in the Canary Islands, OJ L179/22 9 July 2002
- Decision No. 1513/2002/EC of the European Parliament and of the Council of 27 June 2002 (OJ L 232/1 29 August 2002)
- Decision 1230/2003/EC of the European Parliament and of the Council of 26 June 2003 adopting a multiannual programme for action in the field of energy: "Intelligent Energy—Europe" (2003-06), OJL 176/29 15 July 2003
- Council Decision of 10 February 2004 concerning the dock dues in the French Overseas Departments and extending the period of validity of Decision 89/688/EEC, OJ L 52/64 21 February 2004
- Regulation (EC) No 1783/2003 of 29 September 2003 amending Regulation (EC) No 1257/1999 on support for rural development from the EAGGF, OJ L 270/70 21 October 2003
- Council Decision 2006/138/EC of 20 February 2006 extending the period of application of Decision 82/530/EEC authorising the United Kingdom to permit the Isle of Man authorities to apply a system of special import licences to sheepmeat and beef and veal, OJ L54/32, 24 February 2006
- Council Decision 2006/526/EC of 17 July 2006 on relations between the European Community, on the one hand, and Greenland and the Kingdom of Denmark, on the other, OJ L208/28, 29 July 2006
- Joint Declaration by the European Community, on the one hand, and the Home Rule Government of Greenland and the Government of Denmark, on the other, on partnership between the European Community and Greenland, OJ L 208/32 29 July 2006

- Council Decision 2007/249/EC of 19 March 2007 amending Decision 2001/822/ EC on the association of the OCTs with the European Community, OJ L109/33, 26 April 2007
- Commission Regulation 4391/2007/EC implementing Council Decision on relations between the European Community on the one hand, and Greenland and the Kingdom of Denmark on the other, OJ L104/20, 21 April 2007
- Council Decision 2007/249/EC amending Decision 2001/822/EC on the association of overseas countries and territories with the European Community, OJL109/33 26 April 2007

EU Papers

- European Commission Legal Service JUR/CEE/638/62, 16 March 1962, *Legal Status of Monaco, San Marino and Andorra vis à vis the EC*
- European Commission Legal Service JUR: 1086/69, 15 May 1969 on the scope of application of TEC competition rules
- European Commission Note Interne—Article 227, 18 June 1970 concerning the application of Community law to San Marino
- Memorandum on the application of the Treaty to the Continental Shelf, SEC (70) 3095 final
- European Commission Press Note JUR/2827/72/JA, 16 November 1972, *Territories of the Member States*
- European Commission Legal Service JUR/413/74, 18 February 1974, *Territorial application of the agreements signed by the Community with EFTA countries and certain Mediterranean countries*
- European Commission Legal Service JUR(78)D/01681, 17 May 1978, *Territories of Member States to which the EC competition rules apply*
- European Commission Legal Service JUR(83)D/01290 *Etude concernant les raisons pour le statut spécial des Iles Anglo-Normandes et L'Ile de Man*
- European Commission Legal Service JUR(88)D/4014, 22 June 1988, *Application territoriale de la directive proposée fondée sur l'Article 235 concernant le droit vote municipale—notamment Monaco, Andorre, Gibraltar*
- European Court of Auditors, Special Report No 2/93 on the customs territory of the Community and related trading arrangements accompanied by the replies of the Commission, OJ C 47/1, 27 December 1993
- Communication from the Commission: *The status of OCTs associated with the EC and options for "OCT 2000"*, COM (1999) 163 final, 20 May1999
- Commission report on measures to implement Article 299(2): the outermost regions of the European Union, COM (2000) 147, 14 March 2000
- Opinions of the European Economic and Social Committee of 19 July 2005 on the Commission Communication entitled *A stronger partnership for the Outermost Regions* (CES/847/2005) and of 29 May 2002 on the future strategy for the Outermost Regions of the European Union, OJ C221/37, 17 September 2002

- Commission report on implementation of Article 299(2) of the TEC: measures to assist the Outermost Regions, COM (2002) 723 19 December 2002
- Commission Communication of 18 February 2004—Third report on economic and social cohesion COM (2004) 107 final, 18 February 2004
- Communication from the Commission: A stronger partnership for the Outermost Regions COM(2004) 343, 26 May 2004, and Annex SEC (2004) 1030, 6 August 2004
- Communication from the Commission on a strengthened partnership for the Outermost Regions: assessment and prospects, COM (2004) 543, not published in the Official Journal
- Report by the Presidents of the Outermost Regions on the Commission Communication *A stronger partnership for the Outermost Regions*, sent to the European Commission on 17 June 2004
- European Parliament resolution of 28 September 2005 on a stronger partnership for the Outermost Regions—A60246/2005
- Communication from the Commission: *Strategy for the Outermost Regions: Achievements and Future Prospects*, COM (2007), 12 September 2007 and Annex SEC (2007) 507 final, 12 September 2007
- Commission Green Paper: *Future relations between the EU and the Overseas Countries and Territories*, COM (2008) 383 final, 25 June 2008; Commission staff working document accompanying the Green Paper, SEC (2008) 2067, 25 June 2008

Table of Written Questions

- Written Question No 489/73, OJ C49/3, 1974 Response by European Commission to Lord O'Hagen concerning the impact of the Treaty on oil production in the North Sea
- Written Question No 1007/84, OJ C62/34, 11 March 1985 by John Ford to the Commission: the status of Clipperton Island

Table of Selected Cases

- Case 14/74 *Norddeutsche Vieh- und Fleisch Kontor GmbH v. Hauptzollamt Hamburg-Jonas*, [1974] ECR 899
- Case 54-60/76 *Compagnie Industrielle et Agricole du Comté de Loheac v. Council and Commission* [1977] ECR 645
- Case 61/77 *Commission v. Ireland* [1978] ECR 417
- Case 148/77 *H. Hansen jun & O.C. Balle GmbH & Co v. Hauptzollamt Flensburg* [1978] ECR 1787
- Case 91/78 *Hansen GmbH & Co v. Hauptzollamt Flensburg* [1979] ECR 935
- Case 283/84 *Trans Tirreno Express v. Ufficio provinciale IVA* [1986] ECR 231
- Joined Cases C-100/89 and 101/89, *Peter Kaefer and Andréa Procacci v. French State,* [1990] ECR I-4647

- Case 298/89 *Government of Gibraltar v. Council* [1993] ECR I-3605
- Case C-355/89 *Department of Health and Social Security v. Christopher Stewart Barr and Montrose Holding Limited* [1991] ECR I-3479
- Case C-163/90 *Administration des Douanes et Droits Indirects v. Léopold Legros and Others.* [1992] ECR I-4685
- Case C-260/90 *Bernard Leplat v. Territory of French Polynesia* [1992] ECR I-643
- Case C-430/92 *Kingdom of the Netherlands v. Commission* [1994] ECR I-5197
- Case C-363/93 *Rene Lancry SA v. Direction Generale des Douanes* [1994] ECR I-3978
- Joined Cases T-480/93 and T-483/93 *Antillean Rice Mills NV, Trading & Shipping Co. Ter Beek BV, European Rice Brokers AVV, Alesie Curaçao NV and Guyana Investments AVV v. Commission* [1995] ECR II-2305
- Case C-310/95 *Road Air BV v. Inspecteur der Invoerrechten en Accijnzen,* [1997] ECR I-2229
- Case C-171/96 *Rui Alberto Pereira Roque v. His Excellency the Lieutenant Governor of Jersey* [1998] ECR I-4607
- Case C-212/96 *Paul Chevassus-Marche v Conseil régionale de la Réunion,* [1998] ECR I-743
- Joined Cases T-332/00 and T-350/00 *Rica Foods (Free Zone) NV and Free Trade Foods NV v. Commission* [2002] ECR II-4755
- Case C-293/02 *Jersey Potato Marketing Organisation v States of Jersey and Another* [2005] ECR I-9543
- Case C-300/04 *M.G. Eman and* O.B. *Sevinger v. College van burgemeester en wethouders van Den Haag* [2006] *ECR I-8055*

Index

F. Murray, *The European Union and Member State Territories: A New Legal Framework Under the EU Treaties*, DOI: 10.1007/978-90-6704-826-2,

MIX
Papier aus verantwortungsvollen Quellen
Paper from responsible sources
FSC® C105338

If you have any concerns about our products,
you can contact us on
ProductSafety@springernature.com

In case Publisher is established outside the EU,
the EU authorized representative is:
Springer Nature Customer Service Center GmbH
Europaplatz 3, 69115 Heidelberg, Germany

Printed by Libri Plureos GmbH
in Hamburg, Germany